'Transitional space is where finding entwines subject and object in curious, unsettling ways. The evocative verbs *finding, dreaming, playing and analysing* are put through a Winnicottian lens, refracting the clinical alongside the philosophical as objects of play. As we pass through games, spaces and properties of thinking and being, the apparently simple-complexities of DWW inspire the reader as we re-view analytic theory. A page turner indeed.'

Dr Jonathan Sklar, *Training Analyst, British Psychoanalytic Society, UK*

Finding Winnicott

In *Finding Winnicott: Philosophical Encounters with the Psychoanalytic*, Fadi Abou-Rihan expands upon Winnicott's category of the found object and argues that a genuine understanding of the analyst's own thought requires that it be considered in relation to that of another.

The essays in this collection are in dialogue with the work of Freud, Deleuze and Guattari, Laplanche, Bonaventure, Ibn al-'Arabi, and Huizinga; these encounters showcase some of Winnicott's yet unexplored contributions to the questions of subjectivity, time, and language. They weave psychoanalytic theory, clinical vignette and key moments from the history of ideas in order to shed light on our findings regarding, and indeed findings of, desire, on some of the playful but no less compelling ways in which the subject lives, suffers, understands, questions and/or normalizes desire. Chapters span a range of topics including rationales, findings and spaces, and highlight the subject as not only that which finds but that which is found.

With clinical vignettes throughout, this book is vital reading for practicing analysts, as well as analysts in training and students of both philosophy and psychoanalysis.

Fadi Abou-Rihan, PhD is a psychoanalyst in private practice. He lives, writes, and works in Toronto, Canada.

Finding Winnicott

Philosophical Encounters with the Psychoanalytic

Fadi Abou-Rihan

Routledge
Taylor & Francis Group

LONDON AND NEW YORK

First published 2023
by Routledge
4 Park Square, Milton Park, Abingdon, Oxon OX14 4RN

and by Routledge
605 Third Avenue, New York, NY 10158

Routledge is an imprint of the Taylor & Francis Group, an informa business

British Library Cataloguing-in-Publication Data
A catalogue record for this book is available from the British Library

ISBN: 978-1-032-40320-5 (hbk)
ISBN: 978-1-032-39133-5 (pbk)
ISBN: 978-1-003-35248-8 (ebk)

DOI: 10.4324/9781003352488

Typeset in Times New Roman
by MPS Limited, Dehradun

For Antonio Calcagno

Contents

Acknowledgements

This project would not have seen the light of day without Antonio Calcagno's unwavering care and faith. To him and to Paola Melchiori, K. Daymond, Lene Auestad, Jonathan Sklar, Gyongyi Hegedus, Scott McLoad, Ann Scott, Peter Trnka and Zoë Meyer goes my gratitude for the opportunities to learn, write, discuss, present, listen, experiment, publish, play.

An abridged version of *Series* appeared as "Constructions Revisited: Winnicott, Deleuze and Guattari, Freud" in *The British Journal of Psychotherapy* 31.1 (2015):20–37.

An abridged version of *Solitudes* appeared as "On the Micro-Colonial" in *Janus Unbound: Journal of Critical Studies*. 1.1 (2021):83–91.

Preface

Freud considered the dream the royal road to the unconscious and the dream book the jewel in his crown. While only a few of Freud's followers sought to appropriate that crown, many have not hesitated to lay claim to the title of its most deserving guardians and, consequently, to the authority vested by its so-called official story. It is no wonder that, after so many revisions, the story has become as much of authority and access, rivalry and conquest, as of the psyche and its workings.

With his notion of the found object, Winnicott recast Freud's story as one of play and findability, as the story of an animated and vital object that belongs to imaginative living and creative science as much as it does to the nursery or the unconscious. As such, this object far surpasses the typologies of the good and the bad, the fetishistic and the partial, the mythological and the real. Winnicott effectively challenged many of our assumptions regarding the clinic and its theories; in the process, he upended the psychoanalytic and indeed broader cultural orthodoxy founded on the distinction between a subject (in lack) and an object (of satisfaction).

Some will no doubt argue that to the subject belong an inviolable will and a dynamism that the object in its inertia lacks. While this may very well be the case according to certain textbooks of psychology and philosophy, it is not so with respect to the transitional space where Winnicott cultivated many of his insights, where finding entwines subject and object in curious and unsettling ways. This space knows as little of the object as inanimate and unresponsive, that is as dead, as the unconscious knows of death itself—which, at least according to the official story, is hardly anything at all. And if it knows little of the object, it might then make sense to consider that the transitional space would know as little of the other to that object, of its structural and psychoanalytic nemesis, the subject. Foregrounded in that space instead is the verb in its unfolding: finding, dreaming, playing, analyzing. This verb resists the customary view of the transitional as a passageway out of hallucination and into perception or a bridge across which the subject may be guided from infantile omnipotence to mature cooperation and, alongside it, libido from fragmented perversion to disciplined pleasure. Contra the teleology that much of the literature has ascribed to the transitional, finding animates the various elements of its world and invests them with particular yet impermanent qualities.

In assessing the viability of this point of view, three questions present themselves:

- First, how is the Winnicottian perspective furthered when the distinction between subject and object is considered in light of finding?
- Second, what can be said of the production of this distinction, of its inner workings and of its relationship to the phenomenon of playing articulated by Winnicott?
- And, finally, third, what effects does playing have on the ways in which we think and live desire?

In so far as they are psychoanalytic, these questions unravel meta-psychologically—which is to say philosophically—as well as clinically. Indeed, the mind is not simply the implement psychoanalysts may fix should it break down or optimize should it fail to run at full capacity. While one psychoanalytic responsibility is to understand *how* the mind works and engage it on its own terms, another is to understand *that* the mind works, which is to say to grasp the concepts and priorities that transform finding from an occurrence into a way of being, pleasure from a sensation into a principle and language from a messaging tool into a structuring apparatus. Such responsibilities go hand in hand even as interest and avowal vary across individuals and orientations. At the end of the day, philosophy is an integral component of the psychoanalytic field rather than an accidental hazard or a personal fancy. In turn, philosophy may eventually stand to learn a great deal from a practice that reveals it as a passion, no less driven than reasoned.

Chapter 1

Rationales

Within

The texts in this collection constitute a study of the activity Winnicott termed play, the play that unfolds between child and found object. My premise is that this activity is more than an event that the adult clinician observed in his young charges; it is also the object he found and with which he, in turn, went on to play—clinically, meta-psychologically. I take up Winnicott's example and play with his findings, as I believe he did with the child's. I explore the extent to which this very idea of play may shed light on our findings regarding, and indeed findings of, desire—on the playful but no less compelling ways in which we have come to experience, suffer, under-stand, deploy, question and/or normalize this desire. I show that desire is distinct from an innately differentiating marker (as Soul or Drive) of what it means to be a subject, or of a predicament suffered by the subject in ac-cordance with the commands of a pre-existing superordinate law (as History or Structure). Desire is the use the subject makes of the broad spectrum of material, discursive, affective and psychological objects it finds.

Against this background, the subject emerges as altogether different from the vessel or voice of a discernible will that may one day come to recognize its unconscious origins and/or ideological determinants, a will that, in the best of all possible worlds, may manipulate and consume the objects that animate it, the same objects it previously lacked but has since been fortunate enough to acquire. The subject is constituted by finding; it is not only that which finds but also that which is found and is available to be found, repeatedly, by the object, by other subjects and, most poignantly perhaps, by itself.

Instead of a comprehensive introduction to Winnicott and his thought, it is the ambiguity inherent to this reciprocal and at times reflexive finding that I wish to pursue. To this end, I have chosen to focus on a selection of Winnicott's concepts (found object, playing, use) and texts (primarily those collected in *Playing and Reality* (Winnicott, 1971a), the last and, arguably, most philosophical volume Winnicott prepared for publication) rather than on a lifetime abounding with ideas and writings.[1] Regarding the concepts,

DOI: 10.4324/9781003352488-1

while most of the ones I will not tackle (including true and false self and good enough mothering) are rich and, I believe, merit their separate treatments, they tend to operate less prominently in the dynamics I study. As for the texts I privilege, they recast libido as object-finding instead of object-seeking, as per the Fairbairn dictum (Fairbairn, 1963) adopted by much of the object-relations tradition to which Winnicott belongs. Rather than a decisive and synthesizing word, these texts communicate an open process in which finding may be reconfigured beyond the subtle teleology at work in the vast field of Winnicott studies.

Of all that has been written on Winnicott,[2] much has focused on the role of play in his clinical schema.[3] A considerable effort has been devoted to comparative readings, of potential rapprochements and fraught encounters between the analyst and other figures in the field.[4] Less attention has been paid to the intersections between Winnicott's thought and certain currents within the broader philosophical tradition.[5] Lastly, no one, to my knowledge at least, has traced the clinical and philosophical implications of a reflexive study, which is to say of a study that not only fleshes out certain Winnicottian categories but also filters them through a Winnicottian lens. Guided by such reflexivity, much may be gleamed from thinking through psychoanalysis as not only a *setting* or an *occasion for* but also as an *object of* play, as, in other words, an object that is found as well as a theory of finding. In submitting the discipline's concepts to its clinical insights, the texts that follow consider the extent to which psychoanalysis may surpass the clinical observations it finds precisely because it has *found* them, in other words, the extent to which the practice is a creative elaboration of life and work, passion and play as much as it is a descriptive strategy designed to fuel a therapeutic intervention in the service of health. In the process, these texts bridge the gap between philosophy and clinic, theory and practice and hope to uncover a richer and more malleable appropriation than what a critique or application may yield.

This approach is formulated in the spirit of the call Jacques Derrida once issued that psychoanalysts reconsider their theories in light of their clinical concepts and strategies (Derrida and Roudinesco, 2001), that they listen to and appreciate their formulations as they would the musings of their analysands. Derrida's call was not meant to encourage a psychologizing approach that reads into an analyst's body of work the traces of a latent personal history, an approach that effectively marks their or indeed their readers' professional breakthroughs and lacunae as merely the symptoms of otherwise private trajectories. While such a strategy is interesting and potentially quite instructive, it is best suited for the biographers and those who work in the field of so-called applied psychoanalysis. For his part, Derrida called on theorists and clinicians alike to focus on, in this instance, Winnicott as thought, text and technique rather than Winnicott the individual, to open up those spaces where the theory reveals itself as neither cause nor effect, neither produced by nor producing of the clinic, but as produced alongside—which is to say according to procedures akin to those of—the clinic. It should come as no surprise then if and when the playing attempted in these pages emerges as, simultaneously, the focus of a reasoned meta-psychology conjoined with clinical observation as well as the outcome of a meta-psychological playfulness.

The play of a two-year-old with a rag doll constructs a world of pleasure and fancy, movement and care rooted in the situation that comprises the child, the toy and the playing. If this world speaks anything of the provenance, value or characteristics of the toy—whether it is a prized family heirloom or the product of a modern-day Dickensian sweatshop, whether it is made of hand-spun wool or recycled polypropylene—or of how it may measure up to other children's engagement with that toy, it does so either to an outside observer or to the participant in hindsight or as an afterthought. Should the observer/participant choose to bring such factors to bear on the play, they can do so either in the form of reflections and/or limits or perhaps as yet further objects of pleasure and fancy, movement and care. Winnicott often pursued this latter option, participating in the play without losing or even inhibiting his capacity to observe. This two-pronged strategy comes across in the games—linguistic, clinical, theoretical—Winnicott deployed throughout his body of writing, in the pithy yet inviting, confident though not any the less curious style he adopted in order to engage in, as well as advocate for, a measure of creativity and ambiguity.

In this regard, Winnicott's avowed extension of his playful sensibilities from the analytic chair to the writing desk is worth revisiting. In a frank and irreverent introductory passage to his "Primitive Emotional Development" from the mid-1940s, he declared:

> I shall not first give an historical survey and show the development of my ideas from the theories of others, because my mind does not work that way. What happens is that I gather this and that, here and there, settle down to clinical experience, form my own theories and then, last of all, interest myself in looking to see where I stole what. Perhaps this is as good a method as any'.
>
> (Winnicott, 1945, 145)

Eventually, the editors of Winnicott's 12-volume *Collected Woks* (Winnicott, 2016) traced this strategy to a letter the young clinician had written his sister Violet twenty-five years prior to his methodological *aperçu* in which, they observed, the clinician showed a readiness to 'jump across' and 'dive into' the unconscious, to avoid 'a consistently logical sequence of thought in favor of building up a set of apparently unconnected areas [thus] demonstrating the central tenets of psychoanalysis by making intuitive, free associative, barely conscious leaps' (Caldwell and Taylor Robinson, 2019, 4). Tellingly, and in that very same letter, Winnicott had also lauded psychoanalysis for requiring 'hard work and prolonged study' (Winnicott, 1987, 1) while declaring it his 'hobby' (4). There is neither inconsistency nor ambiguity in Winnicott's assessment of the new cure. What comes across instead is the co-occurrence of seemingly conflicting opposites—discipline and excitement, rootedness and serendipity—typically, though erroneously, apportioned between the revering professional and the less conforming (read: less authoritative) hobbyist.

This seemingly uncomplicated sense of divergence betrays the more fruitful and, by the same token, more troubling irreconcilability that animates much of the material in the pages that follow. Its elaboration will reveal it as varying in its resistance to compromise while striking a more unsettling note than ambivalence. Winnicott's account of his method as a playful though arduous thievery is familiar to those of us who track the vagaries of the primary process,[6] a process that admits continuity (in time and space) or boundary (in property and reason) merely as cover and distraction. A case in point: echoing Winnicott's insight into the 'acute instinctual experiences which tend to gather the personality together from within' (Winnicott, 1945, 150), Thomas Ogden understood well thievery's critical function to the individual's coming into being, to their moving from an early fragmentation of the 'this and that' into a fuller experience of an integrated self (Ogden, 2001). Much like what unfolds in a squiggle game, such gathering cannot be scripted; 'It comes and goes' Winnicott acknowledged (1950, 205).[7]

Against a background of the impermanent and interminable, the details of where and to whom a particular component rightly belongs are stripped of their primacy and relegated to the status of the incidental. Needless to say, such considerations are hardly reassuring for those who stake their professional standing on a mastery in matters of aetiology and development, both theoretical and clinical. Winnicott had limited use for such mastery, and perhaps even less for its attendant requirement of completion. He, for instance, declared that an analysand feeling 'contented at the end if everything has been said' is no guarantee that any analytic work has been done. Instead, the satisfaction generated by a full reporting and the confidence at being known by the analyst, and thus integrated in their person, betray a common phenomenon of un-integration and are hardly substitutes for an enduring, though by no means complete, self-integration (Winnicott, 1945, 150). This point is no less relevant to the end of an analysis erroneously marked with completion and exhaustibility than it is to the end of a single analytic session nor, indeed to a completed and supposedly all-encompassing authoritative meta-psychology.

What I find particularly interesting about Winnicott's approach is that it speaks of a work always in progress, drawing on what has already begun ('this and that'), somewhere ('here and there'), curtailed by neither an overarching paradigm nor a disciplinary boundary, of a work that thrives in the abundance of its ideas and origins. This is a porous work whose components (abstractions, techniques and vignettes), gathered under the heading of 'Winnicott' and identified as the benchmarks of what it means to be 'Winnicottian,' are often heterogeneous and idiosyncratic. Eventually, these components make themselves available, to be found, as the 'this and that' and the 'here and there' of future episodes of play and work—psychoanalytic or otherwise—that may have little if anything to do with labels and pedigrees. Such work fosters mobility at the expense of rootedness. That the provenance of its components may be confirmed in retrospect has little bearing on their genuine capacity to move and transform, to lead beyond the familiar, to, in sum, prove Nietzsche wrong when he arrogantly judged that, in the final analysis, 'nobody can get more out of things, including books, than he actually knows' (Nietzsche, 1968, 717).

With this in mind, and as I occupy the position of a reader *of* Winnicott, fully aware of and trying whenever useful to assume that position's associated clinical and theoretical responsibilities, I lay less claim to the authority of that position than I do to the care and movement, fancy and, eventually, hopefully, pleasure I may convey, as I find and play *with* Winnicott.[8] As the reader will no doubt detect the faulty interpretation and misappropriation in what I offer, I do not so much beg their patience or indulgence as I respectfully affirm a right to a margin of freedom, of deviation, of error even, to occupy, as the early Winnicott put it, an 'intermediate area of experiencing' (Winnicott, 1971b. 2)[9] or, as he eventually identified it, the 'conception-perception gap' (Winnicott, 1971a, 151) somewhere between an objectively agreed upon reality or truth of the text on the one hand and a personal flight of hermeneutic fancy on the other, an area without which, as will soon become evident, playing and finding would be, at best, stagnant and, at worst, utterly impracticable.

To this stance the advocates of exegetical rigour will no doubt object on 'legislative grounds' (Franco and Figueiredo, 2016) that the correct understanding of Winnicott has been sacrificed for the sake of a careless liberty. They may warn of the risks that the playfulness I am advocating will sink into either a playing fast and loose with the charged moments in the life of an individual or a form of intellectual gymnastics of interest only to its practitioner and, at best, a handful amongst their audience. Surely, the objection will be raised, the efforts of a theorist attempting to contribute to the understanding of the human psyche and of a clinician charged with the responsibility of alleviating another person's suffering must outweigh, in both subtlety and import, the playful meanderings of a mere child. A healthy degree of reservation, if not indeed suspicion, seems well justified in response to any equivalence drawn between the impromptu drawings of a two-year-old and the meta-psychological cogitations of, say, a fifty-two or sixty-two-year-old, unless, obviously, the latter are as easily reproducible, as superficial and, ultimately, as dispensable as the tracings of a child.

My response to this objection is twofold.

First, I must admit that the thoughts that fill these pages have not been easily producible—my intellect is not as swift or 'playful' as I would wish it to be. That said, I do not consider the qualities of superficiality or dispensability as markers of intellectual and/or clinical inadequacy. Winnicott recommended that psychoanalysis is best served by a practitioner who relinquishes the need to have the final word, a practitioner who occupies the position of an instigator of play rather than of a technician of truth. Such a practitioner must be intellectually and affectively agile; they must tolerate the fact that, within the context of any particular analysis, their every experience or thought is potentially dispensable, that the theories and strategies that guide their interventions, no matter how firmly grounded, are forever subject to a startling upset. Of the squiggle Winnicott understood that it is but an introduction to a complex reality beyond what has been traced on a sheet of paper. As much ought to be acknowledged of psychoanalysis as the access and exploration rather than the depiction or regulation of an inner life.

Second, the playfulness I am invoking here is hardly the carelessness marked as a legitimate concern by the proponents of clinical sobriety. As I have already mentioned and will soon elaborate more fully—for it is my responsibility to do so—what is at stake here is a Winnicottian playfulness that operates somewhere between objective reality and personal fancy. This, I believe, is the playfulness encountered at the limit of the analyst's understanding (Winnicott, 1969, 86–7), the very limit interpretation points to and experience corroborates. In one respect, as it distinguishes the analyst's contribution from the analysand's, this limit safeguards against the dangers of a merger between these two individuals. In another respect, in spite of itself and as is most often the case, this limit belongs to both of the jurisdictions it delineates, to what lies within each as well as beyond it; it is the overlap between the two domains, the analyst's and the analysand's. This then is a third territory whose exploration calls for a new type of responsibility, one that is not only doubled—as in a responsibility to both parties—but also reconfigured as a desire rather than a rightful demand or an onerous imposition.

Without

The essays that follow are inspired by a tradition that straddles the divide between theory and clinic.[10] Inhabiting and assuming responsibility for the divide is hardly ever convenient or innocuous. Indeed, it requires an investment in a form of play whose consequences for both philosophy and psychoanalysis have yet to be fully appreciated. Freud has been broadly recognized as a significant player in this context and subsequently inscribed in the annals of intellectual history as one of its richest, albeit particularly controversial, contributors. Winnicott, on the other hand, and especially among his English-speaking followers, has yet to be accorded much relevance beyond the therapeutic.[11] The essays collected here explore this relevance as they reconsider Winnicott less as an accidental inheritor to a tradition that encompasses both sides of the divide but as one of its major pillars. They will also extend beyond a specifically Winnicottian inquiry since the threshold they inhabit has been a structuring principle to one or the other of three principal currents that have directed much of the history of psychoanalysis.

Though often identifiable as positions represented by separate traditions, these components run through most analytic orientations. The first is marked by collapsing the opposition between the experiential and the abstract. This has often resulted in either (1) a commitment to presumably inviolable meta-psychological axioms and a disregard for, if not outright suppression of, any experiential material that contravenes the doctrine—the unrelenting conceptualisation of female sexuality as passivity and of gender as the primary, if not indeed singular, site of difference is a stark and sad example here; or (2) a reworking of the irreconcilability between the unshakeable theory and the lived yet undisciplined experience as evidence of a fateful and intractably melancholic, angst-ridden and, lest we be too hasty, angst-producing ontological schism.[12]

The second current is marked by the sidestepping of the opposition through a reframing of both the meta-psychology and the clinical outcome(s) as the means toward a presumably greater, more enduring end, of which 'truth'—as championed by science—and 'health'—as mandated by medicine—are among the most favoured instantiations. Subsequently, and in the name of such an end, virtually all that passes under the heading of psychoanalysis (be it a practice, a theory and/or an institution) must be scrutinized, sorted and disciplined. In this current, the seemingly crucial question of whether psychoanalysis is a research method or a treatment modality[13] sets up a superficial dichotomy between two priorities committed less to psychoanalysis and more to the presumably overriding principles of efficacy and verifiability—that a theory be true and/or that its clinical applications be truly curative. While fitting for such disciplines as psychology and psychiatry, efficacy and verifiability, I would suggest, are not necessarily of the highest psychoanalytic relevance. These considerations not only obviate other potentially equally desirable ends, such as pleasure, culture or, for that matter, the pleasure of culture, but also fail to take stock of the more original and indeed fundamental Winnicottian insight that, as a form of play, psychoanalysis belongs to the history of those activities that identify what it means to be human outside of verifiability and independently of utility.

The third and final current is marked by a privileging of the opposition as neither an empirical mishap nor a meta-psychological burden but as a delineation of and an opening onto the porous space in which much of what is properly psychoanalytic actually takes place. Here, both the meta-psychology and the clinical outcomes take a back seat to the processes (free association, play, agility, construction—call them what you will) that produce and sustain the theory, the experience and their effects. In this current, it is the process that takes pride of place as it gives rise to a new set of concepts and experiences that, far from being unambiguous or indisputable, help cross the divide between the various theories and outcomes, schools and orientations and gather them under the overarching category of the 'psychoanalytic.'

This third current recognizes in psychoanalysis a quality that belongs to most other disciplines. At the end of the day, and no matter the disagreements or valuations, the Platonic is no more or less philosophical than the Humean, the Newtonian no more or less scientific than the Einsteinian, and the Gothic no more or less artistic than the Bauhaus. What identifies each as belonging to a particular discipline or tradition is neither its truth nor its consistency, neither its soundness as a theory of how the world works nor its grounding in a doctrinal belief in what that world is good for. In fact, if anything, it is precisely the controversies around such matters that propel and enrich the internal histories of philosophy, science and art as legitimate fields of inquiry. At stake, rather, is a set of tools, a procedural language if you will, which shapes the sensibilities and determines the directions of any particular practice. It is the disagreements over which grammar belongs where and to whom, the disagreements, in other words, over jurisdictions and qualifications, that mark disciplinary territories and determine the criteria of eligibility. While an epistemologist, a surgeon and a sculptor may be in perfect agreement as to what constitutes a human body, it is the deployment of the concept, the scalpel and the chisel that mark the practitioner as a member of one or the other of the professions.

These essays are thus offered as a contribution to the psychoanalytic broadening of the interventionist 'what ails you?' into the more investigative 'what moves you?' They follow Winnicott's dictum that counting always begins with the number 2: there is no such thing as an infant outside of a relationship with a parent, and growth is always contingent on an interaction with a found other. In between the elements of any one duality eventually emerges a third element under whose aegis much of what is human takes place: between work and rest is playing, between hallucination and utility is desiring; and between the play areas of analyst and analysand is analyzing. Gone then are the principles of Freudian one-person psychology; equally gone are the principles of a canonical self-propelling paradigm of the psyche. In the spirit of such arithmetic, a genuine understanding of Winnicott's own thought calls for it to be considered in relation to another thought or, as is the case in the present context, to a host of others. The resulting encounters showcase some of Winnicott's yet unexplored contributions to the questions of subjectivity, time and language. In the process, and in between Winnicott and his interlocutors, a path is traced for a new elaboration of desire and its science.

With this in mind, I want to invoke Gilles Deleuze and Félix Guattari's double-pronged interrogation: 'Given a certain effect, what machine is capable of producing it? And given a certain machine, what can it be used for?' (Deleuze and Guattari, 1977, 3) The interrogation led its authors—the one a philosopher, the other a psychoanalyst—to insist on the primacy of a 'machinic' or 'desiring' production for human nature. Understood in Winnicottian terms, this production is akin to the process that plays, dreams and associates so that it may pursue these activities further and differently. I would like to re-pose the question of finding and play, of machine and effect, while multiplying the question's resources and orientations. Given any two machines—clinical, theoretical, cultural—what can their juxtaposition be used for and what effects can that juxtaposition be made to produce? At stake here is a process that treats of dynamic effects as much as it does of developmental causes, of potential products as well as of hidden aetiologies and of eventual deployments no less than of retrograde analyses. Ultimately, my hope in posing this question is that such effects, products and deployments may not only communicate to us hitherto unexplored yet constitutive theoretical and/or clinical components within Winnicott and his interlocutors, but that, much more crucially, they may shed a light on and, eventually, instantiate desire anew, that they may allow us to do with that desire, and do with it differently, as much as it does with us.

In positing this doubled implication, I take my cue from the 'machines' I am considering, insofar as each, in its own way, has more or less relinquished as artificial and ineffectual the distinction between the functions of theory and practice, observer and observed, analyst and analysand. By the end of his career, Winnicott was unequivocal when he declared that psychoanalysis '*has to do with two people playing together*' (Winnicott, 1967, 38; emphasis in the original), that such a doing takes place '*in the overlap of the two play areas, that of the patient and that of the therapist*' (Winnicott, 1971c, 54: emphasis, again, in the original). Psychoanalysis has thus little to do with one subject developing, interpreting or correcting another's experience according to some externally pre-elaborated path toward truth or health, and everything to do with fostering the playing that takes place 'in between' the two subjects. Psychoanalysis, according to Winnicott, is therefore as much a practice in play and transitionality as it is a theory grounded in such phenomena; it is as invested in consolidating and legitimizing an Ego, a Self or a Subject, true or false, as a found object may be said to consolidate or legitimize a reality, hallucinatory or concrete.[14]

In a similar and equally forceful vain, Deleuze and Guattari identified the principal task of their analytic orientation (*schizo*analysis) as the dismantling of the distinction between a subject that emits a statement and a subject about whom or on behalf of whom a statement is emitted (Deleuze and Guattari, 1977, 271 and 1987, 75–110). 'The schizoanalyst is not an interpreter' they declared (1977, 338). In schizoanalysis there is no subject that imparts to another its accomplishments in knowledge, health or experience; there is only an analytic machine—altogether different from an imaginary projection, as unconscious fantasy, or a real projection, as cure—a recurring factor of production among parts (associations, syntheses, subjectivities) functioning alongside one another and under specific, rather than overarching and 'structuralized' clinical conditions (Deleuze and Guattari, 1977, 1995 and Guattari, 1984). These are the gears that create new gears, alongside preceding ones, indefinitely, even if, or even as, they seem to function in discordant or opposing ways. In sum, 'that which makes a machine [the schizoanalytic *sine qua non*] are connections, all the connections that operate the *disassembly*' (Deleuze and Guattari, 1986, 84; emphasis added).

My investment in highlighting this relay between the post-Freudian project of Winnicott and the supposedly anti-Freudian project of Deleuze and Guattari is hardly in a history of ideas that may bridge the divide between the British and the French, each a tradition that, sadly, has thrived often on recognizing its other only to dispute its legitimacy as fantasmatic and/or mundane, on, in other words, dissociating itself from that other, a history, and by extension a methodology, that would invariably, self-righteously, grant itself the status of an integration or incorporation greater, wiser, or truer than both. Nor is my investment in exposing and clarifying the ways in which each of these two traditions is, after all and presumably, a metaphor for, or, better still, the metamorphozing outcome of the other. I would much rather spare my readers the disappointment and irritation of witnessing their perspectives and convictions dismissed as the derivatives of some previously or elsewhere more convincingly elaborated views. Nor do I hope to facilitate a triumphal coupling of the two sets of disparate texts and strategies with the aim of producing a clinical and/or meta-psychological offshoot—a strange beast indeed—part Winnicottian and part Deleuzo-Guattarian, part post- and part anti-, forever honouring, which is also to say forever hemmed in by, its provenance and heritage. Nor, lastly, is my investment in a utopian 'in-between' that has gripped much of the imagination amongst contemporary readers of both Winnicott and Deleuze and Guattari, an 'in between' whose idealizing advocates, I suspect, must forever keep to their shores lest they drown in the all-too-real and treacherous waters of the *Oceanus Britannicus*.

On this score, although the notion of a topographical 'in between' seems to be precisely what brings both projects in line with one another, the Winnicottian transitional and the Deleuzo-Guattarian *intermezzo* are most fruitful when considered as processes rather than sites. Playing and *bricolage*, the one a basic form of living (Winnicott, 1967, 50) and the other a handyman's tinkering (Deleuze and Guattari, 1977, 1), have little to do with mapped, striated and/or bound spaces and everything to do with lived experiences. Ditto for the 'in between.' Just as Winnicott's theory of play is a theory that plays and a theory that recognizes itself as clinically the site and object of play, Deleuze and Guattari's commitment to the *intermezzo* is grounded in the very fact that the thought they pursued was itself an *intermezzo*.[15]

The essays that follow unpack/enact variations on the theme of the 'in between' they have stumbled upon while charting the waters of various Channels and Oceans separating Winnicott from concepts and categories dear to, among others, Benjamin, Deleuze and Guattari, Huizinga, Ibn al-'Arabi, Laplanche, Bonaventure and Corbin. Once prioritized, counting from 2 opens the door to a number of encounters between Winnicott and figures and/or ideas, both within and outside the psychoanalytic field, through which his thought may be rediscovered. As one party in each encounter elaborates a thought inspired by the other's prompt, a perspective is shifted and a new insight becomes possible. Taken together, the seemingly disconnected, not quite scriptable scenes will hopefully reveal a compelling and useful dynamic, much as in the squiggles Winnicott drew with his young patients, much as in the squiggles desire draws with its subjects.

Itineraries

While each reader may follow their own itinerary, the first of these essays elaborates the motif of *coincidentia* as a grounding for much of what the project as a whole puts forward. It is therefore recommended as an access point for the other texts as they explore some of the category's productions, traversals, implications.

Findings

While often classified as paradoxes, many of Winnicott's penetrating insights are better understood as instances of *coincidentia oppositorum* (Nicolas of Cusa), less enigmatic and less perplexing though certainly not any less illuminating. *Coincidentia* points to the co-occurrence of inextricable opposites, defining and defined by one another, cutting into one another so as to form an indissoluble unity. *Coincidentia* undermines the classic law of excluded middle as well as the appropriation of opposition in the service of a transformative synthesis or compromise. Through this lens, we discern in Winnicott the emergence of a found subject and a subjectivized object, of troubled play, creative drive, solitary analysis and, in a rejoinder to Walter Benjamin, barbaric civilization.

Series

Winnicottian finding is aligned with construction (Freud) and production (Deleuze and Guattari). Together, these seemingly irreconcilable points of view highlight the dynamism of the co-incidence of opposites as potentially less a painful contradiction or tolerable impasse and more as an inclusive production. Two detailed clinical vignettes illustrate how desire is neither a word nor a principle but a vibrant experience that emerges in the proximity of action to emotion, power to dependence, consistency to surprise and disclosure to privacy. Clinically, co-incidence opens onto a lateral rather than an archaeological depth, a depth of field that jettisons the profundity of interpretation in favour of an analyzing construction whose pleasures and conflicts operate beyond repetition and/or recovery.

Solitudes

The core of this essay is a clinical vignette that meets up with a political category where the co-incidence of opposites—implantation and intromission (Laplanche) fantasizing and fantasying (Winnicott)—opens up colonization from the realm of cultures and geographies to that of the most intimate and troubling. As it traces the effects of a desire that co-opts the body and psyche of the one in the service of the other, as per a parent's sexual abuse of a child, the vignette underscores the extent to which we are colonized in the most elemental of gestures and at our most basic, most structural of cores, the extent to which, in other words, we are libidinal in so far as we are colonized and colonized so as to be libidinal. The vignette becomes a prompt for a reassessment of the relational and clinical dimensions of the capacity to be alone, of the entanglement of solitude with loneliness, separateness with abandonment.

Games

With the found object, Winnicott expanded the dyadic in psychoanalysis in favour of a tripartite structure (inner and outer realities as well as the transitional that is in-between). Finding thus becomes the ground for the elaboration of a similar expansion of one of the most central and problematic of analytic polarities—Eros/Thanatos. This expansion highlights *Ludens* (Huizinga) as yet a third drive that animates the psyche. Rather than a frontier, abyss or wall, *Ludens* operates in the space separating Eros from Thanatos as it draws on both for energy and direction. *Ludens* is play once play has been recognized as pleasurable and hurtful, to the point of being cruel, enlivening and deadening, and sometimes even deadly, freeing and dissociating, at the risk of severing, innocent and guilty, to the extent where its guilt may be unfathomable. *Ludens* exposes cruelty as a constitutive component to play, all play, rather than an unfortunate by-product or what is typically associated with the malignant and/or narcissistic. The subject that plays is thus hardly innocent. In the spirit of analyzing the extreme in order to shed light on the everyday, the pictures of Abu-Ghraib detainees from the early noughts illustrate the extent to which *Ludens* endures, how it operates in a space where means and ends collide, where an action does not suffer the lack of justification since it is forever its own justification and, by extension, its own consequence.

Spaces

Winnicott's impression of the in-between as a limbo reveals the time of the found object as an *aevum* (Bonaventure), a time bounded by the absolute (*aeternitas*) on one side and the transient (*tempus*) on the other. Residing in limbo, the found object defies integration as it partakes of both sides of whatever polarity it may seem to join while belonging to neither. Limbo is thus the quintessential *interregnum* (Pontalis), a kingdom between two kings itself without a king, whose logic extends to the four founding components of psychoanalysis (drive, dream, transference and construction). Echoing Freud's thoughts on repression and Lacan's on forgetting, the Winnicottian subject emerges as a product of finding rather than a preexistent agency that simply finds. Persistent simultaneity: the logic of opposites (subject-object, finding-found, satisfaction-frustration, etc.) moves from succession to co-incidence as a more accurate formulation of desire. With this move, the axiomatic position that the unconscious is immune to time makes way for the *barzakh* (Ibn al-'Arabi) as a more useful rendering of the varied timings and imaginings at work in the psyche.

Properties

The scope of the found object is expanded beyond that which is made explicit in analytic theory and practice so as to include that by which both theory and practice may be reformulated. Vital, resilient and ever-decathectable, the found object that is psychoanalysis may now relinquish its fantasy of truth and resolution. As the ground for an experience of exteriority, psychoanalysis waives its claim to clinical neutrality (as indifference) and assumes instead its function as differentiation (as in-difference). Coming to terms with its limits and vulnerabilities is thus precisely what sets psychoanalysis apart from most other theories and therapies; it brings the practice closest to actual human experience and endows it with both clinical empathy and intellectual re-levance.

Notes

1 As evidenced by the recent 12-volume edition of the analyst's collected works (Winnicott, 2016).
2 Further to the countless many that have been published since, Harry Karnac's *After Winnicott* (2007) catalogues more than 1200 writings on the analyst and his concepts; as such, it is an invaluable resource.
3 Tuber (2020), Green (2018), Saragnano and Seulin (2019) and Grolnick (1990).
4 Caldwell (2019), Abram and Hinshelwood (2018), Luepnitz (2009), Hauptmann (2005), Kirshner (2011) and Vanier (2012).
5 The notable exceptions in this regard include Nussbaum (2006), Alford (2000), Bitan (2012), Sell (2012) and Jackson (2017).

6 In a spirit similar to Winnicott's, Lacan once acknowledged: 'I borrow things wherever I find them, whether that upsets anyone or not' (Lacan, 2014, 12). In time, Félix Guattari came to recognize the value of this self-same gesture in an interview given to the French daily *Libération* in 1980. Originally titled "*Petites et grandes machines à inventer la vie*" (Guattari, 1986), this interview was eventually published in an English translation under the apt title 'I Am an Idea Thief' (Guattari, 1995).

7 Named after a technique Winnicott developed in his clinical consultations with children, the squiggle game consists in two players taking turns building on a random line the other had drawn, transforming it into a somewhat recognizable object. In the course of a consultation, Winnicott would engage his young charge over the twenty to thirty drawings produced and help them express troubling thoughts and feelings (Winnicott, 1964-1968). Winnicott resisted presenting the game as a script or a technique; neither a test nor an examination, no two cases can be alike (Winnicott, 1964-1968, 301-03).

8 Jean Laplanche's strategy of interpreting *with* Freud (Laplanche, 2014), rather than approaching him as merely the object *of* interpretation, has been an invaluable guide and inspiration here.

9 "Transitional Objects and Transitional Phenomena," the seminal essay from which this expression is drawn, was drafted in 1951, published initially in the *International Journal of Psychoanalysis* in 1953 and subsequently included in the 1958 edition of *Through Paediatrics to Psychoanalysis* (Winnicott, 1975). The text I will be referencing throughout is the final version that opens *Playing and Reality* (Winnicott, 1971b). Aside from minor copy edits, this last version substitutes the original's concluding brief discussion of Mosche Wulff's paper on fetishism (1946) with two clinical vignettes, almost doubling the length of the text. I will address the first of these cases in detail later.

10 See Henry (1985), Felman and Noel Evans (2003) and Flax (2012) for more on this tradition.

11 Among the many, five references from outside of Winnicottian English-speaking circles illustrate some of the extra-clinical echoes of the analyst's contributions. The Brazilian Winnicott Society's e-print series explores the Winnicott-philosophy-culture connection. In France, Jean-Bertrand Pontalis (1983, 2007) was a driving force not only in translating and disseminating Winnicott's texts but also in giving them a greater philosophical due; as well, Catherine Cyssau and François Villa (2006) put together a collection of essays that interrogate the philosophical underpinnings of Winnicott's concept of 'human nature,' and the bio-physicist Henri Atlan (1993) deployed the psychoanalyst in his study of the relationship between science and myth. In Italy, Paolo Virno (2008) invoked Winnicott alongside Aristotle, Vygotsky and Simondon in his exploration of the connections between intersubjectivity and negation.

12 Perhaps the most poignant illustration of this last tragedy is the Lacanian positing of a Subject by definition outside the realm of the objective while forever subject to the Other, a Subject that suffers the burden of 'something originally, inaugurally, profoundly wounded in the human relation to the world' (Lacan, 1988, 167), a Subject that may undergo a psychoanalytic experience only on the understanding that what awaits it is nothing short of 'destitution' (Lacan, 2001, 252) in the spirit of a Dantesque 'abandon all hope, ye who enter here.'

13 Addressing the manufactured choice between two mutually exclusive options, Winnicott once declared:

> We have to distinguish clearly between what the patient gets out of the treatment and what we get out of it. For the patient, the treatment is not life.

If the treatment is successful, it enables the patient to start, perhaps at a late date, or to make a better start, or to start with better equipment. For ourselves, the work must be interesting in itself, i.e., we must have an interest in our work which is not dependent on getting results. It is very tempting for us to try to copy our colleagues in other professions; the surgeon, for instance, who often saves a life. Much of our work produces a result, but after an interval which is beyond our capacity to hold.

(Winnicott, 1961, 232)

See, as well, the discussions by Lesche (1985), Sandler and Dreher (1996), Leuzinger-Bohleber and Fischmann (2006) and Hinshelwood (2013).
14 While Winnicott adopted the view that psychoanalysis is essentially concerned with the dynamics of selves shielding, harnessing and/or obfuscating one another (Winnicott, 1960), I will soon show how the found object's operations are, indeed, the farthest from such a manoeuvre.
15 This interpretation was first proposed by Vincent Descombes (1979) in reference to the Marxist and Freudian paradigms in between which he situated Deleuze and Guattari's project.

References

Abram, Jan and Hinshelwood, Robert. 2018. *The Clinical Paradigms of Melanie Klein and Donald Winnicott: Comparisons and Dialogues.* London and New York: Routledge.
Alford, C. Fred. 2000. "Levinas and Winnicott: Motherhood and Responsibility." In *American Imago* 57:3. Pp. 235–259.
Atlan, Henri. 1993. *Enlightenment to Enlightenment: Intercritique of Science and Myth.* Translated by Lenn Schramm. Buffalo: SUNY Press.
Bitan, Shachaf. 2012. "Winnicott and Derrida: Development of logic-of-play." In *The International Journal of Psychoanalysis.* 93:1. Pp. 29–51.
Caldwell, Lesley. 2019. *Winnicott and the Psychoanalytic Tradition: Interpretation and Other Psychoanalytic Issues.* London and New York: Routledge.
Caldwell, Lesley and Taylor Robinson, Helen. 2019. "The Enduring Significance of Donald W. Winnicott: General Introduction to the *Collected Works.*" In *Twelve Essays on Winnicott.* Edited by Amal Treacher Kabesh. Oxford: Oxford University Press. Pp. 1–26.
Cyssau, Catherine and Villa, François. 2006. *La nature humaine à l'epreuve de Winnicott.* Paris: Presses Universitaires de France.
Deleuze, Gilles and Guattari, Felix. 1977 *Anti-Oedipus.* Translated by Robert Hurley, Mark Seem, and Helen R. Lane with a preface by Michel Foucault. New York: Viking Press.
Deleuze, Gilles and Guattari, Felix. 1987. *A Thousand Plateaus.* Translated by Brian Massumi. Minneapolis: University of Minnesota Press.
Deleuze, Gilles and Guattari, Felix. 1986. *Toward a Minor Literature.*Translated by Dana Polan. Minneapolis: University of Minnesota Press.
Derrida, Jacques and Roudinesco, Elizabeth. 2001. *De quoi demain.* Paris: Editions Galilée.
Descombes, Vincent. 1979. *Le même et l'autre.* Paris: Les Editions de Minuit.
Fairbairn, Ronald. 1963. "Synopsis of an Object-Relations Theory of the Personality." In *The International Journal of Psychoanalysis.* 44:2. Pp. 224–225.

Felman, Shoshana and Noel Evans, Martha. 2003. *Writing and Madness: Literature/ Philosophy/Psychoanalysis*. Stanford: Stanford University Press.

Flax, Jane. 2012. *Disputed Subjects: Essays on Psychoanalysis, Politics and Philosophy*. London and New York: Routledge.

Franco, Wilson de Albuquerque Cavalcanti and Figueiredo, Luís Cláudio. 2016. "Winnicott's Style and its Implications: A Study on Authorization, Authenticity and Influence in Psychoanalysis." In *Ágora Rio J.* 19:2. Pp. 325–337. Available at https://www.scielo.br/j/agora/a/GGBdmVRqR87rFybcvn6TrFy/?lang=en#B25 Accessed: 15-08–2022.

Green, Andre. 2018. *Play and Reflection in Donald Winnicott's Writings*. London and New York: Routledge.

Grolnick, Simon. 1990. *The Work and Play of Winnicott*. Northdale, NJ and London: Jason Aronson.

Guattari, Felix. 1984. "Machine and Structure." In *Molecular Revolution: Psychiatry and Politics*. Translated by Rosemary Sheed. London and New York: Penguin Books. Pp. 111–119.

Guattari, Felix. 1986. "Petites et grandes machines à inventer la vie." In *Les années d'hiver: 1980-1985*. Paris: Bernard Barrault. Pp. 152–166.

Guattari, Felix. 1995 "I Am an Idea Thief." In *Chaosophy*. Edited bySilvère Lotringer. New York: Semiotexte. Pp. 37–50.

Hauptmann, Bruce. 2005. *Donald Winnicott and John Bowlby: Personal and Professional Perspectives*. London and New York: Routledge.

Henry, Michel. 1985. *Généalogie de la psychanalyse. Le commencement perdue*. Paris: Presses universities de France.

Hinshelwood, Robert D. 2013. *Research on the Couch: Single-Case Studies Subjectivity and Psychoanalytic Knowledge*. London: Routledge and The Institute of Psychoanalysis.

Jackson, Jeffrey. 2017. *Nietzsche and Suffered Social Histories: Genealogy and Convalescence*. London: Palgrave MacMillan.

Karnac, Harry. 2007. *After Winnicott: Compilation of Works Based on the Life, Writings and Ideas of D. W. Winnicott*. London: Karnac Books.

Kirshner, Lewis. 2011. *Between Winnicott and Lacan: A Clinical Engagement*. London and New York: Routledge.

Lacan, Jacques. 1988. *The Ego in Freud's Theory and in the Technique of Psychoanalysis. The Seminar of Jacques Lacan, Book II*. Edited by Jacques-Alain Miller and translated by S. Tomaselli and J. Forrester. New York: W. W. Norton & Company.

Lacan, Jacques. 2001. "Proposition de 9 octobre 1967 ou le psychanalyste de l'École." In *Autres écrits*. Paris: Éditions du Seuil. Pp. 243–259.

Lacan, Jacques. 2014. *Anxiety. The Seminar of Jacques Lacan, Book X*. Edited by Jacques-Alain Miller and translated by A. R. Price. Cambridge: Polity Press.

Laplanche, Jean. 2014. "Interpreting with Freud." In *Seductions & Enigmas: Laplanche, Theory, Culture*. Edited by John Fletcher and Nicholas Ray. London: Lawrence & Wishart. Pp. 55–70.

Lesche, Carl. 1985. "Is Psychoanalysis Therapeutic Technique or Scientific Research." In *Annals of Theoretical Psychology*. Edited by K. B. Madsen and L. P. Mos. Boston, MA: Springer. Pp. 157–187.

Leuzinger-Bohleber, Marianne and Fischmann, Tamara. 2006. "What Is Conceptual Research in Psychoanalysis?" In *The International Journal of Psychoanalysis*. 87:5. Pp. 1355–1386.

Luepnitz, Deborah Anna. 2009. "Thinking in the space between Winnicott and Lacan." In *The International Journal of Psychoanalysis*. 90:5. Pp. 957–981.

Nietzsche, Frederick. 1968. "Ecce Homo." In *Basic Writings of Nietzsche*. Edited by Walter Kaufmann. New York: Random House. Pp. 655–791.

Nussbaum, Martha. 2006. "Winnicott on the Surprises of the Self." In *The Massachusetts Review*. 47:2. Pp. 375–393.

Ogden, Thomas. 2001. "Reading Winnicott." In *The Psychoanalytic Quarterly*. 70:2. Pp. 299–323. Available at https://www.ctp.net/PDFs/ogden.pdf. Accessed: 15-08–2022.

Pontalis, Jean-Bertrand. 1983. *Entre le rêve et la douleur*. Paris: Editions Gallimard.

Pontalis, Jean-Bertrand. 2007. *Le royaume intermédiaire*. Paris: Editions Gallimard.

Sandler, Joseph and Dreher, Anna Ursula. 1996. *What Do Psychoanalysts Want?* London and New York: Routledge.

Saragnano, Gennaro and Seulin, Christian. 2019. *Playing and Reality Revisited: A New Look at Winnicott's Classic Work*. London and New York: Routledge.

Sell, Christian. 2012. "Reading creatively: Why Nietzsche might have enjoyed Winnicott." In *Psychodynamic Practice*. 18:4. Pp. 413–425.

Tuber, Steven. 2020. *Attachment, Play, and Authenticity: Winnicott in a Clinical Context*. Lanham: Rowman and Littlefield.

Vanier, Alain 2012. "Winnicott and Lacan: a missed encounter?" In *Psychoanalytic Quarterly*. 81:2. Pp. 279–303.

Virno, Paolo. 2008. *Multitude: Between Innovation and Negation*. Translated byIsabella Bertoletti et al. New York: Semiotexte.

Winnicott, Donald W. 1945. "Primitive Emotional Development." In *Through Paediatrics to Psychoanalysis: Collected Papers*. New York: Basic Books. Pp. 145–156.

Winnicott, Donald W. 1950. "Aggression in Relation to Emotional Development." In *Through Paediatrics to Psychoanalysis: Collected Papers*. New York: Basic Books. Pp. 204–218.

Winnicott, Donald W. 1960. "Ego Distortion in Terms of True and False Self." In *The Maturational Process and the Facilitating Environment*. London: Hogarth Press and The Institute of Psycho-Analysis. Pp. 140–152.

Winnicott, D. W. 1961. "Notes on the Time Factor in Treatment."In Thinking About Children.London and New York: Routledge. pp. 231–234.

Winnicott, Donald W. 1964–1968. "The Squiggle Game." In *Psycho-Analytic Explorations*. Edited by Claire Winnicott et al. London and New York: Routledge. Pp. 299–317.

Winnicott, Donald W. 1967. "Playing: A Theoretical Statement." In *Playing and Reality*. London and New York: Routledge. Pp. 38–52.

Winnicott, Donald W. 1969. "The Use of an Object and Relating Through Identification." In *Playing and Reality*. London and New York: Routledge. Pp. 86–94.

Winnicott, Donald W. 1971a. *Playing and Reality*. London and New York: Routledge.

Winnicott, Donald W. 1971b. "Transitional Objects and Transitional Phenomena." In *Playing and Reality*. London and New York: Routledge. Pp. 1–25.

Winnicott, Donald W. 1971c. "Playing: Creative Activity and the Search for the Self." In *Playing and Reality*. London and New York: Routledge. Pp. 53–64.

Winnicott, Donald W. 1987. *The Spontaneous Gesture: Selected Letters of D. W. Winnicott*. Edited byRobert Rodman. Cambridge, MA: Harvard University Press.

Winnicott, Donald W. 2016. *The Collected Works of D. W. Winnicott*. Edited by Lesley Caldwell and Helen Taylor Robinson. Oxford: Oxford University Press.

Wulff, Mosche. 1946. "Fetishism and Object Choice in Early Childhood." In *The Psychoanalytic Quarterly*. 15:4. Pp. 450–471.

Chapter 2

Findings

Objects

One plays with the object one has 'found,' an object that, strictly speaking, and as per Winnicott's own examples (blankets, teddy bears, tongue depressors and the like) is a manufactured object. Governed by a myriad of laws and relations, there is rarely anything to this object that is natural or immediate. Though hardly ever a given, the found object is much less found than it is given.[1]

The found object is not something that was once held, assumed, enjoyed, lost, not quite mourned and since, fortunately, found anew. Rather than the remedying of an absence or the conclusion of a sorrow, finding is the encounter with an unfamiliar and benign other; it is the trigger to a host of processes and machinations, not altogether predictable yet, it seems, not all that threatening. Found and finding are the preliminaries to curiosity and exploration rather than the expressions of satiation or finality.

The found object is part of the world of the real—and hence not a mere delusion—while it also belongs to the subject's inner reality. Here, Winnicott set up the triadic topology of an internal life (experienced through desires and fantasies—whether conscious or unconscious), an external reality (accessible via the senses) and, in between, a space of an inherently illusory though tangible and crucial event of 'experiencing' where the found (a.k.a. 'transitional') object and its corresponding phenomena are located (Winnicott, 1971b, 2–3). Topology and function combine in order to disrupt the abstract and intractable duality to whose opposing poles inside and outside are customarily bound. The found object is effectively charged with the capacity, nay the responsibility, to facilitate the subject's passage from the interior to the exterior, from '(magical) omnipotent control to control by manipulation (involving muscle erotism and coordination pleasure)' (9). Developmentally, this is a passage from oral erotism (as the earliest and most rudimentary operation of desire that gives the subject's internal dynamics precedence over all others) to object relationship (as the complex, nuanced and less easily manageable desire in constant interaction with its surround).

DOI: 10.4324/9781003352488-2

Winnicott thus cast the found object teleologically as a bridge over the otherwise insurmountable gap between solipsism and relatedness, limitless delusion and limiting interaction.[2]

The found object is the first other-than-me possession the subject will weave into an already existing personal pattern (3). As such, and notwithstanding its overarching teleology, this object is neither consumed nor assimilated; it holds on to the contours, textures and colours that distinguish it from all other objects—be they real or imagined, good or bad—that make up the tapestry that is the world of the subject that finds it. As well, this object is more than what the subject discovers in order to observe, catalogue and then perhaps reserve for a future time when it may prove beneficial. Much as it provides a measure of reassurance and/or satisfaction (8), the found object is an object in use. I shall return to Winnicott's very specific deployment of the notion of use soon enough; in the meantime, suffice it to say that, as found, an object is far greater than an object of utility, i.e., a tool designed with a specific function in mind, as, for instance, a blanket that covers or a teddy bear that distracts. Instead, the found object is identifiable by three interlocking features: first, it possesses a modicum of vitality evidenced through, among others, warmth, movement and texture (think here of the psychological and affective valance of a child's experience cuddling a teddy bear or running their fingers along a blanket's satiny border); second, it is resilient enough to survive the loving and/or aggressive manipulations of the subject that finds it (bear and blanket must withstand hugging, gripping, tossing, pulling or dragging), with the proviso that, and herein lies its third distinguishing quality, it does not perish or disappear; rather, it is decathected. As it loses meaning, the found object is never truly forgotten—since the feeling about it does not undergo repression; nor is it mourned—since it does not die but merely ceases to be relevant. Henceforth, the object's corresponding phenomena will become diffused and 'spread out over the whole intermediate territory between "inner psychic reality" and "the external world as perceived by two persons in common," which is to say, over the whole cultural field' (5).[3]

Winnicott again took up this assessment of an object depleted yet redeemed in the service of a broader experience in the notes he prepared for a presentation to the Association for Child Psychology and Psychiatry in Glasgow: likened to the old soldier that merely fades away, the found object is the ground of symbolism upon which culture can grow (Winnicott, 1959b, 56–7). Winnicott's logic here may evoke associations to cycles of life, of decay and rebirth. Much like Freud's *fort-da* where the spool is never truly lost but is made to vanish momentarily so that it may reappear, where, in other words, the child confirms for itself the illusion of its power to give life after it has taken it away, Winnicott's decathected found object is spared an unimpressive death as it is incorporated into the soil of a broader and more enduring dynamic. In both cases, seemingly, death's finality is averted and grief is rendered pointless. While they may make sense in the context of most discussions of uses and purposes, these associations are problematic here on two presumably irreconcilable though equally legitimate grounds: first, they elide an account of the all-too-real experience of irredeemable finality in favour of a story of a childhood, nay indeed humanity, in control of its losses and pains, of a nature ever-abounding in its ability to sustain itself on its own detritus;[4] and, second, they introduce an episodic alternation of presence with absence that, as we shall soon see, runs against the constancy of the found and of finding in what it means to be a subject.

Coincidentia

Enter *coincidentia oppositorum*, the co-incidence of opposites. With thematic antecedents stretching as far back as pre-Socratic thought and early Kabbalah, the term was coined by the 15th-century German philosopher Nichols of Cusa and has since become part of the intellectual toolbox of a number of figures from early modern philosophy (Bruno, Leibniz, Hamann) to, more recently, Carl Jung, heir to the psychoanalytic throne turned renegade, Henry Corbin, a scholar of Sufism and frequent presence at Jacques Lacan's seminar, and Gershom Scholem, an authority on Jewish mysticism and close friend of Walter Benjamin's. Colleagues and regular participants at the annual meetings of the Eranos circle in Switzerland,[5] each of these men upheld the concept of *coincidentia* as a core feature of a thought and a world (Wasserstrom, 1999).

The history of *coincidentia oppositorum* is replete with meanings and variations on meanings that extend far beyond the scope of this project. While a theological principle for some and a higher form of intuition for others, the definition I am deploying here strikes a most productive note for the psychoanalytically attuned. Distinct from the oft-invoked logics of duality and conflict, *coincidentia oppositorum* is a major motif in the principal dynamics and phenomena uncovered by Freud. Similarly, as I will soon show, although often classified as paradoxes, many of Winnicott's penetrating insights are better understood as instances of this *coincidentia*, less enigmatic and less perplexing though certainly not any the less illuminating. I would in fact go so far as to say that the category is one of the distinguishing features of the Winnicottian paradigm.

First then, what *coincidentia* oppositorum is not. It is not, as the term would suggest, a coincidence—as in a fortuitous simultaneity in a surround of indifference. Nor is it the oppositional, inter-dependent and/or complementary logic of such couplets as left and right, inside and outside, big and small. Nor is it the duality of potential meanings in one and the same scenario determined by intent or approach, as in the same stairs going up or going down, an individual at one and the same time a parent to one generation and a child to another. Nor, lastly, is it the linguistic contronym (aka janus word) that, depending on the context, may mean one or the other of two opposing designations, e.g., apology, oversight, custom, dissipation, to sanction or to dust. Rather, *coincidentia oppositorum* is the co-incidence of inextricable opposites defining and defined by one another, existing inseparably and only existing inseparably of one another. As per the roots of incidence in the Latin *incidere*, the opposites in *coincidentia* cut in and are inscribed onto each other so as to form an indissoluble unity—hence, at first glance, the logic-defying sense of such instances as the centre located on the periphery and the border lying within. The cutting is a mixing, as in cutting with or cutting into, an intervention (*oppositus*) rather than an excision, a doubling as opposed to a mere bifurcation. No simple metaphor, the inscription is greater than a record produced so that it may reflect a preexisting reality. The inscription produces a reality as much as it claims to merely describe one.[6] It is the site where, as Deleuze and Guattari insisted, something in the order of a subject is discerned (Deleuze and Guattari, 1977, 16), a subject established rather than timeless, one that is as fraught with opposition, as conflicted and troubling as the forces that inscribed it. *Coincidentia* confirms the power of irresolvable contradiction; it undermines the hold of both the classic law of excluded middle (that, at any given point, either a proposition or its opposite may be true) as well as the more recent appropriation of opposition as the ground for a transformative synthesizing repetition, an insatiable *Aufhebung* convinced of its authority yet sadly ever anything more than the season's iteration of the Philosopher's New Clothes.

From the recent history of ideas, consider Walter Benjamin as a figure whose thought was enlivened by the logic of *coincidentia*. 'Even in authors whose picture of the world exhibits mostly reactionary traits he heard the subterranean rumblings of revolution, and generally, he was keenly aware of what he called "the strange interplay between reactionary theory and revolutionary practice,"' so wrote Scholem (Scholem, 1976. 195) illustrating Benjamin's investment in interwoven opposites—historical materialism and Jewish mysticism being among his most central. The motif of co-incidence permeated the picture Benjamin painted of history and its paths, of a radical politics reliant on theology and of a messianic arrest as an opening in the fight against fascism (Benjamin, 1940b, 389, 397, 396). *Coincidentia oppositorum* indeed gave a theoretical grounding for Benjamin's unsparing insight that, rather than occasionally hijacked or polluted by baser human instincts, culture is sustained by an environment of cruelty and desolation, that, in essence, 'every document of civilization is a document of barbarism' (392).

Considering the radical transformations in the technologies of recording and dissemination, it is safe to assume that what one identified as a document when Benjamin formulated his views in the early days of the second world war (Briet, 1951) differs greatly from our present expansion of the category to run the gamut from the seemingly benign line of code to the bombast of the politically crude and cruel. With thanks in no small part to Benjamin and thinkers like him, we have become increasingly aware of the dubiousness of the distinction between a document and what it is supposed to document. Nevertheless, while our judgement of what qualifies as civilized or barbaric has undergone its peculiar transformations, the disjunction between the supposedly inconsonant rubrics comes easily still. It is the illusion of this seemingly self-evident operation that Benjamin exposed.

Benjamin's insight references the ways in which a cultural treasure—a painting, a statue, a sarcophagus—is transmitted from one person to another, one site to another, one culture to another. According to traditional practice, these are the spoils carried in the triumphal processions in which rulers step over those lying prostrate (Benjamin, 1940b, 391). Barbarism fuels their traffic as well as the control exercised over their meanings. We may therefore bask in the genius or beauty of the Rosetta Stone, the Parthenon Marbles, the statue of Rameses II or the Pergamon Altar. Likewise, we may stand in awe of Freud's passion and commitment as a collector of archaeological treasures. We may nevertheless cringe with the sense that, on their way to the analyst's consulting rooms, many of Freud's 3000+ statuettes, rings and scarabs (Greek, Roman, Egyptian or Chinese) may very well have traversed terrains governed by principles less noble than the pursuit of knowledge or the appreciation of beauty—to wit, war, pillaging, illegal transport and black markets.[7] As much has been confirmed of many holdings in the museums of London, Paris, New York and Berlin.[8]

The concern with provenance and travels highlights the lengths to which certain powers go in order to absolve themselves of their cultural crimes. 'We paid for our riches with your blood. Couldn't you at least be grateful for our preserving this beauty on your behalf and for the sake of the world?' Thus goes their absurd though all too familiar plea. In his recent attempt to redeem the looting of the Benin Bronzes, the Oxford art historian John Boardman declared comfortably, and I quote with the requisite trigger alert here, 'the rape proved to be a rescue' (Boardman, 2016, 326). Since, in a similar spirit, though not in quite as cruel a tone, various museums across the Netherlands have vowed to repatriate over a hundred thousand cultural works belonging to former Dutch colonies now that they have been identified as objects of 'involuntary loss' (Boffey, 2020). 'Involuntary loss' is now one of polite company's euphemisms for the fact of theft as a vehicle of culture and its peregrinations.[9] In a parallel move, while observing its own code of *politesse*, the French Senate recently opted to avoid any mention of restitution and spoke instead of 'circulation' as it authorized the return to Senegal and Benin of 'extra-European' works pilfered by French soldiers in the late 19th century.[10]

Lest one be tempted to recruit him in a convenient war that pits a culture's saviours against its desecrators, a game of cops and robbers whose main purpose it seems does not go far beyond vindication and vilification, Benjamin was careful to note that cultural treasures owe their existence as much to anonymous toil as to great genius (Benjamin, 1940b, 392). The intertwining of culture and barbarism is drilled past traffics and histories down to the modes and conditions of production through which a testament to human excellence is also a pointer to suffering and injustice. In this regard, monumentality and patronage provide sharp illustrations. On the one hand, many of the palaces of humanity's gods and monarchs, the walls and highways that mark its landscapes and pace its histories, speak not only architectural ingenuity or aesthetic distinction but also cold-blooded exploitation. One thus counts as part of the legacy of Khufu's Great Pyramid in Giza: 36 thousand deaths; the Great Wall of China: the estimates are in the millions; the Panama Canal: 30 thousand; Qatar's 2022 FIFA stadiums: one can only hazard a guess. On the other hand, in a history that spans from the patronage of the Florentine renaissance to today's international auction circuits, artistic production has proven itself almost entirely bound up in the circulation of capital and the accumulation of wealth by the few at the expense of the many. While culture's contributions to our health, individually and collectively, are no doubt necessary and beyond measure, the belief in culture's innocence and in the possibility that it may be rescued from its less-than-civilized investments remains untenable.

Co-incidences

Introducing Benjamin into a discussion of Winnicott may register as a haphazard choice—a coincidence indeed, rather than a co-incidence—that does little to counter the initial impression that there are hardly any identifiable references in favour of an argument for a relationship between the two figures. Timelines aside, there is instead every reason to believe that such an argument is far-fetched considering, on the one hand, Benjamin's commitment to revolutionary politics, literary theory and most anything by way of nineteenth-century Parisian culture and, on the other, Winnicott's focus on psychoanalysis as a clinic and a vocation. And yet, much like Benjamin, Winnicott understood well culture's complex and troubling undercurrents as he recognized among its components the destructive and so-called criminal alongside the loftiest and most esteemed of endeavours (Winnicott, 1971b, 5). Equally significantly, much like Winnicott, Benjamin was keenly aware of the intertwining of history with psyche, politics with creativity. His exhortation that one ought 'to brush history against the grain' (Benjamin, 1940b, 392) and disabuse oneself of the fallacy of a 'homogenous, empty time' (395), in other words of a continuum of progress filled sequentially with history's events, is as much the stock-in-trade of a practice focused on the unconscious and its murmurs as it is a grounding principle of critical political analysis.

Manifestly at least, and with the exception of a few references in his study on Baudelaire (1940a), Benjamin managed to sidestep the psychoanalytic project. In this respect, he stood apart from many of his fellow members of the University of Frankfurt Institute for Social Research, including Horkheimer,

Adorno and Fromm, who were already integrating Freud's discoveries into their scholarship.[11] Nevertheless, the *coincidentia* Benjamin epitomized meets a foundational counterpart in the psychoanalytic discovery that the unconscious is not simply an other to consciousness existing somewhere alongside it—an idea already in circulation in nineteenth-century clinical circles[12]—but a thought process in a relation of co-incidence with consciousness as its opposite. Thus, Freud's early definition of association as the 'simultaneity of occurrence' (Freud, 1900, 539) morphed into a major leitmotif in his more mature formulations—to wit, the synchrony of the dream processes (Freud, 1900, 576), the inseparability of opposing affects and component instincts (Freud, 1905, passim), the coupling of conscious and unconscious presentations (Freud, 1915a, 201–02), the experience of the uncanny as the frightening familiar (Freud, 1919), the mechanics of disavowal (Freud, 1927), and, last but not least, the disruption in the ego's synthetic functions (Freud, 1940). In shedding light on such a gamut of phenomena and processes, Freud could comfortably assert that the dynamic unconscious he was investigating knows nothing of the negative, that in it 'contradictories coincide' (Freud, 1915b, 296). The door for subsequent generations of clinicians to rethink the psyche beyond logic's classic oppositions is open now that the frailty of the law of excluded middle has been decisively exposed. Among the most notable of these clinicians is Winnicott.

Consider the experience of finding where the subject engages the object as both the target and instigator for myriad dynamics that bear upon the encounter's reality—reconfiguring it, augmenting it, distorting it. As previously noted, for the object to qualify as found, it must possess not only a materiality but a vitality all its own (Winnicott, 1971b, 5); in its finder's mind, it has a life and a history of which the fact that it has been found is an integral part. Thus, for instance, among the many objects available to the child, blanket and teddy bear display activity, production and effect: as soother, friend or partner in play, each intervenes and reconfigures whatever scene the child may have already set. Woven into the subject's psychodynamic structure, the found object is thus an object that has already been, or at least partially been, subjectivized, and subjectivized by virtue of the fact that it has been found. The found object is henceforth the mark of an ontological heterogeneity, an other-than-me far more complex than the favoured Winnicottian 'not-me' (Winnicott, 1971b, 1)—a term which evokes the negation Freud had exposed as an ideational barrier against, in this particular case, the affective engagement finding makes possible (Freud, 1925). In sum, before us is the first Winnicottian co-incidence of opposites, of subject and object as categories that do not exclude or compliment each other but that exist simultaneously in one and the same entity, the subjectivized object, integrating and incorporating one another.

Occupying the transitional space between inner and outer realities, the found object grounds an experience in which the subject foregoes the certainties of hallucination while it disencumbers itself from the ossifying demands of concreteness. Winnicott extended this phenomenon beyond the confines of the subject's earliest and most rudimentary interactions with the world when he reminded us that 'the task of reality-acceptance is never completed, that no human being is free from the strain of relating inner and outer reality' and that it is specifically the 'intermediate area of experience which is never [or, more accurately, in certain circumstances at least, ought never be] challenged' that provides relief from such a strain (Winnicott, 1971b, 13). An inanimate object, an event, a human being, an organization or an idea are among the objects that are found, time and again, precisely because of their capacity to be, and because of the sub-ject's often continued desire for them to be, more than mere objects. One is thus rooted in a geography, shaped by a technology, gripped by an idea, defined by membership in a family, institution or nation. Such found objects usher new meanings and potentials; they trigger certain emotions and justify others after the fact; they precipitate actions and elaborate formations of ideas and groupings. Such objects make movement possible.

The initial intra-co-incidence of subject and object thus leads to an inter-co-incidence: as the subject finds the object, it is also found by that selfsame, by now subjectivized, object, woven into its tapestry and transformed to satisfy its needs. In finding, no subject finds without becoming an object and there-fore found as well as finding. Together, these two basic co-incidences clarify finding as the *sine qua non* of the subject that can hardly count the experience as one among the many it may call upon whenever necessary or convenient. The subject in Winnicott is founded by and as finding much as it is by re-pression in Freud, language in Lacan or speech in Laplanche and Pontalis. Finding is thus brushed against the grain, to use Benjamin's turn of phrase, of a progressivist pattern of finding-playing-relinquishing-decathecting. As the defining quality of the subject, finding also brushes that subject against its own grain, weakening its unity, by doubling its status as object and undermining its autonomy as subject to the will of an other. This is no simple cognitive manoeuvre for what is opened up for the subject here is the prospect of finding itself and becoming its own found object, thus experiencing itself as an other that is neither a self-fashioned hallucination nor a cog in the vast machinery that is external reality (*qua* Biology or History) nor, indeed, as the site for a sustained compromise or reconciliation between these two domains. Found, the subject is animated and resilient even and perhaps most especially, as per the third of its distinguishing features, when confronted with the prospect of its own inevitable irrelevance. Finding's reflexivity thus differentiates a gen-uine ever-transformable understanding from a terminal and static explanation and, in turn, introspection from an inwardly directed cognition, regardless of whether the latter is grounded in a self-serving delusion or in the presumably most authoritative and verifiable of (meta-)psychological proofs. This re-flexivity invests introspection with the potential of an integral, dynamic and mutative knowledge. It is in the context of the analytic relationship where analyst and analysand come to find one another, where each also comes to find, or find again, time and again, themselves that the reciprocity of the transference/counter-transference becomes operative, crystallized and, consequently, functional.

Confounds

Its potential to foster growth notwithstanding, the reciprocity of finding extends the Winnicottian line of thought in a number of uncomfortably challenging directions.

Meant to underscore the mutually defining relationship between parent and child, Winnicott's declaration that there is no such thing as an infant (Winnicott 1960, 39) confirms that not only is a subject grounded in a relationship with another from the very beginning but that crucial for each is a nurturing, soothing and/or exciting relationship with a hopefully 'good-enough' other.[13] While self-evident in principle, this reciprocal expectation of care and reliability at the heart of a functioning relationship, analytic as well as parental, the expectation that the baby be good or analysand be trustworthy for instance, is overridden by, on the one hand, an awareness of the baby's or analysand's genuine limits as to what they may actually be capable of offering and, on the other, a coming to terms with the misconception that parent or analyst somehow require nothing and expect even less in return. A frustration is hence structurally woven into this relationship amongst unequals, a frustration that, at best, calls for endurance rather than satisfaction as, at worst, it opens the door to a host of less than savoury or responsible scenarios—acting out, enactment and projective identification being the most frequent.

Reaching beyond the paradigmatic scenarios of the parental and the analytic, Winnicott insisted on a sobering counterbalance to the seemingly innocuous adventures of finding. Initially formulated in terms of a renunciation and a submission though eventually understood as exteriority, finding carries with it a considerable dose of aggression the subject suffers and may eventually perpetrate. No matter the erotism and pleasure it may yield—one might even say precisely because of the erotism and pleasure it does yield—finding is accompanied by an injurious if not in fact humiliating 'abrogation of omnipotence' (Winnicott, 1971b, 5). That the subject may derive joy or soothing from an object that is not entirely of its own making, an object that exists beyond its absolute control, is evidence of a not quite invulnerable internal world and of a far from self-sufficient set of resources that will require that world to rely on external means in order to safeguard and/or further its integrity—both bodily and psychologically. Operating along the border between primary creativity and objective perception, the found object sets the stage for an experience as rife with frustration and eventually shame as it is with satisfaction and release. Finding is then the burgeoning of the subject's awareness of its lack or failure and therefore the springboard for retaliatory hostility as much as it is for movement and curiosity. Winnicott's insight into the found object's resilience in the face of the aggressive manipulations of the subject that finds it makes it all the more likely that the object survives in spite of the subject's hostility and not simply because of that subject's care. Yet a third co-incidence of opposites emerges at this point: finding is doubled not only in its directionality (inter- and intra-psychically) but in its composition (experimentation-play and shame-aggression) as well.[14]

Winnicott reminds us that the found object serves as the ground for 'the early stages of the use of illusion, without which there is no meaning for the human being in the idea of a relationship with an object that is perceived by others as external to that being' (Winnicott, 1971b, 11). It is on the basis of such a multifaceted experience that rests the subject's ability to recognize and interact with whatever lies beyond the limits of its psychological and material domains. This seemingly axiomatic declaration challenges much of what has been taken for granted regarding that other separate object also known as mother. Indeed, there is much for Winnicott that hinges on the presence of the found object in the life of the individual to the point that, while writing up the clinical illustration of a young boy who adopted a toy rabbit for more than four years, he declared that the rabbit never truly became found because it 'was never, as a true transitional object would have been, more important than the mother, an almost inseparable part of the infant' (Winnicott, 1971b, 7). That, for an infant, something ought to be more important than the mother in developmental matters is a crucial statement from the same Winnicott who persistently brushed the day's psychoanalytic tradition against its paternal grain by underscoring, seemingly above all else, the primacy of the mother-infant relationship. That, in a parallel fashion, and for the analysand this time, something might eventually be more important than the analyst should prove as startling not only to those amongst the Winnicottians who have privileged a nurturing 'motherly' understanding of the psychoanalyst's function, but also to the many, if not most, who have structured the entire process of psychoanalysis around the relationship to the analyst as a parent—regardless of the differences of opinion concerning genders, rearing styles or purposes. Rethinking the analytic process in terms of finding, rather than, say, repetition, displacement and/or resolution, may yet generate its own startling effects.

Culture

The foregoing dynamics presuppose that culture is a process far more complex than, say, a sublimating safety valve for otherwise socially undesirable urges.[15] It is no mere accident that Winnicott raised culture as an issue in the same text where he tracked the found object's itinerary from animation to decathexis and from an individual illusion to a collective experience. In this discussion, Winnicott, curiously, playfully, expanded the scope of culture from the illusory experience of art and religion (Winnicott, 1971b, 3) to include not only dreaming, imaginative living, creative scientific work and philosophy (14) but fetishism, lying, stealing,[16] the origin and loss of affectionate feeling and drug addiction as well (5).

Winnicott's expansion of culture is relevant for a number of reasons. Not the least among these is the fact that the expansion deploys, seemingly quite comfortably, the category of 'creative scientific work,' a category that has steadily and sadly acquired the status of an oxymoron in a therapeutic environment bound by so-called objectively verifiable standards of efficiency and utility[17] at the expense of anything that may hint at unpredictable and potentially unsettling creativity, an environment that reduces the duality creativity-science to an intractable, irresolvable opposition, much as it does to the categories of play and work for instance. For Winnicott, it is precisely under the heading of such seemingly conflicted and contestable dualities that playfulness is inscribed.[18]

Even more relevant in Winnicott's expansion is the fact that, consistent with the third co-incidence of composition (play and aggression), culture's horizons now encompass creativity and theft, passion and apathy, experimentation and compulsion. Located between the hallucinated and the concrete, illusion is the common thread running through all these phenomena. Tellingly, illusion's etymological roots point to the Latin '*illudere*' as the assimilated form of '*in*'- at or upon + '*ludere*'-to play—hence illusion as, literally, playing (Huizinga, 1995, 11). Henceforth, illusion and play may be neither idealized nor derided since both are recognized as producing the destructive as well as the creative and without which, it seems, neither type of activity is possible. This is indeed an illusion and a play without which the human, as a subject that has learned to differentiate itself from all other subjects and species precisely because of its capacity for the sacred, philosophical, researched, subtle and/or imaginative and hence, by extension, because of its capacity for the profane, anti-intellectual, pseudo-scientific, crude and/or destructive—its capacity, in short, for the Winnicottian 'cultural'—would not itself be possible either.[19]

True enough, Freud was committed to empirical authority and judged as 'delusional' (Freud, 1939, 127–132) and '*Meschugge*' (Freud, 1985, 186) the axioms of a psycho-mythology that projects all manner of falsehood onto a nature, a future or a god. And yet, Freud also insisted that knowledge of such projections and mastery of their subtleties must be considered among the subjects required for training in psychoanalysis—as tools rather than truths, to be used rather than revered. Among such subjects Freud counted the history of civilization, mythology, the psychology of religion and the science of literature. Notwithstanding the fact that their viability far exceeds the purview of empirical verifiability, 'unless he is well at home in these

subjects, an analyst can make nothing of a large amount of his material'
Freud insisted (Freud, 1926, 256).

It seems to me that Winnicott's expansion of play onto 'the whole cultural
field' so as to include these selfsame processes mirrors a movement in
Freud's thinking. Whereas Freud wanted to bring cultural anthropology to
bear on the individual's earliest interactions with the familial surround, he
nevertheless tried to situate, expose and interpret the former in light of the
latter. For his part, Winnicott wanted to trace the origins and dynamics of
cultural experience back to the playful interactions between infant and
found object and, as a curative parallel, between analysand and analyst.
What unites both thinkers is the conviction that some universal principle is
invariably at work here: for Freud, it was libido, Oedipus or the repetition
compulsion, as each supposedly predates and structures the history of any
particular individual or phenomenon, while for Winnicott, it was the ubiquity of play in the life of the species, a play of which, incidentally, psychoanalysis, as the analyst himself came to recognize, is but a most recent
though highly specialized form (Winnicott, 1967, 41).

Against this background, the Winnicottian abstraction that identifies the
child's play as the root of culture butts against a theoretical and experiential
limit. Structured around an almost always manufactured and mediated
object, the trinity of child, found object and play may not stand without its
own cultural underpinnings. To think otherwise would be to believe that,
somehow, the child approaches an object in a vacuum, that the approach is
sui generis, shaped by neither temperament nor environment, that the object
in question is without a history that produces it in such a way as to make it
available to the child in the first place, or, last but not least, that the play is
facilitated, monitored and/or interrupted solely by the child and in the absence of an adult whose identity and function have already been defined and
regulated by a broader cultural surround encompassing considerations of
kinship, care, health and law.

If play is the root of culture and culture (as a combination of, among
others, environmental, historical and familial dynamics) is the backdrop
against which play emerges, the circular relation thus forged between the
two phenomena prompts the awkward though presumably inevitable 'what
came first, the chicken or the egg?' question. Often, this circularity is raised
as a challenge to the accuracy of the relation's psychological grounding or
the soundness of its theoretical premise. In the rare case, as with Winnicott
himself, it is appreciated as evidence of a paradox that calls for fortitude and
patience. Indeed, Winnicott prefaced his collection of essays on the subject
of play with the request that such a paradox be 'accepted and tolerated and
respected, and for it not to be resolved' as he went on to identify the kernel
of his own contribution in terms of the request itself (Winnicott, 1971a, xii).
Considerations of priorities, logical as well as chronological, have since been
rendered moot by both evolutionary biology (as a reproductive mechanism,

the egg has been shown to predate the *Gallus gallus* species) and quantum physics (categories such as spacetime and equations of motion have taken over a field previously governed by Aristotelian principles of causality). In some of its subtler moments, the theory has recognized that both answers are legitimate, that the egg predates the chicken and vice versa, that, structurally, childish fancy and parental ideology, individual creativity and mass production have always appeared side by side, in defiance of a pro-gressivist/developmental model, as a *coincidentia oppositorum* of the singular and the collective—the fourth so far encountered.

Use

Winnicott's insight into culture as an overarching category that brings to-gether seemingly irreconcilable phenomena exposes yet another, more striking, fifth co-incidence that inches the psychoanalyst ever closer to the troubling relationship Benjamin drew between civilization and barbarism. Before us is not just an instance of opposites occupying through accident or failure the same coordinates in time and space. Animated by finding, not only is each of culture's components enmeshed with its opposite as we have already seen, but, it is safe to assume, culture as a whole is suffused with its nemesis—barbarism. Indeed, there is nothing to indicate that, once re-cognized as a structuring feature at the elemental level, the co-incidence of opposites does not operate at a much larger, more threatening and certainly more destructive scale. At this point, I will provide a basic outline of this position and leave the explanation of some of its implications to the texts that follow.

This fifth co-incidence of, effectively, presence and absence emerges out of Winnicott's presentation of 'use' (Winnicott, 1969). Having little to do with either consumption or exploitation, use is contingent on the subject recognizing the object as a 'thing in itself'[20] existing somewhere outside of its control (88) and surpassing its projective mechanisms (90). In this schema, Winnicott relegated object-relating to a lesser sophisticated stage of development—identified in terms of the subject as an 'isolate'—while object-use takes centre stage as the manoeuvre that opens the subject onto 'externality itself' (91). Winnicott thus traced for the subject a path that leads from relating to an object, to loving it, to attempting its destruction, to recognizing its endurance. Coming to terms with the limits of its ag-gressive powers in light of the object's tenacity, the subject is henceforth in a position to move one step further along its path and 'use' an autono-mous living object (90), that is to say, a subjectivized object with which it may now establish a richer and more enduring experience.[21]

The seemingly developmental logic of this trajectory is undermined by Winnicott's conjoining of externality with aggression at the very point when an object is in the process of, as he put it, 'becoming destroyed because real, becoming real because destroyed' (Winnicott, 1969, 90). This doubled causal relationship between the subject's experience of an object's materiality and its annihilation, between its presence and absence, upends the classic sequencing of aggression as but a retaliation against a pre-existing deficient and/or non-compliant external reality. Instead, Winnicott advanced that 'it is the destructive drive that creates the quality of externality' (93) thus jettisoning a frustrating external world in favour of a productive inner dynamic as the driving force behind not only finding but aggression as well. Lest we infer that this dynamic of a causative drive privileges a progressive sequence in an out-the-front-door-and-in-through-the-back-window manoeuvre, we need only return to Winnicott's earliest observations of the encounter with the found object in which play's aggressive rough and tumble reveals the wish to destroy as emerging in tandem with rather than as the effect of the experience of the object's otherness—in other words, its status as a subjectivized object.

By consolidating the centrality of play to the analytic process and ravelling finding with ontological heterogeneity—which is to say use, as he understood the term, with destruction—Winnicott soldered aggression to the clinical setting, notwithstanding the latter's curative function. The text on the use of an object might just as well have been titled 'Hate in the Transference.'[22] Identified as the kernel of the relationship between the analytic parties, the transference paves the way, as Freud once put it, from a miserable present to an unhappy future, or, as per Winnicott when he refused to accompany Freud down the path of wariness, from a seemingly indispensable false self designed to preempt the furthering of environmental failures to an ego strong enough to experience id impulses and tolerate their consequences (Winnicott, 1956, 250). Regardless of its itinerary's alpha and omega, the transference is forever steeped in a logic of repetition of wishes and phantasies ('you are to me what I take you to be, what I carry within me, what I demand of you to be'), a repetition whose so-called resolution does little to propel the analysand toward externality. One is in the ante-room, in Benjamin's language (Benjamin, 1940c, 402), awaiting the play that disrupts the familiarity of the transference (positive as well as negative) and allows the analysand to deploy the components of an analysis as one would found objects outside the realm of the purely subjective (Winnicott, 1969, 87). Play is not only a means of disengaging from familiar and futile solutions to long-standing problems; play opens onto settings and scenarios that disrupt the prevalence of these problems as it makes way for potentially different resolutions to entirely unfamiliar and unforeseeable complications (Benjamin, 1940c, 402). This explains and further sustains Winnicott's sense of analysis as greater than a contribution to the repertoire of psychotherapeutic interventions but as a most recent, though specialized, chapter in the rich and ongoing history of play (Winnicott, 1967, 41).

Hence the sixth *coincidentia* of hate and healing and, by implication, the seventh of repetition and play, of, on the one hand, the past coming into the consulting room or, as is the case with a more severe regression, of the present retreating into and becoming the past (Winnicott, 1956, 249) and, on the other hand, of a present, and hence a presence, that go beyond the past and its predicaments but instead enter a time whose possibilities have not yet been entirely decided. This ever-expanding cluster of co-incidences suggests that the nature of the analytic intervention is invariably doubled. Winnicott already understood this doubling in his treatment of the types of transferences corresponding to one or the other of the ways in which the past appears in the session: 'I have discovered in my clinical work that one kind of analysis [re setting] does not preclude the other [re interpretation]. I find myself slipping over from one to the other and back again, according to the trend of the patient's unconscious process' (Winnicott, 1956, 250). A decade later, he reformulated the same clinical duality in terms of the work that brings the patient into a state where they may be able to play and the work that is itself play (Winnicott, 1967, 38).

Among the last of his writings, Winnicott's text on the use of an object repositions relating and, by extension, transference, as a form of relating, to a developmental order not yet capable of tolerating exteriority. As it surpasses the quasi-hermetic transference, use places the analyst outside the area of the analysand's omnipotent control and transforms the analytic experience into something greater than a self-analysis (Winnicott, 1969, 91). With exteriority as the ground of a genuine analysis, Winnicott's text might just as well have been titled 'The Retreat of the Transference and the Onset of Analysis,' thus opening onto the eighth *coincidentia* so far.

Post-

That, as Winnicott was fond of saying, psychoanalysis has to do with two people playing 'together' (Winnicott, 1967, 38) is no guarantee that they are actually playing 'with' one another, much less the same game or according to the same rules. Indeed, there is every reason to believe that, over the course of an analysis, such is not always the case, that analysis as the overlap of the play areas of analyst and analysand (Winnicott, 1971c, 54) is eventually reorganized and experienced as a solitude shared by the psychoanalytic partners. The sharing is as figurative as the overlapping since, strictly speaking, neither can be sustained with programmatic intent; at best, each speaks an affinity recognized mostly in hindsight and/or from the outside.

Winnicott considered the ability to maintain and thrive in such solitude, the so-called capacity to be alone, as among the 'most important signs of maturity in emotional development' (Winnicott, 1958, 29). Given such a status, it is reasonable to assume that this capacity will eventually materialize in the course of an analysis, especially one deemed successful. Deploying 'well-worn' psychoanalytic phraseology, Winnicott likened this capacity to the solitude shared between two individuals lying side by side after intercourse where each enjoys being alone along with another who is also alone (31). Although distinctly un-romantic, which is not to say un-emotive, this post-coital solitude stands in contrast to the other equally well-worn dramas of incest and parricide (Freud) and exasperations over the dead ends of obsessional masculinity and hysterical femininity (Lacan). Winnicott's solitude is configured by neither romance nor sport, neither matrimony (holy or otherwise) nor reproduction; indeed, it is apart from all such concerns. In its midst, Winnicott declared, an impulse and a sensation 'will feel real and be truly a personal experience' (34). The declaration may well strike one as counterintuitive, even fantastical, since, presumably, it is intercourse and its associated pleasures rather than their ensuing collapse that one is tempted to hold up as the expressions of the 'real' and truly 'personal.' And yet, it is in the spent, rumpled and sticky post-coital moments when everything is over and nothing has yet begun that pretence and purpose cease to make any sense; in the at times barely countable and at others interminable seconds of quivering muscles and thumping heartbeats that the worlds of meaning and property recede, as if by magic, into a nebulous background of shadow and dust; in the flash between the dissipating traces of the little-death that is the orgasm where the self had just lost its depth and the yet to be sounded thud of reality that power and its attendant struggles feel the least relevant.

With such a moment as a case in point, the capacity to be alone emerges as the sign of neither a self-imposed retreat, nor a concentrated seclusion, nor even a useful introspection. Rather, this quotidian and yet most telling indicator of maturity is but the produced and yet unproductive hovering and floundering between two inherently different worlds, the libidinal and the pragmatic in this particular case, reverberating with the after-effects of the former while being pressed on, though not quite succumbing to, the latter. Such states make their mark precisely as they constitute a moment that is the least considered or planned for, and hence the least orchestrated or performed. A by-product rather than a goal, this moment bears as little resemblance to the logic of pleasure and pain as it does to that of property and intelligibility.

Not surprisingly, Winnicott went yet one step further as he identified the capacity to be alone as a modest 'liking' (31) or as the 'stuff out of which friendship is made' (33), rather than, say, the ground for a much loftier love, authenticity or wellbeing. One may very well hold the psychoanalyst's restraint here as the courtesy of a quintessentially English reserve that distinguishes itself from the Middle European or Latin passions that have otherwise dominated much of what has transpired across the psychoanalytic field. One may even judge this as the peculiar yet understandable expression of a post-World War II wariness of what the pursuit of too much love, too much authenticity and, indeed, too much 'wellbeing' can elicit. One may also invoke Winnicott's differentiation and subtle favouring of liking as ego-relatedness over love as an id-relationship, be it crude or sublimated (Winnicott, 1958, 31). Much as each of these interpretations holds water, I believe one may grasp yet another aspect of Winnicott's communication by taking it at its face value as well as exploring its finer subtleties; in so doing, one is reminded that a healthy friendship can and often does endure, and perhaps even welcome, the intermittent irrelevance as well as the purposeless hovering that, committed as they are, passions such as love and hate can barely fathom.

In the spirit of post-coital solitude then, it may be said that psychoanalysis unfolds once one's energy has been spent beyond the seduction of interpretation, the resolution of resistance and the deepening of relationship, once, in other words, the playing that makes possible such accomplishments has ceded its place to a purposeless hovering devoid of the need or demand to seduce, arouse or gratify, to convince, be relevant or hold relevant. In the language of the found object, analysis qua friendship is decathexis redux.

Needless to say, the process that culminates in a psychoanalytic moment is most often paved with, among others, the awkwardness of presence, the seduction of insight, the intensity of identification, and the irreverence of humour. Here, we ought not to overlook the occasional but awkward bump, scratch, and hiccup, and, at times, the painful, confusing, or titillating revelation, confrontation, and intrusion. Such are the effects and dangers of the dismantling of resistances and working through conflicts. While all these are steps along the path leading and contributing to the analytic moment, they ought not to be confused with it. On the other hand, while someone like Adam Phillips may pithily propose that psychoanalysis is about 'what two people can say to each other if they agree not to have sex' (Phillips, 2002, xx) and, in so doing, render civil the characterization (as compliment or charge, depending on one's sensibilities) of the practice as a 'mind fuck,' psychoanalysis unfolds once all of one's energy has indeed been spent and the 'sex,' which is precisely what discovery, conquest, nurture, insight and/or resolution are in large part about, is essentially over and done with. At the end of the day, psychoanalysis is not a substitute for the act, sexual, healing, pedagogic or otherwise; nor is it simply that act's sublimation in speech.

Structured around the capacity to be alone, analysis has hardly anything to do with the busness and currency of a playful conquering of resistances, uncovering of truths, and/or remedying of deficits that will come to fill the requisite number of weekly appointments spent by the one in the supine position while the other sits up close behind—which is to say with all that is considered as everyday analytic fare—and everything to do with the ability, again quoting Winnicott, 'to exist for a time without being either a reaction to an external impingement or an active person with a direction of interest or movement' (1958, 34). As such, it is something to which the analyst will be privy intermittently at best, in the form of a metaphorical caress, sigh or wink, and for whose workings and effects only the analysand may truly claim credit, an analysis whose end, assuming one may still afford the term any relevance, is often a vanishing point that bears little resemblance to the drama and/or fanfare of what is commonly held up as a termination proper.

As an expression of the capacity to be alone, analytic solitude stands in stark contrast to the play theory of analysis as an eventful, energetic, engaged, and communicative *entre-deux* in which each of the parties gets to participate, albeit unequally and, more often than not, intermittently. For better and for worse, one rarely gets to choose among the paradigms or dictate their sequence: play engenders solitude; solitude sets the stage for play; meanwhile the one interrupts and derails the other. At the end of the day, and as yet another instance of *coincidentia*, this dynamic propels psychoanalysis beyond the bounds of a programmatic unity.

Notes

1 Beyond the objects that piqued Winnicott's earliest curiosity, recent investigations have explored the found status of such objects as smartphones, tablets and video games (Janssen, 2016; Leroux, 2016; Tisseron, 2017).

2 One may note in Lacan's formulation of his 'Other' an echo to Winnicott's elaborations on the found object and its topology. For Lacan, this 'Other' lies on the edge ('*à la lisière*') between self and other, as no more in the self than outside it and no more in the other than outside that either (Lacan, 1958, 6). For the record, as the president of the *Société française de psychanalyse* and the driving force behind its publications program, Lacan was instrumental in the translation and inclusion of Winnicott's seminal 'Transitional Objects' text in the 'Essais critiques' issue of the SFP's *La Psychanalyse* (Winnicott, 1959a). See Vanier and Vanier (2010) for more on the Lacan-Winnicott connection.

3 While Winnicott was tracking its history from nursery to culture and from psychology to civilization, another version of the found object was already crisscrossing the artistic landscape, from Dada to Surrealism to Pop Art, from John Cage to Karlheinz Stockhausen to Shawn Crahan and from Jeff Koons to Damien Hirst to Tracey Emin. As far as I can tell, a thorough Winnicottian assessment of these traversals has yet to be undertaken; in the meantime, Domenech Oneto's reflections in this regard (2017) are a worthy starting point.

4 I return to a discussion of the found object's supposed immunity to death in *Timings*.

5 Part symposium, part salon, part ritual, the Eranos Circle was founded in the early 1930s by Olga Fröbe-Kapteyn (1881-1962). To this day, it continues its research and conference activities into culture and spirituality through the lenses of, among others, comparative phenomenology, cultural anthropology and symbolic hermeneutics.

6 The examples from the everyday illustrating the phenomenon of inscription as production are all too familiar: a medical report, a title deed and a birth certificate do not simply register a fact; each produces an identity complete with its own history, privileges and limits.

7 On Freud's collecting and collections, see Gamwell (1989), Forrester (1994), Ucko (2001) and Burke (2006).

8 Dan Hicks' *The Brutish Museums* (2020) addresses the history of colonial violence and cultural dispossession perpetrated in the name of research and education and on behalf of the museums of western Europe.
9 The 'involuntary' seems to be growing in popularity at this point; a proposal to describe slavery as 'involuntary relocation' was presented to the Texas Board of Education in June 2022. The proposal was turned down. (Suliman, 2022)
10 France Culture (05.11.2020). "Restitutions d'œuvres au Bénin et au Sénégal: le Sénat donne son feu vert mais critique la méthode." https://www.francetvinfo.fr/culture/patrimoine/restitutions-d-oeuvres-au-benin-et-au-senegal-le-senat-donne-son-feu-vert-mais-critique-la-methode_4169521.html
    Le Monde (16.07.2020). "La France acte la restitution définitive d'objets d'art au Sénégal et au Bénin." https://www.lemonde.fr/afrique/article/2020/07/16/la-france-acte-la-restitution-definitive-d-objets-d-art-au-senegal-et-au-benin_6046342_3212.html
11 That said, many are the compelling arguments in favour of the view that Benjamin was not only familiar with the work done by our man in Vienna but also sharing in its principal sensibilities. Among these I note Stewart (2009), Ley Roff (2004), Kageura (2009), Nägele (1991), Weigel (1996) and Fraga-Levivier (2008).
12 See Ellenberger (1981) and Gay (1987).
13 A classic Winnicottian expression in the context of parenting, the good-enough unseats the exceptional and/or ideal as a sought-after standard: 'The good enough 'mother' (not necessarily the infant's own mother) is one who makes active adaptation to the infant's needs … that gradually lessens, according to the infant's growing ability to count for failure of adaptation and to tolerate the results of frustration' (Winnicott, 1971b). In making room for both care and frustration, the good-enough protects against the illusions of a parent's omniscience and a child's omnipotence.
14 The object that elicits an abrogation of omnipotence in the very moment it pleases is hardly likely to qualify as partner in a perfect and perfectly gratifying relationship. This conclusion stands *contra* the criticism levelled by Lacan when he dismissed Michael Balint's version of object-relations on the grounds that it 'conjoins to a need an object which satisfies it' and, conversely, on its insistence that 'an object is first and foremost an object of satisfaction' (Lacan, 1991, 209). Many Lacanians have since hastily expanded the aim of the same misguided broadside from Balint onto anyone and everyone connected with the object-relations orientation. Lacan's subsequent harsh over-generalizations in the vein of 'wise men's ideas about the perfect object-relationship are based on a rather uncertain conception and, when exposed, they reveal a mediocrity that hardly does credit to the profession' (Lacan, 2006, 203) have not helped matters much either.
15 This is the classic position Freud articulated in, among other texts, '"Civilized" Sexual Morality and Modern Mental Illness' (Freud, 1908) and, eventually, *Civilization and its Discontents* (Freud, 1930).
16 The qualification of stealing as a cultural rather than a criminal and hence, presumably, anti-cultural phenomenon fits well the younger Winnicott's unapologetic self-identification as a thief I discuss in *Rationals*.
17 Needless to say, such standards speak more to the priorities of the day than to the nature and/or purpose of therapy.
18 Illustrating a resistance to this environment, Stephen Heard's is a wistful account of an experiment conducted without an identifiable purpose in mind: 'You'd never get a grant to support such an experiment, and you'd never admit to your

supervisor, your colleagues, or your students that you were doing it. I allowed myself play once, though, and it worked out pretty well' (Heard 2015).

19 Philosophers have often wondered about this differentiation and some among them have gone so far as to question whether it may be nothing but the product of a self-serving delusion. Meanwhile, many scientists are confirmed in their belief that such is precisely the case. (Lab rat science anyone?) It is disconcerting that a far from negligible number of mental health professionals have summarily dismissed the work of the former as a distraction and instead sought in the empirical findings of the latter (re genes, neural networks, brain elasticities and the like) proof of the authority (read justification and efficacy) of their therapeutic procedures. The studies on neurophysiology and psychoanalysis that invoke the one presumably in order to justify and sustain the other continue their influence at a steady pace. (Solms, 1997; Solms and Turnbull, 2002; Talvitie and Ihanus, 2011; Fotopoulu et al, 2012; Cozolino, 2006; Brockman, 2002; Liss, 2006; Beutel, 2003; Hopkins, 2016; Spagnolo, 2018). See Galgut (2021) and Blass and Carmelli (2007) for some counterarguments.

20 Here, Winnicott was deploying a highly contested Kantian term. In the first of his three classic *Critiques* (Kant, 1999), Kant emphasized the difference between the thing in itself (the noumenon, outside of both space and time yet possessing significant causal powers) and its representation (the phenomenon, empirically external although dependent on human perception). Kant went on to distinguish among the representations those that are valid for all from those shaped by specific perspectives and sensibilities (Kant, 1999, A235/B294-A260/B315). It is this latter, potentially no less problematic, distinction that is most operative in Winnicott.

21 Winnicott's deployment of use goes against the foundations of two among the most influential currents in modern philosophy: first, the Kantian, in its resistance to properly distinguish in use the developmental from the moral (Stänicke et al, 2020; Johnson 2014); and, second, the Hegelian, in its insistence on understanding intersubjectivity as a subjugating recognition that eclipses mutuality (Benjamin, 1988; Corradi Fiumara, 2015) and hence, effectively, *coincidentia*.

22 The hate here is in the service of the one that hates and not, as is the case with hate in the counter-transference, a supposedly objective response meant to serve the target of hate (Winnicott 1947). For more on this, see Abou-Rihan (2008, 15-31).

References

Abou-Rihan, Fadi. 2008. *Deleuze and Guattari: A Psychoanalytic Itinerary*. London: Continuum.

Benjamin, Jessica. 1988. *The Bonds of Love: Psychoanalysis, Feminism and the Problem of Domination*. London: Virago.

Benjamin, Walter. 1940a. "On Some Motifs in Baudelaire." In *Benjamin, Walter Selected Writings, 4: 1938-1940*. Edited by Michael Jennings. Cambridge, Mass, London: Harvard University Press. Pp. 313–355.

Benjamin, Walter. 1940b. "On the Concept of History." In *Benjamin, Walter Selected Writings, 4: 1938-1940*. Edited by Michael Jennings. Cambridge, Mass, London: Harvard University Press. Pp. 389–400.

Benjamin, Walter. 1940c. "Paralipomena to 'On the Concept of History'." In *Benjamin, Walter Selected Writings, 4: 1938-1940*. Edited by Michael Jennings. Cambridge, Mass, London: Harvard University Press. Pp. 401–411.

Beutel, Manfred and Stern, Emily et al. 2003. "The Emerging Dialogue Between Psychoanalysis and Neuroscience: Neuroimaging Perspectives." In *Journal of the American Psychoanalytic Association*. 51:3. Pp. 773–801.

Blass, Rachel and Carmelli, Zvi. 2007. "The Case Against Neuropsychoanalysis. On Fallacies Underlying Psychoanalysis' Latest Scientific Trend and its Negative Impact on Psychoanalytic Discourse." In *International Journal of Psychoanalysis*. 88:1. Pp. 19–40.

Boardman, John. 2016. "Review of Britain and the Heritage of Empire, c. 1800–1940 ed. by Astrid Swenson and Peter Mandler." In *Common Knowledge*. 222. P. 326.

Boffey, Daniel. 2020. "Dutch museums vow to return art looted by colonialists." In *The Guardian*. 8 October 2020 https://www.theguardian.com/world/2020/oct/08/dutch-museums-vow-to-return-art-looted-by-colonialists?CMP=Share_iOSAPp_ Other Accessed: 15-08-2022.

Briet, Suzanne. 1951. *Qu'est ce que la documentation?* Paris: Editions documentaires industrielles et techniques.

Brockman, Richard. 2002. "Self, Object, Neurobiology." In *Neuropsychoanalysis: An Interdisciplinary Journal for Psychoanalysis and the Neurosciences*. 4:1. Pp. 87–99.

Burke, Janine. 2006. *The Sphinx on the Table: Sigmund Freud's Art Collection and the Development of Psychoanalysis*. New York: Walker Publishing Company.

Corradi Fiumara, Gemma. 2015. *Psychic Suffering: From Pain to Growth*. London: Karnac Books.

Cozolino, Louis. 2006. *The Neuroscience of Relationships*. New York: W. W. Norton.

Deleuze, Gilles and Guattari, Felix. 1977. *Anti-Oedipus*. Translated by Robert Hurley, Mark Seem, and Helen R. Lane with a preface by Michel Foucault. New York: Viking Press.

Domenech Oneto, Paul. 2017. "L'"Objet trouvé" or readymade and its implications: virtuality and transitionality." In *WRG Magazine* 14. https://wrongwrong.net/article/lobjet-trouve-or-readymade-and-its-implications-virtuality-and-transitionality Accessed: 15-08-2022.

Ellenberger, Henri. 1981. *The Discovery of the Unconscious*. New York: Basic Books.

Forrester, John. 1994. "'Mille e Tre': Freud and Collecting." In *The Cultures of Collecting*. Edited by John Elsner and Roger Cardinal. London: Reaktion Books. Pp. 224–251.

Fotopoulu, Aikaterini et al. 2012. *From the Couch to the Lab: Psychoanalysis, Neuroscience and Cognitive Psychology in Dialogue*. Oxford: Oxford University Press.

Fraga-Levivier, Ana Paula Vieira. 2008. "L'œuvre de construction. Une contribution de Walter Benjamin à la clinique." In *Cliniques Méditerranéennes* 1:77. Pp. 231–247.

Freud, Sigmund. 1900. *The Interpretation of Dreams. In The Complete Standard Edition of the Psychological Works of Sigmund Freud SE. IV-V*. London: Hogarth Press.

Freud, Sigmund. 1905. "Three Essays on the Theory of Sexuality." In *SE VII*. London: Hogarth Press. Pp. 125–243.

Freud, Sigmund. 1908. "'Civilized' Sexual Morality and Modern Mental Illness." In *SE IX*. London: Hogarth Press. Pp. 177–204.

Freud, Sigmund. 1915a. "The Unconscious." In *SE XIV*. London: Hogarth Press. Pp. 159–216.

Freud, Sigmund. 1915b. "Thoughts for the Times on War and Death." In *SE XIV*. London: Hogarth Press. Pp. 275–302.

Freud, Sigmund. 1919. "The Uncanny." In *SE XVII*. London: Hogarth Press. Pp. 217–256.

Freud, Sigmund. 1925. "Negation." In *SE XIX*. London: Hogarth Press. Pp. 233–239.

Freud, Sigmund. 1926. "The Question of Lay Analysis." In *SE XX*. London: Hogarth Press. Pp. 177–258.

Freud, Sigmund. 1927. "Fetishism." In *SE XXI*. London: Hogarth Press. Pp. 147–158.

Freud, Sigmund. 1930. "Civilization and its Discontents." In *SE XXI*. London: Hogarth Press. Pp. 59–145.

Freud, Sigmund. 1939. "Moses and Monotheism: Three Essays." In *SE XXIII*. London: Hogarth Press. Pp. 1–137.

Freud, Sigmund. 1940. "Splitting of the Ego in the Process of Defence." In *SE XXIII*. London: Hogarth Press. Pp. 275–278.

Freud, Sigmund. 1985. *The Complete Letters of Sigmund Freud to Wilhelm Fliess: 1887-1904*. Edited byJeffrey M. Masson. Cambridge: Harvard University Press.

Galgut, Elisa. 2021. "Against Neuropsychoanalysis: Why a Dialogue With Neuroscience Is Neither Necessary nor Sufficient for Psychoanalysis." *The Psychoanalytic Quarterly*. 108:3. Pp. 315–336.

Gamwell, Lynn and Wells, Richard. 1989. *Sigmund Freud and Art: His Personal Collection of Antiquities*. New York and London: SUNY Press/Freud Museum London.

Gay, Peter. 1987. *The Bourgeois Experience: Victoria to Freud Volume 2: The Tender Passion*. Oxford: Oxford University Press.

Heard, Stephen. 2015. "Creativity, Play, and Science." https://scientistseessquirrel.wordpress.com/2015/09/14/on-creativity-and-play-in-science/ Accessed: 15-08-2022.

Hicks, Dan. 2020. *The Brutish Museums: The Benin Bronzes, Colonial Violence and Cultural Restitution*. London: Pluto Press.

Hopkins, Jim. 2016. "Free Energy and Virtual Reality in Neuroscience and Psychoanalysis: A Complexity Theory of Dreaming and Mental Disorder." In *Frontiers in Psychology*. 7:922. https://www.frontiersin.org/articles/10.3389/fpsyg.2016.00922/full Accessed: 15-08-2022.

Huizinga, Johan. 1995. *Homo Ludens: A Study of the Play Element in Culture*. Boston: Beacon Press.

Janssen, Christophe. 2016. "L'objet transitionnel dans un contexte de fragilisation des liens." In *Les nouveaux objets transitionnels*. Edited by Daniel Marcelli and Anne Lanchon. Toulouse: Éditions érès. Pp. 53–70.

Johnson, Barbara. 2014. "Using People: Kant with Winnicott." In *The Barbara Johnson Reader: The Surprise of Otherness*. Edited by Melissa Feuerstein et al. Durham and London: Duke University Press. Pp. 262–74.

Kageura, Ryohei. 2009. "Walter Benjamin and Psychoanalysis: On Dream and Revolution in Benjamin." In *Journal of Social and Psychological Studies*. 2:1. Pp. 6–23.

Kant, Immanuel. 1999. *Critique of Pure Reason*. Translated by Paul Guyer and Allen W. Wood. Cambridge: Cambridge University Press.

Lacan, Jacques. 1958. "Séminaire du mercredi 9 Avril 1958." https://ecole-lacanienne.net/wp-content/uploads/2016/04/1958.04.09.pdf Accessed: 15-08-2022.

Lacan, Jacques. 1991. *Freud's Papers on Technique. The Seminar of Jacques Lacan, Book 1.* Edited by Jacques-Alain Miller and translated by John Forrester. New York: W. W. Norton & Company.

Lacan, Jacques. 2006. "The Function and Field of Speech and Language in Psychoanalysis." In *Ecrits*. Edited by Jacques Lacan Translated byBruce Fink in collaboration with Héloïse Fink and Russell Grigg. New York: W. W. Norton & Company. Pp. 197–268.

Leroux, Yann. 2016. "Les jeux vidéo et l'experience transitionnelle." In *Les nouveaux objets transitionnels*. Edited by Daniel Marcelli and Anne Lanchon. Toulouse: Éditions érès. Pp. 89–104.

Ley Roff, Sarah. 2004. "Benjamin and Psychoanalysis." In *The Cambridge Companion to Walter Benjamin*. Edited by David Ferris. Cambridge: Cambridge University Press. Pp. 115–133.

Liss, Jerome. 2006. "Psychoanalysis and Neurophysiology." In *Ricerca Psicanalitica*. 17:3. Pp. 295–314.

Nägele, Rainer. 1991. *Theatre, Theory, Speculation*. Baltimore: Johns Hopkins University Press.

Phillips, Adam. 2002. "Introduction." In *Wild Analysis*. Edited by Sigmund Freud. London & New York: Penguin Books. Pp. xii–xxv.

Scholem, Gershom. 1976. *On Jews and Judaism in Crisis*. New York: Schocken Books.

Solms, Mark. 1997. *The Neuropsychology of Dreams*. New York and London: Psychology Press.

Solms, Mark and Turnbull, Oliver 2002. *The Brain and the Inner World*. New York: Other Books.

Spagnolo, Rosa (ed.). 2018. *Building Bridges: The Impact of Neuropsychoanalysis on Psychoanalytic Clinical Sessions*. London: Routledge.

Stänicke, Erik et al. 2020. "The Epistemological Stance of Psychoanalysis: Revisiting the Kantian Legacy." In *The Psychoanalytic Quarterly*. 89:2, Pp. 281–304.

Stewart, Elizabeth. 2009. *Catastrophe and Survival: Walter Benjamin and Psychoanalysis*. London: Bloomsbury.

Suliman, Adela. 2022. "Texas education board rejects proposal to call slavery 'involuntary relocation'" In *The Washington Post*. July 1, 2022. https://www.washingtonpost.com/nation/2022/07/01/texas-board-education-slavery-involuntary-relocation/ Accessed: 15-08-22.

Talvitie, V. and Ihanus, J. 2011. "On neuropsychoanalytic metaphysics." In *The International Journal of Psychoanalysis*. 92. Pp. 1583–1601.

Tisseron, Serge. 2017. *Médiations numériques et robotiques en psychothérapie*. Paris: Dunod.

Ucko, Peter. 2001. "Unprovenanced Material Culture and Freud's Collection of Antiquities." In *Journal of Material Culture*. 6:3. Pp. 269–322.

Vanier, Catherine and Vanier, Alain. 2010. *Winnicott avec Lacan*. Paris: Herman.

Wasserstrom, Steven. 1999. Religion after Religion.Princeton NJ: Princeton University Press.

Weigel, Sigrid. 1996. *Body-and Image-Space: Re-Reading Walter Benjamin*. London and New York: Routledge Books.

Winnicott, Donald W. 1947. "Hate in the Contertransference." In *Through Paediatrics to Psycho-Analysis: Collected Papers*. New York: Basic Books. Pp. 194–203.

Winnicott, Donald W. 1956. "On Transference." In *Essential Papers on Transference*. Edited by Aaron Esman. New York: New York University Press. Pp. 246–251.

Winnicott, Donald W. 1958. "The Capacity to Be Alone." In *The Maturational Processes and the Facilitating Environment*. London: Hogarth Press and The Institute of Psycho-Analysis. Pp. 29–36.

Winnicott, Donald W. 1959a. "Objet transitionnel et phénomènes transitionnels, étude de la première 'Not-me possession.'" In *La Psychanalyse*, N°5. Paris: Presses Universitaires de France. Pp. 89–97.

Winnicott, Donald W. 1959b. "The Fate of the Transitional Object." In *Psycho-Analytic Explorations*. Edited by Claire Winnicott et al. London and New York: Routledge. Pp. 53–58.

Winnicott, Donald W. 1960. "The Theory of The Parent-Infant Relationship." In *The Maturational Process and the Facilitating Environment*. London: Hogarth Press and The Institute of Psycho-Analysis. Pp. 37–55.

Winnicott, Donald W. 1967. "Playing: A Theoretical Statement." In *Playing and Reality*. London and New York: Routledge Books. Pp. 38–52.

Winnicott, Donald W. 1969. "The Use of an Object and Relating Through Identification." In *Playing and Reality*. London and New York: Routledge Books. Pp. 86–94.

Winnicott, Donald W. 1971a. *Playing and Reality*. London and New York: Routledge Books.

Winnicott, Donald W. 1971b. "Transitional Objects and Transitional Phenomena." In *Playing and Reality*. London and New York: Routledge Books. Pp. 1–25.

Winnicott, Donald W. 1971c. "Playing: Creative Activity and the Search for the Self." In *Playing and Reality*. London and New York: Routledge Books. Pp. 53–64.

Chapter 3

Series

Constructions

Joyce McDougall once recalled Winnicott declaring: 'Now you know that when you give a small child a pencil and paper, what does he do? He delights in stabbing the paper, making holes in it everywhere; everything that follows after that is sublimation.'[1] I understand Winnicott's declaration as signalling in the child's gesture a moment of appropriation as well as of destruction. With the stab, the child establishes the resilience of paper and pencil as best she knows; she marks both as objects she has found, belonging to her territory, to do with as she pleases. She may stab, crumple, smooth out, draw upon or tear the paper; she may draw with, suck on, toss, and/or retrieve the pencil—and do so repeatedly, in the manner reminiscent of the *fort da* (Freud, 1920, 14–5). Paper and pencil are neither discovered nor observed; they are suffused with the illusory vitality that transforms them from mere objects into the critical components of play of which creativity, aggression and, lest we forget, delight are principal aspects.

Considering finding's reciprocity, the found object is not simply woven into its finder's inner world; it produces an entirely new environment of its own; it builds it and tells its story. And so, as she manipulates paper and pencil, the child enters a world of lines, sounds and textures, of the responses of those around her as well as of the physical sensations she herself is now experiencing, a world to which she now belongs. In this respect, the found object is very similar in both style and function to the construction Freud discussed at the end of his career. In a text thoroughly imbued with the logic of mutually exclusive opposites[2] (Freud, 1937b), Freud distinguished a 'single' interpretation—as a correspondence between one element of the clinical material and a specific meaning—from an 'extensive' construction which promotes a scaffolding, if you will, upon which a host of meanings may hang (261). A construction arranges various one-to-one correspondences into relations of affect, priority and consequence and invests them with the potential to generate even further correspondences. Part of an order higher than that of interpretation, construction mirrors the found object's function as an

DOI: 10.4324/9781003352488-3

in-between that crosses the divide between inner and outer realities. It transforms an individual's world from a constellation of seemingly chaotic drives, objects and fantasies into an external event—often initially encountered through speech—with a conscious, graspable and shareable meaning capable of reconfiguring its psychic and material underpinnings. Construction not only opens one reality up to another, it reconfigures both. That it is a product of the psyche does not diminish its impact on the outside world; 'constructed' as it may be, it is never a delusion whose itinerary and effects are confined to the mind. Though self-evident, the validity of this last statement is all too often lost in the rigamarole of convenient polarities such as truth and falsehood, perception and fantasy.

Freud's distinction between interpretation and construction with regard to definition and agency is not without its difficulties. At this point, I offer two of the more obvious ones. First, and in hindsight, when Freud identified secondary revision as an initial 'interpretation' of a dream's imagery (Freud, 1900, 490) whose purpose is to 'establish order in material of that kind, to set up relations in it and to make it conform to our expectations of an intelligible whole' (499),[3] he was far from identifying a strict one-to-one correspondence between image and meaning; instead, he was describing the construction of a complex though seemingly unified psychological setting. Nevertheless, to have recognized a constructive quality to the dream work only to qualify it as distortion and censorship—since this, after all, is precisely what secondary revision is—ascribes a falsity to construction that Freud, as we shall soon see, was loath to declare. Second, that construction is a dimension to dream work undermines the classic Freudian division of labour between, on the one hand, the analysand's main responsibility for uncovering a repressed though crucial past and, on the other, the analyst's task 'to make out what has been forgotten from the traces which it has left behind or, more correctly, to *construct* it' (Freud, 1937b, 258–59, emphasis in the original). As the analyst constructs what has been forgotten, the analysand, it seems, may only remember. We have since come to appreciate how such a division of labour is itself a most tenuous construction that sustains a myth of analytic expertise and impartiality as it distracts from a subtler and less convenient scenario whereby the analyst claims command of a knowledge—memorable and memorizable, some of which conscious and much often significantly less so[4]—upon which the analysand draws while, in turn, the latter frequently operates as the principal agent of construction—in waking life as well as in dreams.

Such concerns notwithstanding, construction promotes a crossing of the border between inside and outside, the same crossing which, according to Winnicott, amplifies the found object's ability to advance the subject from solipsism to object relationship. Construction is also akin to the familiar thievery of the 'this and that' and the 'here and there' of associations, affects and enactments, not to mention previous constructions, organized onto a structure potentially available for further thievery. It should come as no surprise then that, as it harnesses the achievements of previous efforts and is hence hardly a point of origin, construction is 'always a preliminary labour' (Freud, 1937b, 260) and thus equally hardly a final destination. The emerging picture here is of a series of interconnected constructions—clinical, meta-psychological, and/or experiential—each deploying the effects of its preceding or, if I may be allowed the term, neighbouring[5] constructions in the service of further labour. A construction's status as an in-between, this time in relation to other constructions, is thus re-confirmed.

As is the case with the found object which operates within an intermediate area of experience that ought never be subjected to the demands of reality-testing (Winnicott, 1971, 13), construction is but a conjecture for which no scientific authority is claimed; it may be judged as to its accuracy only in hindsight and, once so judged, it ceases to be a construction and becomes a since verified or falsified hypothesis. Freud further confirmed that truth is inapposite in this context when he acknowledged that he did not require direct agreement from his patient; nor did he argue with that patient if they denied a construction's validity. Instead, Freud advised the clinician to follow the model of 'a familiar figure in one of Nestroy's farces—the manservant who has a single answer on his lips to every question or objection: "It will all become knowledge clear in the course of future developments"' (Freud, 1937b, 265).

Freud's willingness to accommodate uncertainty and his ability to essentially submit, even if but for a moment, to the possibly endless deferral of truth are invaluable, all the more so considering his declaration, only a few lines further down the same page, of his steadfast commitment to the principle of psychoanalysis as the reclaiming of lost memories and incidents: 'The path that starts from the analyst's construction ought to end in the patient's re-collection' (265). Ever concerned with the factual truth of his analytic utterances as well as with the task of psychoanalysis as the filling of historical lacunae, Freud reiterated his judgement thus: 'construction is only effective because it recovers a fragment of lost experience' (268). Alongside the contemporaneous and significantly less self-assured 'Analysis Terminable and Interminable' (Freud, 1937a), Freud's avowal and clarity of purpose here illustrate a thought deeply shaped by complementary antonyms in matters of both concept and process. At this point, I cannot but wonder as to the extent to which the troubling split Freud devoted the text he wrote shortly thereafter (Freud, 1940) pertains not only to the inability of a child's ego to recognize its mother's lack of a penis but also to a style of psychoanalyzing incapable of coming to terms with its findings' lack of truth and finality.

Evocative as they may be of one another, construction and found object seem to occupy significantly different positions in the thoughts of their originators. While the opposition between interpretation and construction is central to 'Constructions in Analysis,' at stake in that text is the equally crucial ground upon which the opposition is built—namely, the clinical valuation of a truth uncovered over the means of its uncovering, of the original (as *arche*[6]) over the provisional, of fact (be it psychic or material) over fiction. It is in terms of this valuation that Freud distinguished himself from the archaeologist for whom, he believed, construction was 'the aim and end of his endeavours,' all the while insisting that, for the analyst, construction is only in the service of a recovery of history on the road to health (Freud, 1937b, 260). For Winnicott, meanwhile, it is precisely the found object and its attendant categories of transitionality and play, of means rather than ends (or sources and origins, for that matter), of all that is comforting yet exciting, precarious yet reliable, actual yet magical that lays the ground for psychoanalysis as a 'form of playing in the service of communication with oneself and others' (Winnicott, 1967, 41). Truth thus opens onto an experience as the *arche* pursued no longer points to genealogy but to a playing.[7]

Series Producing

At this point, I allow myself a conjecture and a thievery à la Winnicott in the hope of elaborating further on what construction may contribute to an analysand's so-called recovery. I want to juxtapose construction and found object with a perspective that, much like Winnicott's, promotes process over product. Hardly ever agreeable no matter the circumstances, thievery involves a border crossing as it retrieves an object from its original and supposedly rightful habitat and places it somewhere where it does not belong. It should therefore come as no surprise that the perspective I have in mind has tended to be all too easily, though I believe erroneously, judged—no less by many of its advocates than by its detractors—so anti-psychoanalytic as to be thoroughly unwelcome, and unwelcoming, of any consideration within contexts such as the present one.

Released in the early 1970s, Gilles Deleuze and Félix Guattari's *Anti-Oedipus* was deemed a *tour de force* by some and an embarrassment by others. Deleuze and Guattari took Freud at his word and in the strictest of senses as they deployed the theory of a *dynamic* unconscious in order to show that production rather than representation is the fundament of human existence. They distilled reality, both psychic and material, to its most elemental components and uncovered a 'universal primary production' (Deleuze and Guattari, 1977, 5) that animates a complex network of producing, recording and consuming machines. Thus, instead of a stage upon which a pre-scripted Oedipal drama is re-enacted in all its glory, the unconscious is a factory 'at work everywhere, functioning smoothly at times, at other times in fits and starts … . What a mistake to have ever said *the* id. Everywhere *it* is machines—real ones, not figurative ones … with all the necessary couplings and connections' (3, emphasis in the original).

Deleuze and Guattari's view of production as the grounding of what it is to be human—*their* version of the *arche*—is no more abstract or all-encompassing than, say, Winnicott's promotion of playing as universal or, for that matter, Freud's designation of the human in terms of one dramatic couplet (incest and parricide) or a seemingly more benign other (love and work). Neither is Deleuze and Guattari's point of view any less meta-psychologically compelling or experientially viable than the other two. Seen through the lens of primary production, desire does not simply elicit a fantasy (in the form of a dream, a hallucination or a symptom) of a lost object—the object it strives to consume. Desire produces a flow (as object, relationship and/or dynamic) that far surpasses the meta-psychological and clinical dimensions of lack. Take, for instance, the child's stabbing of paper with pencil. This stabbing reveals not only aggression and play but also the attempt to set into motion an assemblage of machines in the guise of seemingly inert objects (paper, pencil), body parts (fingers, hands, eyes, ears, mouth) and intensities (destroying, manipulating, playing) whose effects (squiggles, holes, thumps, squeals) may not be as scriptable or summarily discountable as the categories of sublimation or displacement might suggest. What we have instead is a production governed by three syntheses, as Deleuze and Guattari called them: (1) a connection that extends the series (paper and pencil and hand and mouth and ear and …); (2) a disjunction that, for every element in the series, multiplies the scenarios in the direction of which it may unfold (drawing or stabbing or crumpling or tossing or sucking or crying or laughing or …); and (3) a conjunction that gathers all that preceded it and imbues it with an 'always preliminary' function, construction or subjectivity, often recognizable as insight or revelation (so that's what it is—an aggression, an enactment, a game, an annoyance; so that's who I am—a player, a scribbler, a noise-maker).

These three syntheses of production recapitulate the principal mechanisms of displacement (metonymy), condensation (metaphor) and secondary revision (construction) Freud (and Lacan) identified as the mechanisms by which unsettling primary wishes are distorted so that they may be represented anew in palatable forms (Freud, 1900, 339–508; Lacan, 2006). However, these syntheses exceed their Freudian and Lacanian antecedents insofar as they reveal dreams, parapraxes and symptoms as no simple distortions but as the means by which new sounds, images and objects are produced; they are proofs not only of the fact of the unconscious but of its complex inner productions—of its dynamism. These syntheses echo the agile passages and relays mounted by the found object, be it between self and other or nursery and culture. Much like the machine which produces a flow that gets intercepted and incorporated into another's production, the weaving of subject and found object is forever deployed in the service of further illusion and creativity.

This continuous dynamic is the reason why the Deleuzo–Guattarian syntheses assert as little a claim to truth as do Freudian constructions and

Winnicottian found objects.[8] Seen through their lens, desire is extra-ordinarily fluid; its code pays little heed to finality or truth. What the syntheses prioritize instead are the connections between the machines, the disjunctions they make possible and the conjunctions to which they may lead—all, again, in the service of further relays and productions. In this context, the analytic cure ceases to revolve around the integration of a truth or the attainment of a compromise between conflicting priorities. Rather, the cure is defined in terms of an agility that helps navigate an expanding network of relays, of a production fostered, multiplied, a production that, as Guattari later put it, yields 'a boost of virtuosity, like a pianist, for certain difficulties,' generating 'more freedom, more humor, more willingness to jump from one scale of reference to another' (Guattari, 1995, 14).[9]

Just as much as the Winnicottian found object is far from inert, the process Deleuze and Guattari identified is hardly of a traffic in the inanimate and consumable. At stake here is the production of an entire schema of production, recording and consumption, a production of needs and de-mands, of exchanges and circulations—a production of production, of, in sum, a construction that not only crosses the boundary between hallucina-tion and reality but also between the individual and the collective, the psychic and the ideological. This production of production sustains Deleuze and Guattari's contribution to the ongoing analysis of the relationship be-tween discourse and reality. No matter the source (psychological, familial, legal, scientific), a theory of desire, normalcy or health is never a reflection and always a production and a manipulation of what it intends to elucidate. Broadly speaking, the discourses on infantile sexuality (whether aberrant or banal) and gender identity (whether biological, cultural or a manifestation of some yet-to-be-verified combination thereof) are among the most familiar illustrations of this production. The more specifically psychoanalytic de-ployment of this understanding exposes the Oedipal edifice as hardly the timeless immutable structure in which the subject may seek refuge or forever be doomed to misfortune. On the contrary, Oedipus is as much a directive as an observation, as much the effect of a practice (social, political, clinical)—its product—as it is its premise.

Amplifying this perspective beyond the confines of Oedipus, an account, any account, may emerge as reaching past the province of descriptions and ex-planations, as a theory may be shaped by its own psychological discovery—in the form of an instantiation, an endorsement and, more compellingly at times, an injunction in favour of that discovery. This is why the undisciplined text of *Anti-Oedipus* where Deleuze and Guattari first elaborated their 'machinic' un-conscious is best understood as the enactment of a process and a structure, as the voice of less an attempt at a restrained 'clinical' observation and more a conjoining of an observing perspective with its point of concern. Rather than a critique of the Freudian-Lacanian edifice, *Anti-Oedipus* is the 'becoming-unconscious' of psychoanalysis—the communication of analytic principles and techniques reworked according to the productive dynamics attributed to the unconscious. (Abou-Rihan, 2008, 36–40). Seen in this light, Winnicott's playfulness—theoretical and textual—is best appreciated as more than a reasoned strategy or a personal leaning, or, better still, as both a strategy and a leaning that have been coloured by the playfulness they describe. Winnicott's is a communication that carries within its logic an instantiation of and empathy with its object.

Clinically, the flow of words, slips and sounds, of queries, interpretations and silences is the effect of processes of association and construction at work in the intervener (be it the analyst or the analysand). This flow is experienced by both parties as a construction that has gathered whatever components are at hand, insinuated itself into the series of associations and exerted its own ability to reconfigure, invest, derail, produce and/or inhibit further associations. Much like the analyst, the analysand listens to and is often transported by their own words and corresponding worlds into a fresh memory ('I just remembered …'), a useful hypothesis ('I wonder if …'), a new insight ('I can see how …') or a sharp detour ('It just struck me that …'). As intervening is no mere uncovering of a meaning or a desire, associating is no simple enumeration or reporting. Each utterance is a machine that reconfigures the machines and series that preceded it; it invests them with new meanings and propels them in different directions, helps them produce further associations or altogether stifles them. Within a particular series, each association points to a construction that is always a reconstruction, situated between two machines, one a presumed origin and the other a hoped-for destination, an animated and animating measure tracing a complex multistationed path between hallucination and fact.

Obviously, there is much that remains to be said about this seemingly though rarely tidy cycle of associations, constructions and syntheses as it unfolds within and between each of the two analytic partners. For the time being, I offer two clinical vignettes in order to illustrate some of the ways in which constructions can be intimately connected to an analysand's sense of self and of the analysis in which they are engaged—in other words, some of the ways in which constructions are produced, deployed and lived as found objects and as syntheses.

Series Touching

Halfway through the third year of her treatment, Helen was beginning to disengage from a long-standing logic of opposites she always felt as heavy and stifling. Since her early teens (she is now in her mid-forties), she had lived a determined, responsible and measured 'public self' that harnessed most of her resources in the service of, on the one hand, a successful career as a family physician and, on the other, more crucial, hand, a protective shield for a reclusive and vulnerable 'private self' tormented by overwhelming confusions, fears and compulsions. Along with the compartmentalization of public and private, Helen separated much of what she faced into various sets of dual realms consistently at odds with one another: action versus emotion, professionalism versus vulnerability, efficiency versus pleasure.

Shortly after beginning her analysis, Helen contemplated the possibility of occupying the position of 'patient' in relation to me as her 'doctor.' Though she found that possibility somewhat reassuring insofar as it held the promise of relief from her difficulties, she effectively rejected it as undermining her sense of herself as the physician; in her world, there is only room for one such character in any given relationship; to ascribe that character to someone other than herself—in this case, me, who, at this early stage in our work, was unverified as to both character and abilities—would risk her forsaking her public self and loosening her hold on the private self she so desperately needs to monitor and protect. Not surprisingly, my suggestion that, together, she and I could engage in a process in which neither assumes the authority of an expert and both are, as it were, explorers—my suggestion, in other words, that she and I could be actively, albeit differently, responsible for the work—she declared thoroughly inadmissible.

And so, for the first two years, much of the material Helen brought into the sessions revolved around her conflict as to which of her two 'selves' was 'healthier' and more 'valuable' and which was more in need of a 'clinical intervention.' Considering how she had constructed her dilemma and how she was experiencing herself through it, Helen was mainly interested in exploring the underlying causes of the difficulties borne by her private self, in the manner of a surgeon who, ideally, would perform a clearly established and well-proven therapeutic procedure that would excise any and all pathology. She frequently reported on such difficulties as if she were presenting at a case conference and would seem to solicit my advice as she would that of a colleague with whom she was consulting; evidently, it was safe enough for her to engage with me only when twice removed from her material.

Frustrating as she found it, I chose to abstain from privileging either of Helen's so-called selves. My resistance both to colluding with her rationalizing defences and to forcibly accelerating a full disclosure of her affects, to, in other words, endorsing one or the other of the constructions she had elaborated, was the rudiment of my analytic presence with her. Instead of intervention, it was presence I thought best to provide. Or, rather, I chose presence as my major intervention. With this presence as background, Helen's persevering nature and sense of responsibility, her (loath as she might have been to admit it) compliance with the professional and authoritative weight she had already invested in that presence, led her to assume the task of securing the frame of the analysis as she welcomed the higher frequency of our sessions, the use of the couch and my encouragement that she not censor herself and speak whatever came to mind.

That her professional public self gradually became the very precondition and means for accessing whatever of her private self ailed her, that, in other words, her mutually disjunctive synthesis gave way to a connective dynamic, did not correspond in Helen to the simple assumption of the previously rejected position of patient; an altogether subtler construction, and its attendant components, began to unfold. One day, she told me about the 'strange and unique' dream she had had the night before. She had lain in bed after a long day at work, closed her eyes and begun to see herself in a field awash with grey—nebulous yet unthreatening. On one side of the field, she discovered 'action,' and on the other, 'emotion'—the most recent iteration of the two selves she had constructed and carried within her for much of her adult life. She reported that both selves were so close she could 'touch' them. Sandwiched between the acting 'doctor' and the feeling 'patient,' she became the 'observer,' she interpreted. After a brief pause, she told me that she felt excited about this newfound 'intermediary' zone and yet was a bit apprehensive about now having to manage and care for three selves instead of two—'as if, to begin with, there was anything simple about that,' she quipped, her voice conveying worry and enthusiasm, exasperation and humour. I asked her to say more and she responded by describing how calming the field of grey was to her; it allowed her to look around with curiosity, to not be carried away by the pressures of either doing or feeling, which she associates with other colours. 'I wonder if you feel you can be more patient when you're the observer,' I commented. 'I feel like I can move closer or farther away. It's about scale now; from afar it all looks very small; up close and it's the size it actually is.' I understood this as Helen assuming for herself a measure of control over how near she will be willing to get to her material at any given moment. This control, in turn, spoke to the measure of her ability to protect herself against the likelihood that whatever material she was approaching might prove overwhelming. Helen was now following an analytic pace that was neither programmatic nor erratic; she was more patient with herself as a patient yet less predictable, less urgent.

Another pause produced Helen's association to the idea of a 'virtual space,' which she had come across during her days in medical school. This, she explained, is the space between an organ and its outer lining, a space typically so infinitesimally small that it is often merely hypothesized, a space that becomes actualized and detectable in the case of, say, a pathology that comes to fill it. 'You sound like you see yourself as the pathology,' I said. 'More like a growth,' she corrected, 'and now I can touch the two sides of me,' emphasizing yet again the tactility she had introduced at the beginning of the session. To my ears, Helen's voice at this point carried with it both a hint of relief at having finally reached a less rigid and more comfortable position, as well as some excitement as to what that position might eventually afford her.

Helen's construction of herself was no longer governed solely by such mutually exclusive disjunctions as public/private, doctor/patient, action/emotion. In refiguring her polarities as inclusive, she was undoing the rigidity of the two-count logic her syntheses had suffered; she was gaining access to the observer dimension she had not previously explored and was beginning to assume responsibility for herself as, simultaneously, healing doctor, suffering patient and touching observer. In so doing, she was opening onto the possibility of further 'growth,' eventually and otherwise; her ability to count to three extended the syntheses further still, beyond any triangular limits, toward incorporating additional connections and/or disjunctions. In sum, Helen's touching conjunction ushered a qualitative change that, first, reconfigured the elements of her previous polarities as amongst her various possibilities rather than the components of her ineluctable fate and, second, afforded her a mobility she could use to modulate her emotional responses to her material.

No doubt, Helen's proliferation of selves and positions manifestly excluded me as her analyst as it instituted, yet again, both her independence as a competent and pragmatic healer as well as her isolation as a private, even secretive, sufferer. As with old found objects, constructions get decathected; they rarely ever die. Nevertheless, the emergence of her 'observer' self served not only a defensive manoeuvre against the dangers of proximity and the telltale signs of a production gone awry, but also the signal of a decathexis of the found object that I had become at that particular stage in the analysis and a reorganization of the syntheses in the service of new relays and possibilities. Helen's process, its materials and mutations, what she spoke, sorted, utilized or discarded, what made it possible for her to 'touch' herself without either a demand for approval or a request for guidance, took place in the context of the analytic relationship. Her touching herself and experiencing a modicum of excitement, if not, indeed, pleasure, in both the touching and its display, was something that she, as far as I could tell, had not previously been able to accomplish. She was finding herself as someone more than either a reasoned healer or a private sufferer; she was making room for a touching, touched, pleasuring, pleasurable, observing, not to mention exhibiting, self upon which much of the next stage in her experience, analytic and otherwise, would hinge.

Series Sliding

Mat, a graphic artist in his early thirties, offers another illustration of the process of constructions unfolding and reproducing in the course of analytic work, though in this particular context at a much faster pace and in the span of a single session. The setting, here, is from the first year of our work, when Mat found himself in the midst of a difficult struggle with experiences of proximity and rejection.

Mat began the session with the announcement that a dental emergency would require the kind of medical attention that could drain his limited finances and undermine his ability to pay for his treatment. As I silently wondered about the announcement that his mouth was effectively out of analytic commission, Mat wondered aloud about whether I would accommodate his situation with a sliding-scale fee schedule, even if only temporarily. (Evidently, analyst and analysand are not always on the same page.) At the beginning of our work, Mat and I had addressed some of our options in the event of his analysis becoming vulnerable to a change in his already precarious fortunes. In my attempt to explore with him how best to deal with the situation, I revisited a question I had raised during one of our earliest sessions—the question as to why, considering his limited means, he would opt for an analysis with a clinician who was not covered by the government-run health insurance plan.[10] In his response, Mat offered a series of explanations, each a construction that spoke a layer or an aspect of his fantasy regarding himself and his work with me.

The first of these constructions—or, more accurately, the second, since, by his request, Mat had already constructed himself as someone who, among other things, was in some justifiable need of assistance—hinged on three seemingly distinct factors: (1) though in effect 'free of charge' to the patient, the practices of MD psychoanalysts are typically associated with long waiting lists; (2) Mat is wary of analysts with medical training as he had previously had a couple of unhelpful encounters with members of their ranks—he had felt with them as if he were nothing but a 'wound' to be expediently cleaned and sutured; (3) understanding psychoanalysis as a relationship between two individuals, Mat not only did not want his suffering to be reduced to either a malady or an accident but wanted to engage and be engaged in a more thorough, subtler and ultimately more enduring process than any other type of therapy might allow. His impression of what I could offer, from the information he had gathered about me prior to our sessions as well as from our earliest encounters, confirmed for him that I, unlike my medically trained peers, would be an appropriate companion in such an endeavour. In sum, Mat not only chose me, he found me.

As the session progressed, I kept quiet and Mat took time to ponder the situation. After a pause, his pride, as a delayed response to the humiliation likely triggered by his request for financial assistance, was activated; that same pride was then deployed as a hook for his next construction. With much conviction, he declared that he was a 'full and independent' human being, that, while he may suffer certain weaknesses, he possesses strengths that make him quite capable of handling the practicalities of life, of taking care of his needs and of procuring for himself whatever services he may require, 'thank you very much!' No sooner had he finished speaking than he acknowledged being struck, and doubly so, by the dubiousness of his declaration; it rang suspiciously 'libertarian' to his left-leaning political ear.

Moreover, it ran counter to his request for my help in, manifestly at least, alleviating the genuine strain on his finances: 'If I'm that independent, I wouldn't be asking for your help, would I?'

With this ostensibly rhetorical question, Mat was not only recognizing his dependence, he was also asking me to validate it for him and, in a more subdued, though to my mind at least, more crucial sense, to help him refute it in the hope of quieting his wounded pride. His question was not a query but a demand that I engage in an internal struggle that had less to do with fees and finances and more with autonomy and relationship, a struggle from which it seemed no party could emerge unscathed, let alone victorious. As I maintained my quiet, Mat moved on to his next construction. He told me that his payments to me confirm a 'business' aspect to our relationship and to whom and to what each of us is within it. The payments, he explained, mitigate any possible claim, manifestly on my part but implicitly by either of us, that the work we were undertaking could be filed under the category of 'help,' a category that, for Mat at least, is much too 'Christian,' and hence much too familiar, for his liking. Insofar as they are in exchange for my services, his payments underscore my own practical, and thus undeniable, investments and interests. 'The helper must derive some sort of return; otherwise, the help doesn't make any sense,' he said.

With this latest construction, Mat's confidence began to make way for a disquieting indignation. His reference to the familiarity of religion led him to the memory of an encounter with a cleric with 'clinical aspirations' when he was in his early twenties, roughly a decade earlier. At the time, he had been feeling particularly isolated, distressed and short on resources; the cleric's offer to lend support and understanding—without any financial compensation—was more than welcome. The support eventually paved the way for a friendship and, during a weekend stay at a retreat, culminated in what Mat now describes as a 'sad and all-too-predictable scene'; he had allowed himself to be enticed into joining this man of faith in bed, although, soon after the caresses had begun, he put an abrupt but firm end to the entire episode. At this point in the session, Mat was again struck by what he had just said; he took a moment to tell me that he found his compliance with the cleric's advances 'curious' and assured me that he would be quite willing to explore what it might mean for his sense of himself as a heterosexual man later in the analysis. For now, what was pressing for him was his need to let me know that he would accept nothing I might offer in the spirit of 'help' or 'generosity;' our relationship was to remain an exchange between two equals.

In response to this series of constructions built upon associations, requests, avowals, injuries, memories, fears and denials, I proffered one of the hypotheses I was beginning to formulate. I suggested to Mat that he wanted to put me in my place as someone who is paid for services rendered and he in his as a consumer of said services, that he wanted us to relate to one another in a more meaningful way than that of a 'business' exchange but feared that his wish carried with it the threat of a betrayal that might be as rife with pleasure as with danger. By this time, our session had come to its end and, as he was getting ready to leave, he turned to me with a smile and responded: 'Sure! But I still want you to slide as low as you can.' The analysis continued, and so, needless to say, did its seductions.

Constructions Revisited

As the analysand associates, the analyst listens not only to what is being said but also to the manner in which it is delivered, the associations it triggers, the detours it generates, the gaps it bridges—essentially, to the analysand's deliberate though by no means always conscious constructions of a life the analyst will re-construct in an ever preliminary way for him- or herself, for the analysand, the colleague, the audience and/or the reader, all in light of what has already been heard, felt, thought, repressed and/or constructed.

The first implication here—essentially a corroboration and variation on some of what Freud has already advanced—is that a construction need not be an accurate observation, a comprehensive summary or a coherent abstraction in order for it to be useful or justifiable. At its best, a construction is generative; it infuses whatever material may have preceded it with the possibility of new meanings and propels that material in unfamiliar directions; subsequently incorporated into that very same material, it will itself be redefined and redirected by future constructions. This is the logic followed by Helen's newly minted tripartite assemblage. What is of analytic import here is neither an accurate depiction of a personality structure nor a universal principle of mental functioning. What invested her latest construction with significant clinical power was her deployment of her assemblage, her ability and willingness to foster its associative flows and pursue some of its implications, in other words, her openness to its potential to move her closer to her desire to touch, to speak and to know. Mat's constructions followed a similar logic insofar as each paved the way for the one that followed, toward what could eventually emerge less as the truth of what he ultimately desired (women, men, both or neither) and more as an expression of the varied ways in which he did desire (the to and fro between intimacy and solitude, the seemingly reticent seductions, the vigilance, the caution, the dare ...).

I hold this implication to be equally applicable to the analyst's constructions. Helen took up the 'patience' and 'pathology' I had proffered, added them to her mix which she refined, corrected and steered in a direction that eventually led her back to the tactility with which she had opened the session. Although other clinicians faced with the same material might have responded quite differently, my interpretation at the end of my session with Mat proved to be as legitimate a construction as any not so much because it touched upon a truth but because it elicited a parting smile and an agreement that were revealing in spite of their dismissiveness as much as by their charm, a smile and an agreement that facilitated Mat's closing request that I slide, a request that spoke a multifaceted desire that had directed much of the session's material, a desire no longer lying in wait or lied about, safe-guarded or disavowed, a desire no less enjoyed than feared, a desire, by virtue of the fact that it had already made its appearance on the analytic scene, was most likely to be terribly feared.

The second implication here is that, no matter how benign, careful, caring or insightful, no matter how therapeutic (at least according to those that equate the term with some or all of the preceding qualifiers), the analyst's construction is, in the manner of the child's stabbing of paper with pencil, an intervention in the most immediate and explicit sense of the word and hence, among other things, an interference, a rupture, a tear. As such, an inter-pretation cannot simply facilitate a 'joining in' in the analysand's state of mind, mirroring, twinning or merely colluding with it, as some psychoanalytic clinicians—most notable among them Kohut and the Kohutians—have ad-vocated.[11] Rather, an intervention is inevitably constituted by, among other things, an aggression and a delight that the analyst would be remiss to disavow or repress. Experiencing my silence as that of a withholding expert who, presumably, could alleviate her troubles but instead refused to align himself with either side of the conflict she suffered caused Helen much frustration; and I, the supposed expert, could not have found myself any closer to the proverbial but all-too-hollow 'this hurts me more than it hurts you' line of defence. As for Mat, he was not entirely off the mark when, as he subsequently informed me, he had heard my reposing the question regarding his choice of an analyst whose services are not covered by a government-financed program as a criticism as well as the sign of a curiosity about whatever else he might have had to say. Moreover, and though it might have been insightful or reassuring, my intervention at the end of the session summing up his desires and pointing to their associated fears was, at least in part, my not quite benign attempt to rein in a session that was a bit too crowded and a bit too fast for my own comfort. The fact that, at times, Helen and Mat found me withholding, aggressive, even dismissive was not without its consequences. I have already suggested that Helen's move toward an internal observer self was facilitated by her sense that, at least temporarily, I was not meaningful or relevant to her pursuits. Mat's parting wish that I, as opposed to my fee, slide as low as I could conveyed not only an erotic note but a wish that I prostrate myself and become available to him as the object he could look down on rather than face as the competent and confident analyst I believed I was.

No matter the empowering constructions they help elaborate, the analy-sand's associations foster their own troubling delight and aggression. Helen's newfound growth is not without its painful undertones; her task of having to fend for 'three selves' rather than two could more than likely exert its own peculiar toll, and her proximity to her emotions allowed her an intimacy that, though welcome, could become overwhelming, an intimacy that, while it expressed a sense of ease, exacerbated the need for vigilance. Such vigilance was, in turn, not only a response to a potential moment of aggression but an aggressive manoeuvre insofar as it disciplined, inhibited, whatever of her resources might otherwise and eventually contribute to ease. On the other hand, Mat spared himself neither the pleasure nor the discomfort of tearing through the seemingly coherent presentation of his own position, first in relation to his claims of self-sufficiency, and second in relation to his avowed heterosexuality. Equally aggressive was his wish to limit the scope and value of his relationship with me to that of an exchange of services for a fee that would simultaneously frustrate his desire for intimacy as much as it spared him its dangers.

The third implication is that finding's principle of reciprocity—namely, that whenever a subject finds an object, it finds itself being found by that selfsame object and incorporated into its world—is no less true of constructions than it is of blankets and teddy bears. A construction is a foreign and differentiating entity that founds a space in the analysand from which an other may emerge. No simple observation or hypothesis, structure or law, this other belongs to a living, moving, demanding, constructing, founding and producing voice. Helen not only 'found' a tripartite structure in her inner world, she found herself found by it, produced anew through its opportunities and expectations; while she may have been somewhat less encumbered by her previous constraints, she was nevertheless weighted down by a fresh set of looming responsibilities. Mat had to rediscover himself constantly in the constructions revealed by his associations; his ever-varying sense of who and how he was—the offshoots of his conjunctive syntheses—mutated in the process of being found and reproduced by members of various professions (doctors, analysts, dentists, clergymen), by political affiliations (libertarian, left) and/or by identitarian categories (heterosexuality, homosexuality, questionning). Constructions are not passive or lifeless realizations that Helen and Mat encountered over the course of their analytic experiences; they are found and founding objects with their own worlds and destinies; they are the conjunctive syntheses that redraw flows and reconfigure identities.

These two vignettes' logic and unfolding may be familiar to many who have gone through an analytic experience and are comfortable with its detours and nuances. There is material in them that may serve as added justification for a number of popular theories of stages, splits, self-states or perversions, for the nature of *jouissance* and the mechanics of the transference, and, indeed, for the anti-oedipal—or at least non-oedipal—dynamics and nuances otherwise distorted or obscured. At the end of the day, these vignettes shed light on Helen's and Mat's particular psycho-geographies and idiosyncratic modes of travel across their respective terrains. In the process, the vignettes offer up something far more useful, far more human than a theory or a pattern. They show how, given certain circumstances, desire emerges as neither a word nor a principle but as a vibrant experience—speaking, associating, seducing, touching, sliding—an experience that encompasses mind and body, memory and affect, economy and power, an experience that produces anew all of these polarities in ways that have little to do with either accuracy or consistency, an experience, in sum, much less concerned with science than with life, or, rather, an experience that is concerned with science as life.

This experience is located in a space that opens up when the two elements of any given dyad or polarity are juxtaposed to one another. Desire is triggered in the course of this juxtaposition. Both Helen and Mat are headed toward a space that lies between two supposedly incongruous categories, a space made possible by these categories and yet—precisely because of their incongruity—presumably excluded from their logic. Helen and Mat move toward, get stuck in, fear, abandon themselves to and/or relish the proximity of action to emotion, power to dependence, consistency to surprise, normalcy to inversion, disclosure to privacy. It is their movement toward this space that kick-starts the cycle of associations, constructions, findings and syntheses. Their taking hold of that space, their being held, and, at times, even gripped by it, invigorate their doubts and potentials, insecurities and experimentations. This is the transitional space Winnicott elaborated, the space of play that butts against reality on one side and hallucination on the other, the same space that Deleuze and Guattari thought belongs to both sides of the divide (Deleuze and Guattari, 1991, 25). This is the space for which the elements of the framing dyads are necessary supports rather than insurmountable hindrances, and into which, as we shall soon see, such elements often seep, eventually confusing and even becoming confused with one another. One need neither tolerate nor disavow, neither suffer nor sublimate, neither bridge nor sink into this space. Once again, this is a space that is lived.

Skins

A construction belongs to the space of the found object. It is sustained by reality, so as not to be useless, and freed up by hallucination, so as not to be devastating. Though it requires both reality and hallucination, it is restricted to neither; it is less a demarcation that, even when flexible or moveable, holds on to its function as a differentiation or a severance, and more a *coincidentia oppositorum* whose effect is a vital and resilient found object, an assemblage of machines both produced and producing. However, insofar as it is a reciprocal finding that invokes proximity and a being-together in a space of unremitting contradiction, a construction is a confound—it mixes, confuses and perplexes; it unhinges the very balance of a hierarchy that would tolerate, deny or overcome *coincidentia*; indeed, it is contingent on that co-incidence. Construction is thus tantamount to seeing simultaneously through two eyes that cannot but be positioned differently. This seeing opens onto a depth of field, lateral and topological rather than vertical and archaeological, a depth that skims rather than plummets, that touches, as in Helen's case, or slides, as in Mat's. This depth of field runs afoul of the profundity that has been a point of pride for much of psychoanalysis, the same profundity that sustains the pursuit of truth as an earnest un-covering and reinforces the prevalent though simplistic reduction of curiosity to a trifling voyeurism.

Interestingly, despite his privileging such profundity, Freud often resorted to metaphors of skins and surfaces in order to articulate a different dimension to his clinical inquiry. Among these I cite three of the most familiar.

First, Freud repeatedly insisted that the psychoanalytic understanding of infantile sexuality is based on a direct observation of the most elemental, indeed most superficial events in a child's life: sucking, touching, urinating, defecating (Freud, 1905, 1916). Infantile sexuality is not discernible only by specially trained adepts; it is on display for all to see, assuming that they want to see it and have it be seen. The humiliation that results from the failure to have seen the most obvious, the humiliation born out of wilful blindness perpetuated by those who possess visual acuity, feeds the antagonism toward any claim to the offending nature of a sexuality that has been in full view all along. Rather than a straightforward contradiction, the blindness of the sighted here is yet another co-incidence of opposites that produces a realization and potentially generates different emotional responses, including, but not limited to, rage, contempt and relief.

Second, Freud declared that, at any given stage in its development, and for all its intricacies, a drive is but the outcome of the most recent volcanic eruption; once buried and now exposed, eventually hardened from contact with air, homogenous, complete unto itself; it is the outermost layer of lava enveloping whatever may have come before it (Freud, 1915, 131). Among others, the metaphor evokes the dynamic sequence of a tectonic shift that produces a flow which enshrouds a history precisely as it brings forth previously buried material that will reconfigure a terrain and the ways in which it may be inhabited and/or traversed. Not surprisingly, partial as it may be to depth and cover, such a sequence is lively and prolific enough to displace the image of an obscured and immutable bedrock drive in search of the forever-lost object in favour of the fluid, produced as well as productive machines advanced by Deleuze and Guattari.

The third and last of Freud's surface metaphors I cite belongs to his earliest assessments of the scope and limits of dream interpretation. That Freud could declare, in the span of a couple of pages, that he had 'completed the interpretation of a dream' (Freud, 1900, 118) and that, subsequently, he would not pretend that he had either 'completely uncovered' its meaning or that 'its interpretation is without a gap' (120–21), that he could acknowledge in one and the same sentence the fact of a 'tangle of dream-thoughts which cannot be unravelled' while asserting, with a confidence that lacks any hint of irony or awkwardness, that such a tangle 'adds nothing to our knowledge of the content of the dream' (525) are the types of contradictory statements we have grown to rely on as fodder for debate and controversy in both clinical and academic circles. Freud's own attempt at rescuing his position from its structural tenuousness is what is most telling for the current purposes. Interpretation must acknowledge the fact of a 'concealed meaning,' Freud insisted in his discussion of the Irma dream; it cannot proceed beyond an 'unplumbable' point of contact with 'the unknown' (111n1);[12] as with every dream, it must arrive at its 'navel' as the passage that 'has to be left obscure' (525). It is only along the skin that dreamer and interpreter may travel. Henceforth, the lure of depth and verticality must give way to 'the intricate network of our world of thought' (525).

Freud's investment in surfaces and topologies calls into question his insistence on an unbridgeable gap between psychoanalysis and archaeology, two disciplines that otherwise seem to share much in terms of sensibility and process. Setting aside the veracity of Freud''s claims regarding disciplinary methods and priorities[13] and focusing instead on their import in matters of analytic technique, it seems to me that, in spelling out his clinical division of labour, Freud was setting a prescription against the overvaluation of construction as, essentially, a perversion of the psychoanalytic process that derails it from its proper aim by privileging one of its components at the expense of all others. However, as the vignettes with Helen and Mat make abundantly clear, construction is not merely a tool among the many at one's disposal; it is the fundament of their analytic experience, much as interpretation, play or production are recognized by the standards of other paradigms. Neither an offshoot nor an afterthought, construction is a generative dynamic; it propels further associations and sets the ground for interpretations that may seem discrete and self-contained but invariably belong to a much larger and subtler network of interpretations from which they are often severed. In the process, construction reconfigures the very subject that gave it its initial momentum as it shifts that subject's perspectives and expands its possibilities. To put it differently, and following Deleuze and Guattari who recognized production as the production of production rather than the production of any one particular product—as, in other words, the production of the ever-renewing and ever-renewable conditions and processes of production, recording and consumption—construction pertains less to a construct's hoped-for ability to recover a lost history and more to the process of constructing itself. Prioritizing construction—archaeology's shortcoming as per Freud's account—is thus hardly a perversion of an otherwise developmentally mature or structurally sound clinical process; it is the recognition of the dynamic that undergirds that process, of construction as the construction of construction—of association, of interpretation, of, in sum, analysis.

That construction operates under the category of series rather than destination is a principal reason why the transference and counter-transference are less discrete states than way stations on an itinerary traversed by both parties in the analytic process. That the construction of construction is responsible for fuelling the analytic motor implies that the transferential dynamic is a product of construction as much as it may be its source and foundation. This dynamic is grounded in a doubled finding—an animating, disrupting, cathecting-decathecting process—rather than in a projection or reenactment. More specifically, it is one of reenactment with an exteriority that charges the psychoanalytic process with potential as it allows each of the parties to place the other outside the area of subjective phenomena (Winnicott, 1969, 87). In any given analysis, the analyst recognizes the inevitability of the various features of the found and the constructed to their function, as diverting rather than repetitive, as constitutive rather than resolvable. The transference is no inevitable carryover from a history that has not been fully worked through but an object found at a particular moment and hence harnessed in the service of a specific construction. Helen and Mat have driven this message across often enough. In turn, my counter-transference has been greater than a subjective response to their so-called transferential projections or inducements. It has been defined by the ways in which I have found myself being constructed by them rather than simply in whether or how they may have upset me, fed my narcissism, triggered any of a myriad of my not fully worked through unconscious scenes or dilemmas. I have carried this counter-transference not only with each separately but also in the overlapping margins and in the times when I have been with neither yet very aware of both.

At this point, we might be content to carry the parallel between constructions, machines and found objects no further; Helen and Mat, on the other hand, and in subtle though distinct ways, insist that we press on. Both her touching and his sliding betray a modicum of unmitigated, unsublimated, unrepressed pleasure, often mistaken for residue or by-product, but, in fact, a principal component of the playful machinery of self-discovery, insight and analysis. Alongside the pursuit of a respite from the misery of isolation, the debilitation of fear or the paralysis of vigilance, it is this pleasure that sustains the continued cathexis, the libidinal investment, not so much in this or that construction, hypothesis or theory as clarifying or useful, but in the act of constructing, hypothesizing and theorizing. This pleasure attaches less to the found object and more to the finding as discovering and playing, less to the construction or understanding by the analyst and of the analysand, for instance, and more to the activity of analyzing in which both may participate, an activity that, in the by-now familiar words of Winnicott, belongs to the 'imaginative living and creative scientific work' of culture (Winnicott, 1971, 5). A construction is as lasting as it is useful, pleasurable; neither refuted nor repressed, it eventually becomes irrelevant. We again find ourselves in the transitional space between reality and fantasy, efficacy and gratification, the space in which a construction is as much an analytic teddy bear or blanket to be played with, hugged, dragged, tossed, or curled up under as it is an empathic insight, a curative intervention or a meta-psychological formulation.[14] As much might thus be true of that other instance of construction, the transference/counter-transference couplet, and indeed of psychoanalysis itself.

For the time being, and as we await the eventual decathexis of construction and analysis, we may seek reassurance, as Freud once did, in the belief that a number of dreams occurring in one night need be nothing more than attempts, expressed in various forms, to represent one meaning (Freud, 1911, 94) and that, likewise, Freud's, Winnicott's and Deleuze and Guattari's contributions to our understanding of construction, their meta-psychological dreams so to speak, are but seemingly irreconcilable variations on the same meaning that fuels the impetus toward analysis, a meaning that presses upon as it confounds us. Be that as it may, it is in the interstices between these dreams that we may eventually discover that the will to analyze belongs to the unconscious as a desire as much as it currently stands as a means to uncovering its mechanics or elucidating its theories.

Notes

1 Winnicott made this statement in response to Sidney Stewart's query regarding the archaic sources of the creative impulse. To the best of McDougall's recollection, the exchange took place at a London meeting (1953?) of the International Psychoanalytical Association. (McDougall, 2003, 26–7)
2 Among the more notable of these one counts repression/recovery, recollection/interpretation, analyzing/being analyzed, transference-less archaeology/transference-laden psychoanalysis, construction as aim/construction as means.
3 Freud reiterated the same idea about secondary revision when he traced its roots to 'an intellectual function in us which demands unity, connection and intelligibility from any material, whether of perception or thought, that comes within its grasp; and if, as a result of special circumstances, it is unable to establish a true connection, it does not hesitate to fabricate a false one' (Freud, 1913, 95).
4 Aside from the authority arrogated through training, both formal and experiential, one may consider here the gamut of counter-transferential dynamics communicated through the analyst's constructions—conscious and otherwise.
5 As per Deleuze and Guattari's discussion of *voisinage* (Deleuze and Guattari, 1991, 25).
6 Less an origin in time, *arche* here is the often unspoken first principle from which an order may follow and according to which it acquires meaning.
7 Hinting that the *arche* in question pertains not only to a phenomenon made manifest through psychoanalytic research but to the phenomenon's researchers and theorists as well, Winnicott declared 'it must be of value to the analyst to be constantly reminded not only of what is owed to Freud but also of what we owe to the natural and universal thing called playing' (Winnicott, 1967, 41).
8 Deleuze and Guattari will continue to downplay the category of truth throughout their collaborative enterprise and in a number of different contexts. Among their

more notable claims is that philosophy secures its function through the exclusive right of concept creation (1991, 13) independently of any so-called scientific value (111).

9 In regards to the clinic, the literature on Deleuze and Guattari's highly ambivalent relationship to psychoanalysis, especially its Freudian and Lacanian branches, is rich. I offer the following as starting points for a more extensive study: Abou-Rihan (2008), David-Ménard (2005) and Holland (1999). As far as I know, and aside from Gary Genosko's brief observations (2002), no thorough elaboration of the connections between Deleuze and Guattari and the Winnicottian paradigm has yet been published.

10 In the province of Ontario, and as of the time of this writing, psychoanalysis and most forms of psychotherapy are fully covered by the government-run health insurance plan when undertaken with a medical doctor.

11 See, for instance, Kohut (1977), Kohut and Wolf (1978), Teicholz (1999), Siegel (1996) and Bacal (1990).

12 Derrida identified this 'beyond' as 'the place where desire for death and desire *tout court* call for and speak the analysis they prohibit' (Derrida, 1998, 24). This is where both the resistance to the psychoanalytic process as well as the cover psychoanalysis deploys for its own procedural limit, the resistance of the psychoanalytic process itself, meet.

13 While a fair treatment of the relationship between psychoanalysis and archaeology is beyond the scope of this text, I offer Schmidt (2001), O'Donoghue (2004), Thomas (2009) and Corcoran (1991) as worthwhile explorations.

14 Much like the found object that is eventually decathected, the machinic assemblage is eventually brought to a standstill. Indeed, Deleuze and Guattari insisted on a moment of 'anti-production' at the heart of the productive process, a moment at which, once it has become too organized, too predictable, the assemblage halts and its flows cease (Deleuze and Guattari, 1977, 8). In the language of *Anti-Oedipus*, this is the 'body without organs,' which is neither an interruption nor a culmination but a moment among many in a series, like a child's stabbing of the paper, punching of the teddy bear, tossing of the rag doll or tearing of the satiny blanket—a moment of repulsion, of the assemblage not working or needing to work differently, a moment, hence, generated by all that preceded it, itself unproductive yet contributing to what has yet to come (including a turning away or a returning)—a moment, in other words, and not a finality. Likewise, a construction is relinquished for another that might seem more useful, more clarifying or even more pressing.

References

Abou-Rihan, Fadi. 2008/2011. *Deleuze and Guattari: A Psychoanalytic Itinerary*. London: Continuum International Publishing/Bloomsbury.

Bacal, Howard. 1990. "Heinz Kohut." In *Theories of Object Relations: Bridges to Self-Psychology*. Edited by Howard Bacal and Kenneth Newman. New York: Columbia University Press. Pp. 225–273.

Corcoran, Lorelei. 1991. "Exploring the Archaeological Metaphor: The Egypt of Freud's Imagination." In *The Annual of Psychoanalysis, Volume 19*. London and New York: Routledge. Pp. 19–32.

David-Ménard, Monique. 2005. *Deleuze et la psychanalyse*. Paris: Presses Universitaires de France.

Deleuze, Gilles and Guattari, Félix. 1977. *Anti-Oedipus*. Translated by Robert Hurley, Mark Seem, and Helen R. Lane with a preface by Michel Foucault. New York: Viking Press.

Deleuze, Gilles and Guattari, Félix. 1991. *Qu'est-ce que la philosophie?* Paris: Edition de Minuit.

Derrida, Jacques. 1998. *Resistances of Psychoanalysis*. Translated by Peggy Kamuf, Pascale-Anne Brault, and Michael Naas. Stanford: Stanford University Press.

Freud, Sigmund. 1900. *The Interpretation of Dreams*. In *The Complete Standard Edition of the Psychological Works of Sigmund Freud SE*. IV–V. London: Hogarth Press.

Freud, Sigmund. 1911. "The Handling of Dream-Interpretation in Psycho-Analysis." In *SE XII*. London: Hogarth Press. Pp. 91–96.

Freud, Sigmund. 1913. "Totem and Taboo." In *SE XIII*. London: Hogarth Press. Pp. 1–161.

Freud, Sigmund. 1915. "Instincts and their Vicissitudes." In *SE XIV*. London: Hogarth Press. Pp. 109–140.

Freud, Sigmund. 1916. "Introductory Lectures to Psychoanalysis." In SE XV–XVI. London: Hogarth Press.

Freud, Sigmund. 1920. "Beyond the Pleasure Principle." In *SE XVIII*. London: Hogarth Press. Pp. 7–64.

Freud, Sigmund. 1937a. "Analysis Terminable and Interminable." In *SE XXIII*. London: Hogarth Press. Pp. 216–253.

Freud, Sigmund. 1937b. "Constructions in Analysis." In *SE XXIII*. London: Hogarth Press. Pp. 257–269.

Freud, Sigmund. 1940. "Splitting of the Ego in the Process of Defence." In *SE 23*. London: Hogarth Press. Pp. 275–278.

Genosko, Gary. 2002. *Félix Guattari: An Aberrant Introduction*. London: Continuum International Publishing.

Guattari, Félix. 1995. "So What?" In *Chaosophy*. Edited by Sylvère Lotringer. New York: Semiotexte. Pp. 7–25.

Holland, Eugene. 1999. *Deleuze and Guattari: An Introduction to Schizoanalysis*. London and New York: Routledge.

Kohut, Heinz. 1977. *The Restoration of the Self*. Madison: International Universities Press.

Kohut, H. and Wolf, E. S. 1978. "The Disorders of the Self and their Treatment: An Outline." In *International Journal of Psychoanalysis*. 59:4. Pp. 413–425.

Lacan, Jacques. 2006. "The Instance of the Letter in the Unconscious, or Reason Since Freud." In *Ecrits*. Translated by Bruce Fink in collaboration with Héloïse Fink and Russell Grigg. New York: W. W. Norton & Company. Pp. 412–443.

McDougall, Joyce. 2003. *Donald Winnicott The Man: Reflections and Recollections*. London: Karnac Books.

O'Donoghue, Diane. 2004. "Negotiations of Surface: Archaeology within the Early Strata of Psychoanalysis." In *Journal of the American Psychoanalytic Association*. 52:3. Pp. 653–671.

Schmidt, Dietmar. 2001. "Refuse Archaeology: Virchow—Chliemann—Freud." In *Perspectives on Science*. 9:2. Pp. 210–232.

Siegel, Allen. 1996. *Heinz Kohut and the Psychology of the Self*. London: Routledge.

Teicholz, J. G. 1999. *Kohut, Leowald, and the Postmoderns: A Comparative Study of Self and Relationship*. Hillsdale, NJ: The Analytic Press.

Thomas, Julian. 2009. "Sigmund Freud's Archaeological Metaphor and Archaeology's Self-Understanding." In *Contemporary Archaeologies: Excavating Now*. Edited by C. Holtorf and A. Piccini. London: Peter Lang, Pp. 33–45.

Winnicott, Donald W. 1967. "Playing: A Theoretical Statement." In *Playing and Reality*. London and New York: Routledge Books. Pp. 38–52.

Winnicott, Donald W. 1969. "The Use of an Object and Relating Through Identification." In *Playing and Reality*. London and New York: Routledge Books. Pp. 86–94.

Winnicott, Donald W. 1971. "Transitional Objects and Transitional Phenomena." In *Playing and Reality*. London and New York: Routledge Books. Pp. 1–25.

Chapter 4

Solitudes

Take One

To Be Alone

My springboard here is a classic essay of Winnicott's from the late 1950s in which the psychoanalyst marked the capacity to be alone as emblematic of neither a fear nor a wish but of a freedom from withdrawal, a freedom deemed in the opening lines of the text as 'one of the most important signs of maturity in emotional development' (Winnicott, 1958, 29). While venturing into a conceptual and clinical territory that, in due course, came to be more freely his, Winnicott began his presentation of the ground for the distinction between solitude and loneliness (more on this later) by deploying an admixture of the Freudian and Kleinian terms of his day, as if to reassure all parties concerned that, for all intents and purposes, he was not straying too far afield from the double-sided tradition that had set root in British soil, as if, in drawing on proximate elements in the established paradigms of Anna Freud and Melanie Klein, his thought was neither unique nor threatening, as if, at the end of the day, neither it nor, by extension, its author was, at least theoretically, alone.[1] And so, early in the essay, Winnicott declared:

> It could be said that an individual's capacity to be alone depends on his ability to deal with the feelings aroused by the primal scene. In the primal scene an excited relationship between the parents is perceived or imagined, and this is accepted by the child who is healthy and who is able to master the hate and to gather it in the service of masturbation. In masturbation the whole responsibility for the conscious and unconscious fantasy is accepted by the individual child, who is the third in a three-body or triangular relationship. To be able to be alone in these circumstances implies a maturity of erotic development, a genital potency, or the corresponding female acceptance; it implies fusion of the aggressive and erotic impulses and ideas, and it implies a tolerance

DOI: 10.4324/9781003352488-4

of ambivalence; along with all this there would naturally be a capacity on the part of the individual to identify with each of the parents. (31)

Winnicott went on to describe the capacity to be alone as 'either a highly sophisticated phenomenon that may arrive in a person's development *after* the establishment of three-body relationships, or else it is a phenomenon of early life which deserves special study because it is the foundation on which so-phisticated aloneness is built' (30, emphasis in the original). Given this re-cognition that a defining capacity may develop either pre or post the moment of so-called Oedipal triangulation, one is justified in positing the non-Oedipal as a Winnicottian descriptor—with the caveat that the 'non-' is understood in terms of a differentiation rather than a straightforward negation. One may thus be further justified in identifying this capacity as a precursor to the Deleuzo–Guattarian challenge of the Oedipal as the psychodynamic threshold *par excellence*.

What is at stake in sophisticated aloneness is a rather enjoyable capacity to become un-integrated, to flounder, to be in a state where there is no or-ientation, to 'be able to exist for a time without being either a reaction to an external impingement or an active person with a direction of interest or movement' (34). Such a state submits to neither cause nor effect, neither se-quence nor hierarchy, neither intention nor goal. As it reinforces the central motif of transitionality elaborated in the present pages, the capacity to be alone runs counter to the developmental spirit of the ego psychology and object relations schools dominant in Winnicott's time; instead, it meets up with the subsequently developed and much less historicizing or progressivist Deleuzo–Guattarian notions of 'plateaus' and 'body without organs.'

For Deleuze and Guattari, the 'organs' the body without organs forgoes are not the material components of physiology but such categories as erogenous zones and cognitive functions according to which the various body parts have been structured, periodized and, eventually, organized, all in the service of the so-called natural and innocently self-evident truths of science or culture. In essence, the body without organs is a structural in-between bordered by two hierarchies, relations of production or systems of meaning that may be as different from one another as, say, fantasy and reality, pleasure and practi-cality, but that are nonetheless equally unacceptable because of their fixity and determination. In the face of such structures, the un-organ-ized body refuses to participate or facilitate; it 'presents its smooth, slippery, opaque, taut surface as a barrier. In order to resist linked, connected, and interrupted flows, it sets up a counterflow of amorphous, undifferentiated fluid' (Deleuze and Guattari, 1977, 9). Such a floundering body is neither a residue nor a meta-phor, neither a purpose nor a destination; it is unproductive, unengendered, unconsumable (8).

With the body without organs emerge the clearer echoes between the Winnicottian state of being alone and the limbo-like qualities of suspension and purposelessness of the Deleuzo–Guattarian plateau, between being alone and being in the middle. In what have since become the familiar Winnicottian terms of transitionality, Deleuze and Guattari thought the plateau a 'continuous, self-vibrating region of intensities whose development avoids any orientation toward a culmination point or external end' (Deleuze and Guattari, 1987, 22). Far removed from the stasis frequently registered as accomplishment though more often than not experienced as stagnation, the plateau is a plane of continuous intensity, of attention captured and sustained, of focus shifted, de-centred; such is a plane of time passing, devoid of the anguish or hope that carry the hint of an end or resolution, of another time or, better still, of a time that is other, of a time installed, of a time endured.

To Leave Alone

A healthy capacity to be alone in one party in any given dyadic relationship can flourish on the condition that it be met with the equally healthy capacity to leave alone in the other. After all, an infant can hardly be expected to enjoy a healthy solitude should mother or father, or anyone else for that matter, be ever- and over-attentive. Similarly, an analysand is unfortunately and inevitably deprived from experiencing sophisticated aloneness (Winnicott, 1958, 30) as a positive component of the psychoanalytic experience when the analyst is forever preoccupied with their own presence and/or relevance.

Clinically, the capacity to leave alone is most manifest in contexts that are already quite familiar. Though varying in degree, the ability to tolerate the silence in or of a session, a weekend, a summer break or, eventually, a termination illustrates a capacity to move on willingly, comfortably, patiently and with little by way of harmful remorse or anxiety—in sum a decathexis—as much by the analyst as by the analysand—of an other, a relationship and a practice. In the case of the analyst, the structure and contexts of the capacity to be alone are considered par for the course; all the while, many a principle of metapsychology or a standard of technique is harnessed in order to cover over a mourning process that has gone awry[2] and, more to the point here, a resistance to the demands of a letting go. Consider, for instance, the analyst who tolerates a termination knowing full well that, as is inevitably the case, not all has been revealed or resolved—that while certain analytic tasks may yet be undertaken it is up to the analysand to assume the choice, responsibility and timing for such endeavours. This analyst is far different from the one who not only imposes him or herself as the fulcrum of the analytic process—*qua* transferential target, affective fount, or relational pivot—but further insists on being sufficiently internalized as, among other things, benign superego or transmuting selfobject[3] by the analysand and goes on to mark this internalization as the *sine qua non* of a healthy termination. This analyst's 'you may legitimately leave me on the condition that you take me with you, on the condition that, effectively, you become me' is nothing short of a psychic DNA implantation, a branding and a legitimation that may have as much to do with the analyst's refusal to come to terms with the finitude of their relevance as it does with a concern for the analysand's continued wellbeing.

Presumably, the capacity to leave alone is both a challenge and a requirement the analyst will have already fulfilled in their own analysis but whose appearance on the current analytic scene ought to be coordinated in relation to the analysand's so-called matrix of transference (Winnicott, 1958, 33). In privileging the capacity to be alone, Winnicott is ever so subtly though not any the less determinedly directing the clinician to recognize those moments when the analysand is sufficiently capable of sustaining an independent analytic position, when, in other words, not only is that analysand capable of being left alone but is in actual fact leaving the analyst alone as well as behind where they belong, psychodynamically as well as physically. With the capacity to leave alone, Winnicott is radically and in one fell swoop unsettling the firm and long-held view that the analyst is the principal object at whom all manner of transferential scenarios, including, and especially, those that unfold in silence and/or stillness, are directed, that, as Freud had once insisted, whatever components are in need of treatment must first and foremost be re-directed toward the figure of the analyst (Freud, 1912a, 100) and indeed coincide with it (104), that it is precisely this type of libidinal transfer that converts the analytic consulting room into a clinical 'playground' (Freud, 1914a, 154)[4] on which is freely though safely enacted and potentially worked through much of what has been suffered and/or repressed. Winnicott is here challenging an orthodoxy that has sustained many an analyst's sense of their primacy in all matters clinical, a primacy that may be rivalled only by the one that Freud had attributed to His Majesty the Baby (Freud, 1914b, 91).

Should such undermining, or indeed dethroning, not be challenging enough, I understand Winnicott to be further enjoining the analyst to not simply step aside while keeping a watchful eye in case an intervention is necessary or helpful but, much more significantly, to actively call upon their own capacity to be (left) alone—presumably honed through the training analysis—and leave alone the analysand with whom they have been engaged. Winnicott is effectively, though quite likely unwittingly, asking that the analyst, unlike the responsible parent, occupy less a 'reliable' yet unobtrusive presence somewhere in the background and more a tenuous middle position between presence and absence, a position that, as with all things 'middle,' partakes of both of these modes while being reducible to neither. This is what the philosophers have typically termed 'becoming,' a hovering between two states of being or, more acutely, between a state of being and a state of nothingness. This is what we have also come to understand as transformation, as, in other words, the process through which one forgoes what one is for the sake of something that one is not. Clinically, we recognize this as the experience of forgoing one construction for another, without being quite certain that that other is sure to follow or that whatever may eventually come next in the series is necessarily any the more illuminating, useful or satisfying. Critically for the analyst, the capacity to leave alone is grounded in the capacity to leave oneself alone, to let go of what one holds dearest, of, among other things, one's construction of oneself as analyst, of one's ability to construct, not to mention empathize and/or understand. Thus, hand in hand with the commitment to change and discovery go uncertainty and doubt, a very real prospect of failure and a vacuous aspect to any version of confidence.[5]

In a parallel manner, the analysand's capacity to leave alone is most manifest in those moments when they have already let go of the idea of being, or having been, 'in' analysis in favour of not so much the experience of analyzing but the ability to go about their life analytically—as an organic and un-self-conscious presence that may remember and speak an analytic process without feeling defined, confined, or, heaven forbid, refined by it. Eventually, the experience of undergoing, or having undergone, an analysis seems to culminate less in the mastery of a technique than in the broadening, branching off and away, the displacement and even sublimation of the impetus to play onto other domains and according to other modalities—onto 'the whole cultural field,' as Winnicott was fond of saying. At stake then is hardly the task of negotiating, bridging, or suffering the classic opposition between thinking and acting, observing and participating, doing and having done since there is no lasting opposition to speak of here; rather, there is a conjunction of the various components of these and similar polarities, their arrangements and juxtapositions and, eventually, the recognition and sorting through of whatever temporary dynamics and identities they may foster.

In sum, the capacity to leave alone is the clinically challenging, emboldening, frustrating, and at times downright paralyzing co-incidence of presence and absence, attention and distraction, commitment and indifference that is psychoanalysis. That such a co-incidence may prove to be impossible, paradoxical, narcissistically injurious, embarrassing, arduous, laughable—in all these terms' varied nuances—or perhaps even relieving to the person of the analyst is secondary to the experience it opens up to the analysand. The capacity to leave alone is the ground neither for an existential crisis that culminates in helplessness or cynicism nor for grief in the face of irrevocable loss. This capacity is not scriptable, teachable, or transmissible as a skill; nor is it an enigmatic, unspeakable, and unspoken talent; it addresses neither a lack that ought to be remedied nor an ineptitude that might be surmounted through guidance and practice. The capacity to leave alone is rather intermittent, sporadic; it speaks and acknowledges a limit, an inevitable failure that demands humility. Rather than the indifference of decathexis, it is the effect of the recognition of a practice and the investment in a process unfolding beyond, on the other side of, and elsewhere other than the self. It is the handing over to some other what one has created, some other in whose hands a creation may continue on living, in those hands that are trusted not to destroy but sustain, deploy, play, and further. And so, rather than apathy, the relinquishment characteristic of the capacity to leave alone is instead saturated with openness as purpose. The capacity to leave alone thus speaks a trust—rather than the certainty—that what is left alone may survive or that, conversely, the one doing the leaving may survive, even if that which is left may not. Instead of abandonment or abnegation, it is a relinquishment that neither the self-sufficient hallucination nor the all-encompassing concrete reality—indeed neither the lover nor the enemy—can accommodate; it is the relinquishment that might be more appropriately attributed to the friend or neighbour who occupies a separate space—outside yet close enough.

The analyst's work reaches a point when it becomes irrelevant precisely when it achieves its aim, not when the analysand has finally internalized well—in other words, learned—the tricks of the analytic trade and can hence venture out into the world capable of handling any situation that might call for an analytically informed insight or intervention, but rather when that analysand no longer needs to enlist the analyst into their cause, when they cease to care so about what the latter thinks, when the moment of recruitment and its attendant seductions has in effect passed. This is precisely the moment at which the analysis is unfolding, an analysis the analysand will experience 'alone' while in the presence of another and hence an analysis to which the analyst will be privy intermittently at best, as someone who may be close by but is equally 'alone.' as per Winnicott's post-coital scenario (Winnicott, 1958, 31).[6] Though precipitated by both individuals, this is an analysis for whose workings and effects—plays—only the analysand may claim credit, an analysis that has as little to do with teaching as it does with parenting, curing, or absolving, an analysis whose end is hardly ever available to the analyst and concerning which the most one can say is that it is a vanishing point in the direction of co-incidence rather than a definitive separation from the 'unwell.'

My conclusion hence goes against the classic Winnicottian view that psychoanalysis is the overlap between two areas of play, the one belonging to the analyst and the other to the analysand (Winnicott, 1971, 54). Such an overlap is eventful, energetic, engaged and communicative; it is hardly spent; it is akin to an awkward *entre-deux* where each of the parties participates often unequally and sometimes even intermittently. If an overlap is at all a factor here, then it ought to be understood less as the result of collaboration or co-construction and more, once again, as the overlap of presence with absence in which each of the two participants is implicated. Drawing on Winnicott's infamous post-coital metaphor, the analytic moment emerges as the least orchestrated by-product of the manifest and overarching formal frame that is 'psychoanalysis.' This moment has little to do with the challenge and excitement of a collaborative remedying of deficit or overcoming of trauma; it carries no glamour and is hardly the reason for a victory lap; here, there is even less cure or systemic and ever-lasting transformation.

A number of conclusions unfold from this material: (1) the psychoanalytic moment, strictly speaking, the moment of aloneness, is but a moment that cannot be sustained over long periods of time since either of the two worlds neighbouring it will eventually come calling;[7] (2) this moment is not terminal; rather, it is episodic; it will be forsaken for other moments and then revisited, hopefully on many occasions, or at least on as many occasions as are needed or valued; and (3) this moment is a radical departure from all that came before it, made it possible, and shaped it; like the transference, as Freud would have it, its advent is abrupt rather than gradual.

A fourth and perhaps most unsettling conclusion is inevitable. It might make structural sense to premise the potential for a mature capacity (to be alone) in the analysand on the presence of a complimentary capacity (to leave alone) in the presumably already mature analyst. It might also be developmentally consistent to cast the analytic dyad in terms of a nurture that facilitates the teaching or replication of either or both of these capacities by the one party and of the other. The dynamic of the one in pursuit of a quality or way of being that is available to or in the other persists. The reality of the analytic situation is such as to render this dynamic thoroughly suspect. Not only does the dynamic falsely imply that the analysand may only hope to be as healthy as, and never more than, the analyst and that, somehow, the analyst is in a position to instil in the analysand something that the latter does not already possess, to fill a psychologically constitutional gap, to remedy a lack or resolve a deficit. Much as Winnicott described the foundation of sophisticated aloneness in both pre- and post-Oedipal terms, the capacity to be alone and to leave alone must therefore be accounted for in both pre- and post-clinical terms. One ought to say as much of the capacity to play, to find or to flounder. Indeed, Winnicott insisted that the task of the therapist is to make sure the patient is already in possession of this capacity to play before 'psychotherapy' proper can begin. The boundary separating pre- from post- in a psychoanalytic context is hence not quite solid; it is significantly porous and quite likely less static than one would assume.

Take Two

Primal Goliath

I want to give him a name, one that extends beyond the clinical conventions of the arbitrary and anonymizing initial, a name that safeguards the confidentiality of the analytic space as it sheds light on the why and the what spoken within.

I will call him David, in reference to the biblical figure of the humble shepherd who slays Goliath with a slingshot, of, in another version of the story, the child that defeats the aggressor while the adult tasked with that same responsibility stands helplessly by, of, according to yet a third of the story's versions, a defender that fights a foreign enemy who, as it turns out, is actually a blood relative.

In his younger years, David also went by a name chosen for him by his maternal grandfather and used solely by the beloved forebear: Jake. David has chosen that same name for the dog he recently adopted. He now welcomes canine Jake to share his bed for a couple of hours every night in a small room in the basement while Amelie, David's exceptionally light sleeper wife, spends her nights alone in the main bedroom up the stairs. Thirty years prior, David/Jake had his bedroom in the basement of his parents' house. Back then, it was mother who slept seemingly unawares in the matrimonial bedroom on the second floor while, two levels below, father sexually assaulted his son during regular nocturnal visits.

This chapter in David's life started when he was eight years old and lasted till he reached puberty five years later, by which time his father lost all sexual interest in him. Throughout that period and the decade that followed, David maintained a silence around the assaults, a silence he wore as a badge of honour and a testament to his resilience. '*The baby that never cried*,'[8] the one that '*never really needed any attention*,' as he was already cast in the family story, the baby that most likely recognized the futility of crying as a means of getting any attention, grew into a self-reliant recluse.

In his late teens, David accepted at face value his father's confessed remorse for the assaults; he believed he could now put his history behind him as he prepared for a university education away from home. On his own, he sank instead into a depression for which he initially sought professional help but eventually medicated with the heavy use of alcohol. He endured his suffering through active isolation: he lived alone, worked the late night shift, preferred pornography to lived sexual relations and spent most of his free time immersed in video games. He also reclaimed his isolation as a point of pride, as proof of self-sufficiency, even superiority, as much as a preemptive strategy against unwelcome intrusion. In time, he went to graduate school, travelled a fair bit and eventually returned to his home city and completed specialized professional training.

Fast forward to when, in his mid-30s, David's world fell apart, again, when his father committed suicide with a gun to the head a day after he was arrested for sexually assaulting the neighbours' grandson. For David, the basement could not have been any more welcoming. You see, in this version of the biblical confrontation, the enemy was never vanquished; the punctuation that is the slingshot, or bullet, to the head simply marks the end of one iteration as it makes way for another. It may then be more useful to understand David's struggle as less with isolation *per se* as with the company he must keep. Goliath has not been slain and David is no hero. Each is a 'man of the in-between'[9] and has no one other than his enemy for company. *'I am not my father; I will not repeat his ugly deeds ...' 'No, no. I am very much like my father; I am as guilty as he is ...' 'I am as broken; I must redeem us both by resisting the impulse that prolongs the tragedy ...'* David feels alone with his desire. What he hopes for from me, his analyst, and what he has consistently identified as his aim for his analysis, is that I not stand idly by but sustain him as he occupies this 'in-between' so that he may take charge over his desire and keep it confined to the realm of fantasy.

In one respect, it makes a lot of sense to attribute to the abuse David endured at the hands of his father much of the suffering and struggles he went on to experience. The depression, isolation and substance use, to name but a few of the components of his adult life, fall in line with a seemingly unambiguous chronology of causes and effects. This chronology recalls Freud's formulations of psychopathology in terms of a theory of seduction whose clinical and political failings have impeded many a study of childhood sexual abuse. In order to sustain a theory initially grounded on a presumed event though ultimately formalized around an unconscious fantasy, Freud adapted Ernst Haeckel's famed 'ontogeny recapitulates phylogeny' principle and advanced the view that sexuality's vicissitudes in the life of the individual replicate an evolutionary path leading back to an all-powerful primal father, a Goliath as in David's case, who is 'killed, eaten, resuscitated, and retroactively reigns over everyone' (Lepoutre, 2016, 63).

On the one hand, the scientific foundations for Freud's overarching parallel between species and individual have been shown to be erroneous and misleading (Gould, 1985). On the other hand, we would do well to remember Foucault's lesson that the agencies of domination and the systems that constitute the subject across different contexts are not homologous (Foucault, 1976, 121–35), that power is not exercised uniformly no matter the relationship (parent/child, state/citizen, ruler/ruled) and that neither is the father a mere representative of the state nor is the latter an extrapolation of a father figure on a scale larger than the family's.

Recognizing that the passage from one context to another is hardly ever frictionless, I want to explore the structure that makes it possible for a desire to co-opt and redraw the psyche of one individual in the service of another—as per a parent's abuse of a child—the structure on the basis of which a micro-colonizing relationship is built. I want to elaborate a dynamic that is neither the miniature nor the outcome observed against the background of pre-existing social and economic formations, even as these latter have often configured the colonizer-colonized relationship in familial and sexualizing terms. Rather than focus on sexuality as fashioned by overarching structures (be they moral, legal, economic, reproductive), I want to address sexuality as producing and sustaining such structures, sexuality as not simply an effect or a target but a bedrock and a driving force.

Implantation/Intromission

Thinking sexuality as installing rather than merely instantiating or submitting to an overarching colonial dynamic calls for a reassessment of Freud's theorizing of seduction even though his developmental account of libido, both intra- and inter-psychically, is suffused with the colonial logic of conquest and discipline, efficiency and return. The reformulation proposed by Jean Laplanche under the heading of a 'general theory of seduction' (Laplanche, 1987, 89–148) seems to me to be more explanatory and more useful in this context. Ever the winemaker,[10] Laplanche the psychoanalyst recast seduction as an 'implantation' of sexuality and thus a foundational stage in the formation of the unconscious. In so doing, Laplanche shifted the register of the inquiry into seduction from a whether or not to a how and when, hence further complicating some of the polarities dear to the heart of psychoanalysis and, indeed, the larger culture: activity/passivity, source/aim, nurture/nature, perpetrator/victim.

As Laplanche saw it, the infant does not come into the world with a pre-formed unconscious replete with drives and fantasies. Rather, it is in the general seduction that takes place in the asymmetrical relationship between adult (parent, sibling, caregiver …) and infant that a psychic structure is set up. While it tries to make sense of relatively clear dynamics of preservation, adaptation and attunement, the infant must also reconcile with signifiers originating in the adult yet 'enigmatic' to both sender and receiver. These signifiers pertain to the repressed components of the adult's own sexuality as they are triggered by the interaction with the infant; the implantation they precipitate occurs unbeknownst to the adult and is therefore beyond their choice. Hence, the breast—actual, displaced or fantasized—is not just nourishing, stimulating or withholding for baby, it is more than simply good or bad; it is shot through with the adult's own often unconscious excitement and desire. Ditto, among others, the gentle caress, the melodic coo and the soft sway as each such gesture exceeds its intended function and communicates beyond its manifest meaning.

Both infant and adult are thus actively, albeit differently, involved in an implantation that is neither deliberate nor necessarily malevolent. As they impact the infant, the adult's subtle pleasures do not run counter to or at the expense of a fledgeling libidinal essence. Instead, and herein lies Laplanche's radical contribution to the classic metapsychological position, it is the impact of the unacknowledged and baffling signifier originating in the adult that constitutes the foundation upon which an infant's psychic apparatus is built. Thus, what sustains the infant's ability to make sense of that signifier and integrate it after its own fashion is a budding ego; the effect of the infant's failure to develop a full mastery and symbolization of this signifier denotes a process of repression and an incipient unconscious; and, finally, whatever exceeds the infant's ability to fully 'translate' the sexually imbued signifier, the residue that gets repressed, is the source-object of the drive, a permanent feature and a constant source of excitement and frustration. As a 'generalized' theory of seduction, implantation describes a structuring process rather than a pathological dynamic: though forever translating and forever symbolizing, a human being does not always already belong in the world of the unconscious; it erects that world in its infancy as a dynamic solution to a surround it does not, and cannot, always comprehend.

Some may find it reassuring to think Laplanche's reformulation of seduction in terms of a care that, at times, may go awry, a care that, given the proper resources, is teachable, trackable, correctable. Two aspects to implantation must remain unsettling. First, since, at bottom, it is a confrontation with the fact of an enigma, implantation is fodder for, on the one hand, an Aristotelian sense of amazement and wonder in the face of a world to be discovered and enjoyed and, on the other hand, an unavoidable experience of doubt, of incompletion, of a limit as to what can be understood and metabolized. As products of implantation, the formation of the unconscious and the subsequent structuring of the psyche are hence possible only on the condition of failure as well as success, of injury, as some would say, as well as growth. Second, implantation recruits more than what is supposedly healthy or pleasurable of the adult's unconscious and its desires. The sincerest of intentions and the most responsible of child-rearing practices notwithstanding, the interaction with the infant recruits as much of the adult's ambivalence, narcissistic gratification and toxic projection as it does his or her benign eroticism. Before us are not mutually exclusive best and worst case scenarios but the most common, indeed inevitable, and coextensive components of the interaction between one unconscious and another. What the infant translates into its ego and what remains untranslatable in its unconscious are never exclusively wondrous and/or innocuous. Garden variety implantation which lends the psyche its dynamic topography is invariably accompanied by 'intromission' as the violent variant that stymies growth as it installs elements that short-circuit differentiation and resist metabolization (Laplanche, 1992, 358).[11] At stake then are both an invitation, an encouragement, a welcome into a world of pleasure and care as well as an unyielding territorialization and a hindering implantation for the benefit of one unconscious at the expense of another. In both dynamics unfold before us a conflictual acculturation, an installation of divided identities and prescriptions regarding objects, aims and means.[12]

The simultaneity of implantation with intromission calls up the classic psychoanalytic recognition of a quasi-ubiquitous co-incidence of opposites in terms more foundational than complementarity, compromise or ambivalence. Thought processes (primary, a-rational, unconscious versus secondary, common sensical, conscious), drives (binding and life-affirming Eros contra destructive and de-linking Thanatos), principles (pleasure as minimization of tension against reality as deliberation and deferral) are among the building blocks of a complex psychological apparatus that exceeds the familiar patterns of opposition and resolution. At the end of the day, Laplanche's reformulation of seduction as the origin story of an unconscious produced through implantation and intromission extends further this co-incidence and helps reveal the extent to which we are colonized in the most elemental of gestures at our most basic, most structural of cores: we are libidinal in so far as we are colonized and colonized so as to be libidinal.

The fact that, presumably, seduction may start out in the most caring of implantations does not shield it from intromission; nor does that fact exclude it from colonization. Instead, it is colonization itself that is opened up beyond the logic of presence and absence and onto a spectrum of timelines, modes and intensities. We may now rethink what we typically understand by colonization as a re-colonization: rather than the infliction of a traumatic injustice on an otherwise innocent and unblemished organism, before us is the driving of wedges into pre-existing splits (the enigmatic, the un-metabolizable) and the harnessing of certain components intrinsic to, in this particular context, the child's psychosexual structure and dynamics in order to make way for a new re-colonizing intromission in the service of the colonizer.

If sexual assault is a re-colonization, then one can only guess at the complex chain of past seductions that paved the way for a scenario where a father abuses his child while the mother does not or cannot recognize what is taking place under her roof. David's early history must be placed in a context that incorporates the conditions that produced the construction of *'the baby that never cried'* as well as the ends to which it was, and continues to be, deployed. No matter how thorough or earnest the retrograde analysis, elements of this history that belong not only to David but to his parents as well—separately and as a couple—shall remain forever inaccessible, un-translatable. By that same token, no matter how competent or responsible, the clinician must contend with a factor of the enigmatic (endemic as well as inherited) as it permeates the analytic relationship and shapes it as yet another link in the chain of seductions.

Of one thing we can be certain, the more insidious an intromission, the deeper the reach of the subsequent colonization. After many years of analysis, David can conjure only the vaguest of terms to express his feelings regarding what transpired in that childhood basement bedroom. *'Maybe paedophilia is an orientation and father couldn't help himself.' 'After all, he was married to a narcissist; she chose not to take care of him.' 'Come to think of it, neither of them could be trusted with anything; they put down both of my dogs while I was away on a school trip; they couldn't bother to give them their meds.'* There is sorrow when David speaks of his dogs, anger at the mention of mother, yet hardly anything beyond a most tepid disappointment with father. Aside from certain classic defences (displacement, intellectualization, splitting) and the dissociative tenor typical of a victim of repeated trauma, David's reticence may be attributed to a number of factors: while he does not share his father's choice of sexual object, he recognizes his is not alto-gether within the realm of the 'normal' either; as far as he is concerned, maintaining a two-decade silence over the abuse he endured burdens him with the lion's share of the responsibility for the pain suffered by his father's other victim(s). As the shame and guilt generate more silence, the reenact-ment in the clinical setting of a formative mistrust, a resourceful self-reliance and a wish to protect the other from possible harm mean that, again, David must confront his Goliath on his own, often outside the analytic space. I may provide him all manner of valued support; I, however, may not take part in his struggle.

Take Three

Being With

Much as these concerns complicate the relationship David and I have, they remain, in principle at least, more or less grist for the analytic mill, poten-tially given their due and perhaps even surmounted. And yet ... Recognizing the extent of our work and its enduring positive effects for him and ac-knowledging, with the requisite humility, that another clinician may very well do otherwise as well as better, my sense is that part of David's re-colonization is enclosed within an intractable intromission and may remain forever unspoken, if not indeed unspeakable—which, of course, is not to say un-lived. Over and above what grooming, collaboration and guilt typically produce in such scenarios, David's silence points to a limit past which it seems to me his analysis, with me at least, may not venture. There is, however, something that can be said as to the ways in which this limit keeps David company, the uses it serves and the moves it affords.

With roots in both implantation and intromission, David's being with his limit structures his sense of self and his sexuality; it speaks to his way of being with himself, an other or a group—of belonging, failing or refusing belonging. While there is much that may be said of the affective qualities to each of these modes, I, at this point, would like to concentrate on the me-chanics of fantasizing and fantasying as elaborated by Winnicott (1971), on how they engage implantation and intromission and, in the process, make way for particular styles of being with—solitude and loneliness.

Implantation is the course of a signifier translated, repressed, recovered, re-translated, dismantled and rebuilt, anew; it is the polysemy of symboli-zation where meaning and possibility are created. This is what Winnicott identified as fantasizing in all its manifestations (e.g., dreaming, playing, finding), as a poetry that builds layer upon layer of meaning and an ima-ginative planning that precipitates and looks forward to action as much as it is shaped by it (Winnicott, 1971, 35). In contrast, recognizing in the in-dividual what Marx had identified in group ideology and Nietzsche in nihilism, and echoing phantasying from the English rendition of Freud's reference to a split-off thought activity (Freud, 1911c, 222), Winnicott described fantasying as lacking in poetry, as the dead end of a stark scene where little, if anything, happens, or rather where the thing that does happen is the prevention of anything of substance from ever happening. This is what Deleuze once called the reactive (Deleuze, 1962). Fantasying is an isolating activity that drains objects and relations of their possible meaning as it reduces them to ossifying procedures—think the idle daydreaming of the perfect and perfectly satisfying life (talents, careers, partners, finances ...) in the face of a painful, disorganized and/or fleeting reality. As a counter to the diverse and unpredictable, fantasying installs a numbing and repetitive dissociation (Winnicott, 1971, 27) which Dominique Scarfone has since identified as a paradigmatic precursor to intromission (Scarfone, 2005).

The distinction between fantasizing and fantasying is a distinction between solitude, aka the capacity to be alone (Winnicott, 1958), and loneliness, between an openness to the generative and unfamiliar and the seemingly self-sufficient yet in fact deadening. Sense, theoretical, societal and political, would rather such categories stand apart from one another. Experience tells a different story.

Fantasying is no mere malady. David's loneliness revolves around an endlessly repetitive confrontation with a Goliath that will not die, indeed a Goliath that must not die since his death can only be the outcome of a violent act of self-mutilation. When colonizer and colonized are entrenched in the same psychic space, the cost of their conflict is borne primarily by the colonized. Of porn and video games, each is an engagement with someone else's fantasy and, in David's case, evidence of his reluctance to nurture his own inner world. In conjunction with the bouts of excessive drinking, these are also his ways of placating and numbing his nemesis, of keeping him confined to the basement. As at once toxin and remedy (*pharmakon*), each reinforces the walls of Goliath's prison, secures his confinement and guarantees that the enemy shall remain caught in a consuming struggle to an ever-deferrable death.

Taxing as it may be, Goliath's confinement and the fantasying it requires make it possible for David to engage in a world other than his enemy's, to fantasize outside the constraints of monotony and futility, abuse and mistrust. And, with the help of Jake, fantasize he does, Lest we forget, the basement belongs to the child beloved by his grandfather and to the cared for canine as much as it does to the abuser and victim in this story. It is to Jake that belong both the responsibility and the relish to sustain a playful solitude which Winnicott understood as a 'freedom from withdrawal' and an ability to 'relax' whereby an impulse and a sensation 'will feel real and be truly a personal experience' (Winnicott, 1958, 34).

David's version of this experience is an elaborate construction project. While a quintessential metaphor for the unconscious, the basement is his '*mission central*' for a complete renovation of the house guided by both creature comforts and, as a nod to that other construction paradigm, *'Russian engineering'* by whose standards impermeable boundaries are paramount. Still, David is at his most comfortable as he fantasizes and plays, somewhere between illusion and utility. He delights in formulating ever-changing plans, he thrives in the searches and researches for tools and materials, often with little regard for timelines or practical ends. He takes pride in pursuing his project with as little help as possible from the outside, without, however, entirely retreating from his relations with others. It is in the context of these that his solitude thrives. This is evident in both the analysis and his daily life where separations and extended breaks from those he now considers standard fixtures (e.g., wife and analyst) are triggers for the most intense and most debilitating of symptoms.

Metapsychologically, recall that we are in the realm of relational implantation/intromission—rather than Freudian one-person psychology—and in the realm of fantasizing, emblematic of the capacity to be alone, itself possible only within a dyadic relationship. After all, an infant and an analysand can enjoy being alone because parent and analyst are reliably yet unobtrusively present somewhere in the background. Tellingly, the capacity to be alone in one party in any given relationship flourishes when it is met with the other's capacity to leave alone, to accompany without intrusion or meddling. Since we are considering parents who were once children and analysts who were once analysands, their present capacity to leave the other alone is an outcome of earlier experiences of having been alone in the presence of a preceding other (parent and/or analyst), of having been left alone by that other and, most critically, of having left that other and disconnected from them, of having done so in, hopefully, the healthiest of ways, of, in other words, parents who, as children, snuck away from their parents' gazes, of analysts who, as analysands, left their analysts alone as well as behind where they belonged.

Solitude in the one is hence contingent on an attitude in the other whose aetiology is slightly more nuanced and a bit less innocuous than caring unobtrusiveness in the other. The aetiology of the capacity to leave alone incorporates an inevitable though at times ethically and clinically troubling element of disconnection, escape or neglect. Such an element is often overlooked or explained away as a foible or failure. Supposedly, the analyst who nods off, double books, forgets or misspeaks, the analyst who, in other words, slips and fails to be present with the analysand in their solitude, hasn't been trained enough or analyzed enough. Perhaps. Equally likely however is the possibility that such an analyst, and indeed every analyst, does not simply leave alone, let be, make room or give room for the other to grow but indeed cannot but abandon, avoid, neglect—idiosyncratically, purposefully or indifferently, as, hopefully, they had done in at least two of their most formative relationships.

At this point, little, I believe, may be gained from an enumeration of the ways and consequences in which I have abandoned David—little, that is, beyond the potentially supervisory. Instead, the fact that I have, at times, left him has fuelled further David's wish to leave, both in fantasying—thus sustaining the family story of the baby that never cried in confirmation of its sense of the futility of calling out for care and attention—and in fantasyzing—as a means of fine-tuning the myriad though solitary ways in which his playful renovations may unfold. Among other things, fantasyzing and fantasying are thus relational operators: while the one may enact and/or welcome implantation, the other is also a response to and a defence against intromission.

In David's case, and perhaps in all of our cases, the other whose unobtrusive presence makes fantasizing possible is not exclusively a so-called good other. Drunk and distracted, Goliath remains at bay; sober, he may neglect his victim and leave him alone every so often. As with any colonizer, his longevity is premised on his colonizing fantasy of separateness and superiority, the same fantasy that, perhaps unintentionally but no less critically, opens for the colonized some room beyond pain and duress.

Notes

1 The complicated relationship between being alone and leaving alone, between solitude and distancing, is also under scrutiny here.
2 For more on mourning and termination, see Craige (2002), Murdin (1999) and Schlesinger (2016). See also Knafo (2017) on termination's persistence throughout the analytic process rather than in its concluding stages and as a constitutive dynamic instead of a mere concern.
3 In the debates regarding the roots of psychic pain and the means of treating it, Kleinians and Kohutians are often seen as occupying opposing sides in the conflict (among the drives) versus deficit (of care). Nevertheless, many members from both groupings endorse a quasi-economic process of analyst-produced procedural and emotional goods whose consumption/internalization facilitates for the analysand their journey toward mental well-being.
4 In his presentation of Freud's writings on technique, Ellman (1991, 60–1) rightly notes this playground as a precursor facilitating Winnicott's understanding of the analytic process as occurring at the crossroad between the activities of the two participants.
5 While, in true Freudian fashion, we analysts tend to refrain from extending any guarantee regarding the duration or success of our interventions to prospective analysands, many of us rarely doubt our capacity and commitment to be present, to endure, to witness, to remember, to, in sum, hardly if ever abandon. In the process, we declare ourselves inured to the psychic laws of compromise and the inevitable realities of the parapraxis; we, presumably, never forget, mix up, neglect, misplace or misspeak. Infallible, we remain forever on guard and on point. Or at least we aim to.
6 Interestingly, this moment of the analyst's aloneness jives well with an observation Winnicott made in passing, between parentheses no less, under the heading of research: 'Psycho-analytic research is perhaps always to some extent an attempt on the part of an analyst to carry the work of his own analysis further than the point to which his own analyst could get him' (Winnicott, 1947, 196).
7 Any two worlds will do here: utility and hallucination, work and rest …
8 Unless otherwise stated, the italicized text is David's.

9 This, as suggested by certain versions of the Goliath account, is where the warrior came forward to bring to a close the battle between Israelites and Philistines as the two armies encamped across from one another (Yadin, 2004, 380–81).

10 The Laplanche family owned Chateau de Pommard (Burgundy) from the 1930s onward. Along with his wife Nadine, Jean Laplanche managed the winery for decades, until the couple sold the property in the early 2000s.

11 The decision to render the French '*intromission*'—dating back to the 15th century and meaning the introduction of one object into another—as its English cognate is unfortunate; the latter is nowadays associated with penile-vaginal penetration and leads the reader of Laplanche in translation to the conclusion that the psycho-analyst was specifically referencing a sexual scenario (Zeuthen and Hagelskjær, 2015; Harris, 2018). Laplanche was rather addressing the broader phenomenon of an intrusion that stands in the way of growth, the same one that plays a role in the formation of the super ego as a 'foreign body that cannot be metabolized' (Laplanche, 1992, 358).

12 Cf. Butler, 2014.

References

Butler, Judith. 2014. "Seduction, Gender and the Drive." In *Seductions and Enigmas: Cultural Readings with Laplanche*. Edited by J. Fletcher and N. Ray. London: Lawrence & Wishart. Pp. 118–134.

Craige, Heather. 2002. "Mourning Analysis: The Post-Termination Phase." In *Journal of the American Psychoanalytic Association*. 50:2. Pp. 507–550.

Deleuze, Gilles. 1962. *Nietzsche et la philosophie*. Paris: Presses Universitaires de France.

Deleuze, Gilles and Guattari, Felix. 1977. *Anti-Oedipus*. Translated by Robert Hurley, Mark Seem, and Helen R. Lane with a preface by Michel Foucault. New York: Viking Press.

Deleuze, Gilles and Guattari, Felix. 1987. *A Thousand Plateaus*. Translated by Brian Massumi. Minneapolis: University of Minnesota Press.

Ellman, Steven. 1991. *Freud's Papers on Technique: A Contemporary Perspective*. Northvale: Jason Aronson Press.

Foucault, Michel. 1976. *L'Histoire de la sexualité*, vol. 1. Paris: Gallimard.

Freud, Sigmund. 1911c. "Formulations on the Two Principles of Mental Functioning." In *The Complete Standard Edition of the Psychological Works of Sigmund Freud (SE)* XII. London: Hogarth Press. Pp. 218–226.

Freud, Sigmund. 1912a. "The Dynamics of the Transference." In *SE* XII. London: Hogarth Press. Pp. 99–108.

Freud, Sigmund. 1914a. "Remembering, Repeating and Working-Through: Further Recommendations on the Technique of Psychoanalysis II." In *SE* XII. London: Hogarth Press. Pp. 145–156.

Freud, Sigmund. 1914b. "On Narcissism: An Introduction." In *SE* XIV. London: Hogarth Press. Pp. 67–102.

Gould, Stephen Jay. 1985. *Ontogeny and Phylogeny*. Cambridge: Harvard University Press.

Harris, Adrienne. 2018. "Sexuality as Enigma, Emergent from Otherness and an Agent of Interpellation." In *Psychoanalysis Today* 8. https://psychoanalysis.today/en-GB/PT-Articles/Harris144994/Sexuality-as-Enigma,-Emergent-from-Otherness-and-a.aspx Accessed 15-08-2022.

Knafo, Danielle. 2017. "Beginnings and Endings: Time and Termination in Psychoanalysis." In *Psychoanalytic Psychology*. 35:1. Pp. 8–14.

Laplanche, Jean. 1987. *Nouveaux fondements pour la psychanalyse*. Paris: Presses Universitaires de France.

Laplanche, Jean. 1992. *Le primat de l'autre en psychanalyse*. Paris: Flamarion.

Lepoutre, Thomas. 2016. "From the Myth of the Primal Word to the Test of the Family Romance." In *Research in Psychoanalysis*. *21*:1. Pp. 62–69.

Murdin, Lesley. 1999. *How Much Is Enough?: Endings in Psychotherapy and Counselling*. London: Routledge.

Scarfone, Dominique. 2005. "Laplanche and Winnicott meet … and survive." In *Sex and Sexuality: Winnicottian Perspectives*. Edited by L. Caldwell. London: Karnac Books. Pp. 33–53.

Schlesinger, Herbert. 2016. *Endings and Beginnings: On Terminating Psychotherapy and Psychoanalysis*. London: Routledge.

Winnicott, Donald W. 1947. "Hate in the Countertransference." In *Through Paediatrics to Psycho-Analysis: Collected Papers*. New York: Basic Books. Pp. 194–203.

Winnicott, Donald W. 1958. "The Capacity to Be Alone." In *The Maturational Processes and the Facilitating Environment*. London: Hogarth Press and The Institute of Psycho-Analysis. Pp. 29–36.

Winnicott, Donald W. 1971. "Dreaming, Fantasying, and Living." In *Playing and Reality*. London and New York: Routledge Books. Pp. 26–37.

Yadin, Azzan. 2004. "Goliath's Armor and Israelite Collective Memory." In *Vetus Testamentum*, 54.3. Pp. 373–395.

Zeuthen and Hagelskjær. 2015. "Practicing Psychoanalytic Theory in the Field of Child Sexual Abuse." https://www.ipa.world/ipa/IPA_Docs/Katrine%20Zeuthen. docx Accessed: 15-08-2022.

Chapter 5

Games

Publisher's note: this chapter contains references to sexual assault, discrimination, violence, and death.

Jurisdictions

Much has been said of the painful leisure designed to serve pleasure and foster experimentation, of the sadism justified by principle or whim, of the brutality held in check by adulthood and/or civilization. As much has been said of the cruelty enacted by ordinary people under extraordinary circumstances. In this last context, while supposedly showing how certain situations move one to become abusive and brutal, Milgram's Obedience to Authority experiments and Zimbardo's Stanford Prison Experiment speak the pervasiveness of cruelty in the language of a science that can only address the phenomenon's how but never truly its why. Both scenarios treat cruelty in situational terms and reinforce the bias that assailant and victim share alike in an injustice perpetrated by some external agency, be it a malevolent politico or a misguided scientist. The irony here is that such experiments are, indeed, experiments, i.e., make belief scenarios that mimic reality while differentiating themselves from it. As their participants play at being interrogators or prison wardens, their make belief slides into the suspension of disbelief as the experiment and experimenter help produce a character that captures all too well a cruelty at the essence of the human. Much remains to be said of this cruelty, not only as an unmediated and gratuitous infliction of pain beyond the limit of what reason or common sense can conceive, but as a foundational component to exciting, precarious play, of a cruelty whose effect is a fear that hardly ever speaks. In the process, perhaps and eventually, something may be said of a fear that defies the symbolic, of a fear born not only from the encounter with sheer cruelty but also from the confrontation with that cruelty's playful core.

In his now classic treatment, Johan Huizinga identified play as a creative innocence operating 'outside the antithesis of wisdom and folly, truth and falsehood, good and evil' (Huizinga, 1995, 6). Huizinga nonetheless appreciated the extent to which play is agonistic and war is indeed play: 'Ever since words existed for fighting and playing, men have been wont to call war a game'

DOI: 10.4324/9781003352488-5

Peace	War	Total War

| | Play | |
| | Good | Evil |

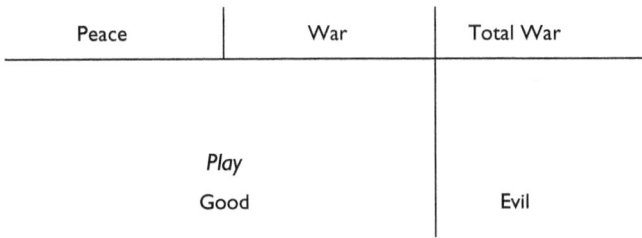

Figure 5.1 Play schema 1 (Huizinga).

(89). Distinguished from both peace and the criminal violence that is 'total war,' war presupposes ludic rules and requires 'a sphere whose members regard each other as equals or antagonists with equal rights' (89). Play then is hardly confined to the times of peace, to the nursery, family room, schoolyard or therapist's office; it extends into periods of great strife; it is the differentiating marker of a just and legitimate war as opposed to a war that is 'total.' Play is hence less outside the antithesis of good and evil as it is the territory whose boundary encompasses the one and delineates it from the other (Figure 5.1).

Huizinga's expansion of the scope of play to include outright conflict fits well a psychoanalytic sensibility that has already wrested the nursery, family room, schoolyard and therapist's office from the illusions of peace and harmony. And yet, this expansion is complicated by the sense that it may be predicated on an idealization of war as an honourable resolution of otherwise irresolvable disputes, a perplexing idealization considering the publication of Huizinga's study in 1938 was bookended by two world wars that had as much in common with the 'total' as with the just and justifiable. More challenging to this expansion is the fact that the wars we now suffer—the wars on terrorists, criminals and infidels—exhibit a cruelty that operates far outside the ludic rules of war while becoming evermore beguiling, incomprehensible and numbing precisely because of its playful lure. Witness in this regard the video-simulation reporting on war, the delivery of extra-judicial death sentences via remote-controlled toy-like drones, the mediatic performances of the adherents of most warring factions and, last but not least, the training of military and intelligence personnel through game-inspired technologies, technologies to whose seductions late adolescence, which often seems an emotional limit-state for many recruits, is highly susceptible.

Contra Huizinga, there is an integral relation between play and cruelty epitomized most strikingly by unjustifiable and indiscriminate war. This relation exceeds what might be sustained by either the logic of the usurpation of the many by the few (the ever-reliable 'few bad apples' hypothesis) or that of unreasonable means justified by reasonable ends (Figure 5.2).

In what follows, I would like to further the elaboration of the unsettling and perhaps obscene though foundational connection between play and cruelty

Peace	War	Total War

Play

Good | Evil

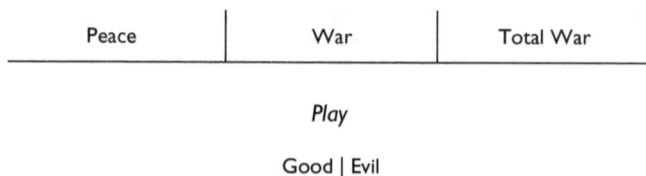

Figure 5.2 Play schema 2 (modified).

rather than on the ways in which the former may inadvertently slip into the latter or even be deployed purposefully as its instrument (Illouz and Prétou, 2018). Where ethical theory and cultural history butt against moral atrophy or intellectual impasse, psychoanalysis exposes a most uncomfortable but no less real dimension to the human psyche: its capacity for cruelty is ubiquitous, exciting, precarious, gratuitous; it belongs to the Freudian pleasure that lies beyond the principle and to the Winnicottian transitional that simultaneously sustains and disavows it. In effect, psychoanalysis uncovers a structural relation between play and cruelty that implicates us all as it extends beyond the temporary, extreme or aberrant. Though this relation may leave little room for hope, it leaves even less room for indifference.

According to Huizinga, play stands consciously outside ordinary life; while not quite serious, it absorbs the player intensely and utterly. Play is an activity 'connected with no material interest, and no profit can be gained from it. It proceeds within its own proper boundaries of time and space according to fixed rules and in an orderly manner. It promotes the formation of social groupings which tend to surround themselves with secrecy and to stress their difference from the common world by disguise or other means' (Huizinga, 1995, 13). Monetary considerations aside, one might have to make an effort here to remind oneself that Huizinga was referencing play rather than the practice of psychoanalysis which, for some of us at least, stands outside the daily requirements of earnestness and utility while subject to its own rules regarding locations, protocols, exclusions, legitimations and confidences. And what Huizinga was not referencing explicitly is precisely what Winnicott had in mind as he underscored the ubiquity of play in the life of the species and identified the analytic space as one of its more specialized arenas. It is also worth remembering here that while Huizinga's attention was focused primarily on the subcategory of games with its rules and procedures, Winnicott's concern was with the broader and more organic phenomenon of playing; while significant, this distinction does not distract from the main points advanced here.

Justifications

As Huizinga spoke of play's grounding in illusion (11), Winnicott located playing in the illusory yet tangible transitional space between hallucination as primary creativity and reality as objective perception. Huizinga's view that play is exempted from the categories of truth, wisdom and morality is paralleled by Winnicott's by now familiar assertions regarding the immanent neutrality of playing and of whatever may occur under its aegis (Winnicott, 1971, 12).

However, Winnicott extended playing beyond the antithesis of 'wisdom and folly, truth and falsehood, good and evil;' the phenomenon is constitutive of all of culture and its foibles, contradictions and follies, including not only artistic creativity and appreciation, religious feeling and dreaming, but also lying, stealing, the loss of affectionate feeling, drug addiction and obsessional rituals (Winnicott, 1971, 5). By extension, in the clinical setting, playing may be evidenced not only in the creative decoding of slips and dreams, the freeing pursuit of fantasies and associations; it also belongs to the suffering of interruptions and resistances, deadlocks and acting outs, regressions and negative therapeutic reactions. By an even further extension, in the broader political context this time, playing operates not only in the arena of democracy as the medium for creative solutions to otherwise intractable problems; it is also at work in, among other things, censorship, confinement, deprivation, abuse, torture and murder (Figure 5.3).

In line with the psychoanalytic approach of understanding the extraordinary in order to shed light on the extremely ordinary, I offer the pictures some US military personnel took of the men they detained at the Abu Ghraib Prison in Iraq between October and December of 2003. Once made public, the pictures and the circumstances that produced them generated controversy and soul searching in some circles (Hersh, 2004) while in others the extreme was dismissed as mundane and unimpressive, as per some political commentators' justifications that there was nothing to see here beyond 'what happens everyday at an American fraternity' (Crowley, 2009) or simply, in reference to the actions of some among the female recruits, 'babes' in 'need to blow off some steam' (Wildau and Seifter, 2004). The then president of the United States delivered what has been accurately described

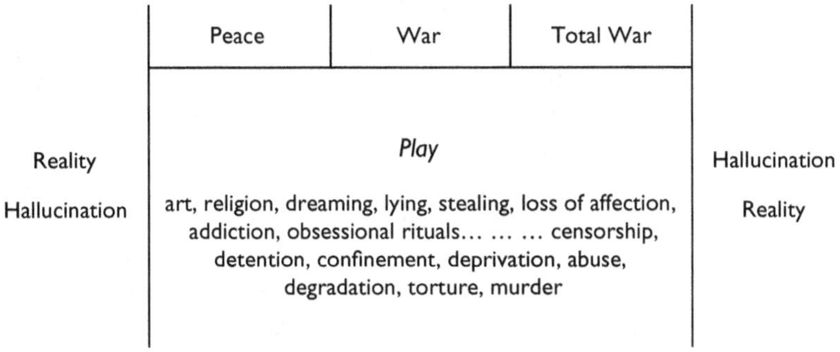

	Peace	War	Total War	
Reality		*Play*		Hallucination
Hallucination	art, religion, dreaming, lying, stealing, loss of affection, addiction, obsessional rituals... ... ... censorship, detention, confinement, deprivation, abuse, degradation, torture, murder			Reality

Figure 5.3 Play schema 3 (Winnicott).

as a 'simulated atonement' with which he sought to skirt accountability for his role in the crisis (Shepard, 2009). The events have since been summed up with a glib, perfunctory and unimpressive, or perhaps exceptionally impressively vacuous admission 'we tortured some folks' proffered a little over ten years after the fact by another president of the United States (Rampton and Holland, 2014), the same president who, five years prior and upon the initial disclosure of the brutal interrogation techniques used by the Central Intelligence Agency, advised against dwelling on the past since 'nothing will be gained by spending our time and energy laying blame' for it (Mazzetti and Shane, 2009). Ta-Nehisi Coates promptly, and accurately, interpreted this statement as signalling that a 'particular' group was not in any danger of being held accountable for a 'particular' past (Coates, 2009), that, in other words, the past in question and its attendant injustices may not be that troubling or in need of redress after all.

The photographs are among the thousands suffused with torture, physical and psychological, that 'began with the lower downs, and was simply ignored by the higher ups' (Rejali, 2009, p. 412).[1] They depict practices designed to 'open up' or 'soften' their targets for upcoming interrogations by the intelligence personnel. Meanwhile, as most everyone from the US Senate down to the interrogators themselves knew but would only admit much later (United States Senate Select Committee on Intelligence, 2014, Danner, 2004, Greenberg and Dratel, 2005, Fair, 2016), these practices and the tortures they led to could rarely if ever yield any so-called actionable intelligence.

Alongside the official rhetoric that swung from legitimation to denial ran the reality in which guards and interrogators alike designated the photographs as moments of 'play' that was 'funny as fuck' or' 'fun as hell'' (Phillips, 2010, 194, 66–7 and Ricks, 2007, 278) for those that took them, of play whose moments and characters were staged and shot in the open spaces of the prison, in full view for all to see,[2] collected and distributed amongst the rank and file without much caution or concern, all the while guarded against the prying eyes of the outside world that, presumably, could not or would not understand their supposed light-heartedness and appreciate their innocence. A prosecutor in the 2004 court-martial of former Abu Ghraib guard Ivan Frederick remarked: 'When you look at those photographs and you hear the testimony, nobody appears to be angry. In fact there's laughter in the background.' Frederick responded: 'It's a game, Sir.' (McKelvey, 2007, 17)

And when, at Abu Ghraib, pictures were not enough of a distraction for those in charge, they were supplanted by all manner of wordplay. Original coinages and neologisms become the order of the day (monstering, compliance blow, tactical questioning and manipulative self-injurious behaviour); those in charge gave themselves innocuous titles (innkeeper, babysitter and condition setter) as they assigned their prisoners corresponding designations (guests and ghosts) while singling out a few with the privilege of a nickname, as children do with their favourite toys (Shank, Dr Claw, Slash, Mr Burns, Big

Bird, Swamp Thing, Piggy and Twitch). The nicknames made the prisoners more familiar than their numeric designations ever could; they turned them into cartoon characters, comfortable and yet unreal. 'It was jail but, you know, you can still laugh in jail, "[Sergeant Hydrue] Joyner said. 'It's not a crime, I hope.'" (Gourevitch and Morris, 2009, 100).

Take 'Gilligan,' for instance, an Iraqi detainee who was initially accused of the murder of two US military personnel though identified by Specialists Megan Ambuhl and Sabrina Harman, from among the prison staff, as a 'pretty decent' and 'funny, funny' guy, the kind you would want to take home (Gourevitch, 2008). In a photograph that encapsulates much of what The Abu Ghraib scenario now stands for,[3] Gilligan is shown standing on a box with a bag over his head, believing that the wires around his fingers, toes and penis are live and that he will be electrocuted should he step down. He is eventually relieved of his ordeal once the scene is photographed from different perspectives. Though in time found innocent of the charges for which he had been arrested, he was not released, as per the Abu Ghraib detention policy in place; instead, he was given extra meals for helping around the prison (Gourevitch, 2009 p. 176).

In yet another photograph,[4] Military Police Specialist Charles Graner and his girlfriend Private First Class Lynndie England pose grinning behind naked and hooded detainees piled one on top of the other. Graner wanted to keep the detainees together 'to control them, so that they are all in one area.' England offered 'We would joke around, everyone would laugh at the things we had them do' at her psychological assessment as part of the military inquiry into the Abu Ghraib prisoner abuse mere months after the discovery of the photographs (Nelson, 2004, p. 4). Specialist Jeremy Sivits complied with Graner's request to take the shot because he was just a 'nice guy' who tried 'to be friends with everybody,' who tried 'not to have anybody mad at [him].' (Gourevitch and Morris, 2009, 190–99).

In the meantime, Specialist Harman flashes a bright smile and signals a thumbs-up for the camera as she hovers over the body of a detainee who had been tortured to death the night before.[5] 'I kind of picked up the thumbs-up from the kids in Al Hillah,' a city 100 km outside of Baghdad where she had been posted previously; 'whenever I get into a photo I never know what to do with my hands, so I probably have a thumbs-up because it's just something that automatically happens. Like when you get into a photo you want to smile.' Twenty other photographs were eventually found in which Harman appears in the identical pose—same smile, same thumbs-up: bathing in an inflatable wading pool, holding a tiny lizard, standing at the foot of a wall that bears a giant bas-relief of Saddam Hussein, fooling around with a buddy who is giving her the finger and flashing a tongue stud, holding a tiny figurine of Jesus, holding a long, phallic melon, mounting the ancient stone lion of Babylon at the ruins of King Nebuchadnezzar's city, leaning over the shoulder of an MP buddy who is holding a Fanta can on top of which sits a dead cat's head (Gourevitch and Morris, 2009, 75) and, again, as in this case, hovering over the body of a detainee who had been tortured to death the night before.

In yet another of the emblematic photographs,[6] Private First Class England poses as the man collapsed on the floor, 'Gus,' also known as 'Mr Burns,' is, she claimed, complying voluntarily; 'I'm just kind of holding the tie-down strap. You can see the slack on it. I know people said that I dragged him, but I never did. After Graner was done taking the pictures, he put the camera back in his cargo pocket, walked over, took the strap from me, and I guess Gus wanted to cooperate then, so he took it off of his neck, and he dragged him up, and he took him to his cell. That was the end of that event' (Gourevitch and Morris, 2009, 137).

In an interview she gave six years after the photographs were made public, Private England disclosed that the naked man in another picture[7] had been masturbating for 45 minutes in a four-hour-long *mise en scène* in celebration of her 21st birthday. She insisted to her interviewer that she had nothing to apologize for since all she had done was stand in the pictures. With a lop-sided smile, she declared: 'Saying sorry is admitting I was guilty and I'm not. I was just doing my duty' (Jones, 2009).

It seems that England's duty belongs to a world in which one individual transforms another to mere flesh, denying them the possibility of experience, a world of torture in which, as Jean Améry once put it, 'man exists only by ruining the other person who stands before him.' (Améry, 1980, 35) Initially, the detainees in these pictures were stripped of any subjectivity as they were manipulated and posed as lifeless objects. Gradually, their pictures shifted from the register of documentation (of the supposedly professional, playful, normal or quotidian) to that of display and exhibitionism, of directorial license and voyeurism (Gourevitch and Morris, 2009, 145–9), our voyeurism included. The men are charged with exaggerated sexuality, as in England's birthday scene, reinforcing the racial stereotype, with the requisite taste for bondage, as per Mr Burns above, or homoeroticism[8] meant as a humiliation that, presumably, befits their status. Conversely, they are displayed as prey, as in the imagery of big game hunting; their objectification comes hand in hand with a trophiism and a triumphalism reserved for the noble among nature's creatures; these men will henceforth belong to a wild and ferocious species whose capture accrues its hunter much glory.

Ludens

Homo Ludens (*Man the Player*, or *The Playing Man*) is how Huizinga chose to title his study. In his honour, and in keeping with the tradition of giving old things new names, even Latin ones, in the hope of thinking them differently, I will adopt *Ludens* (as in the gerundial playing, instead of *ludus*, the noun) to highlight a grounding connection between playing and cruelty, a kinship obfuscated by the fantasy that playing somehow belongs to a wholesome lineage (innocence, pleasure or creativity, with the occasional scraped knee or bruised ego), a fantasy that spares the phenomenon a reckoning with its troubling roots and investments in cruelty, in favour of, say, mere vicinity or accidental slippage. At this point, I will not take on the task of a disquisition on the cruel, its origins or nature; nor will I expound on the category's ethical nuances or status as a breach of eternal laws or (a) sovereign('s) rights. Rather, I will highlight the cruelty of *Ludens* with the understanding that no category is legitimate ground for a worn 'us versus them' demarcation, that whatever category one may wish to invoke in this context obtains in all humans, that the standard of psychological health is not the absence of any such category but the extent to which the subject, who, marked by it, is nevertheless capable of a modicum of love and work. In spite of all their differences, this understanding applies to Freud, Klein, Lacan, Winnicott and, indeed, any psychoanalyst worthy of the designation. As we all possess a psychotic core, are perverse in varying degrees, exhibit schizoid organizations, split, project and get ensnared by the powers of the imaginary, we all participate in playing that is not always or entirely innocent, in playing that is indeed *Ludens*.

Play, Huizinga pointed out, 'interrupts the appetitive process. It interpolates itself as a temporary activity satisfying in itself and ending there' (9). Against play's presumed transience and much like cruelty, *Ludens* endures; it contains its own course and meaning; it has no external purpose and serves no other function beyond itself. It is neither need nor demand; it is not discharge, distraction, compromise or displacement. If it were any of these, it would make room for reason or return; it however needs neither. *Ludens* operates in a space of indeterminacy, or rather in a space that has no use for anything other than its own determinacy, a space of the gratuitous where means and ends collide, where an action does not suffer the lack of justification since it is forever its own justification and, by extension, its own consequence. The cruelty at stake seeks, sustains and enlivens itself, deliberately rather than compulsively; it thinks itself through and cares for itself as it cultivates and refines its strategies and procedures. In the face of this cruelty, reason (as pedagogy, reform or insight—even of the psychoanalytic kind) is not so much a failure, as it is futile and unsustainable.

Ludens populates its domain with the right agents and objects; these will in turn follow the appropriate procedures. Every game has its rules, and rules are sustained and refined through repetition; and no game can afford to be a one-off attempt. In turn, the repetition is deployed both in the service of mastery through re-inscription and as the occasion for finer and more original variations. The examples in this regard are aplenty; the serial murderer or rapist who specializes in a particular population, location or *modus operandi*, the terrorist who plants dozens of car bombs all over the city in order to sow as much pain and destruction as possible, the interrogator who deploys the same torture techniques on one detainee after another all operate not only with the presumed intent of perpetrating the greatest amount of harm and horror but with the equally ludic purpose of sustaining and refining their games' internal consistencies as well as a command over their relations with an excluded outside. In reality, the immediate victims are often mere peons here; the opponents and rivals are ultimately the police, the state or fellow interrogators.

Speaking of the outside, *Ludens* qualifies much of what lies beyond its territory as inferior, uninitiated, dispensable. This exceptionalism enters a reciprocal and sustaining relationship with secrecy. Huizinga again: '[play] loves to surround itself with an air of secrecy. Even in early childhood the charm of play is enhanced by making a 'secret' out of it. This is for us, not for the 'others'. What the 'others' do 'outside' is no concern of ours at the moment. Inside the circle of the game the laws and customs of ordinary life no longer count. We are different and do things differently' (12). Inside the game and outside 'the antithesis of good and evil,' hence beyond; an exemption from rules and oppositions that *Ludens*, the entity beyond, grants itself; an authorization to move beyond and install an opposition between itself and all other oppositions; and, finally, an immunization against both good and evil with the threat of a 'trauma' should the procedure fail or its legitimacy be questioned. This last threat, it should be noted, is forever imminent since the logic of the 'for its own sake' portends both a freedom from any responsibility to the outside as well as a dead end that marks a danger to its subject's long-term sustainability.

And so, as far as the Abu Ghraib pictures are concerned, one detects in the background to all the avowals of harmless playfulness the feeble attempts at justification: body pyramids as a way of gathering people in one area; thumbs-up as the natural and uncomplicated response to a lens, no matter who or what else is in the frame; simply standing there, doing one's duty or wanting to be nice ... While designed to impress, entertain, seduce and intimidate—more so fellow military than detainees—the fact that the cruelty was deliberate, persistent and often repetitive in its pose and turn of mind betrays its self-propelling dynamism. The 'us versus them' demarcations at Abu Ghraib were not between captors and captives since the latter could barely be recognized as human: 'You see these Iraqi people ... They're just the stock detainee. Like a movie prop' (McKelvey, 2007, 17). The demarcations were between the captors and the world outside, the rest of the US military and the civilians back home, the world that, so the story goes, might not appreciate how awful, awfully hard or awfully boring it all was for the personnel at Abu Ghraib who, poor souls, risked being further 'traumatized' by any misunderstanding.

A logic of exclusion, of inside and outside, within and beyond, envelops the polarities of wisdom and folly, truth and falsehood, good and evil. This is precisely what we witness at Abu Ghraib, the suspension of judgement, or at least a category of judgements, on the part of the so-called players as the

Civilian Life | Abu Ghraib

Wisdom | Folly
Truth | Falsehood | Outside — Beyond
Good | Evil

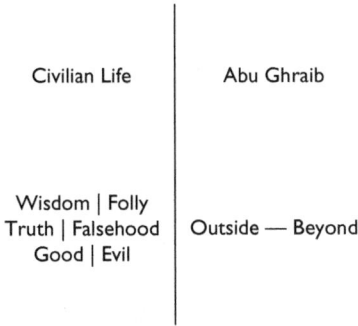

Figure 5.4 Exclusion as beyond.

activities that would have otherwise been restricted or censored are re-habilitated and freed up, outside of convention and beyond the norm (Figure 5.4).

At this point, I move to reframe what I have already presented in psy-choanalytic terms and, in return, attempt a reframing of the psychoanalytic. I want to redraw the schema of exclusion so that the outside and beyond are not elsewhere—above or away; they are rather proximate; they stand be-tween the terms of the polarity they seem to evade. They, in fact, shape the polarity and sustain its tensions, not simply as a barrier or frontier (Figure 5.5), but as an entirely distinct intermediary realm (Figure 5.6).

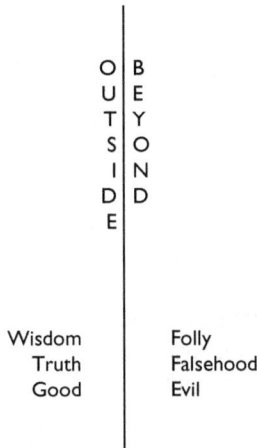

```
O|B
U|E
T|Y
S|O
I|N
D|D
E
```

Wisdom   Folly
Truth   Falsehood
Good   Evil

Figure 5.5 Exclusion as internal distinction.

```
                    O
                    U
                    T
                    S
                    I
                    D
                    E

                    B
                    E
                    Y
                    O
                    N
                    D


Wisdom              Folly
Truth               Falsehood
Good                Evil
```

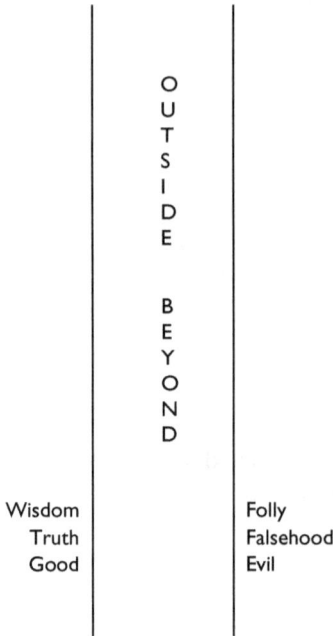

Figure 5.6 Exclusion as internal territory.

The correction I am proposing is grounded in the fact that, while it may have often indulged in a penchant for triangulation (mother/father/child, id/ego/super-ego, imaginary/symbolic/real), psychoanalysis submits much of its concern to a foundational logic of the in-between. The discipline's topography is invariably of three simultaneous though distinct domains, each with its own set of rules and investments and of psychoanalysis as a sustained appreciation for and intervention in the *interregnum* between the contradictory first and third, requiring and required by both, partaking of both in terms of materials and dynamics although belonging to neither. This is true enough of the drive, dream, transference and construction, of, in other words, the four polyvalent pillars of psychoanalytic theory and practice and so much so that it would be legitimate to qualify psychoanalysis as primarily a theory and a clinic of the *interregnum*.

Freud stripped the humours and souls of whatever ontological and therapeutic privilege they had enjoyed in previous centuries and advanced in their place the drive as lying on the frontier between the mental and the somatic. In the language of 'Instincts and their Vicissitudes' (Freud, 1915), the drive is no mere static line drawn between the various structures and agencies; it is 'the psychical representation of the stimuli originating from within the organism and reaching the mind, as a measure of the demand made upon the mind for work in consequence of its connection with the body' (Freud, 1915, 121–22). Freud's topography here must allow for a legitimate reversal of this biological point of view and recognize the drive as equally the psychical representation of the stimuli originating from within the mind and reaching the organism, as a measure of the demand made upon the body for work in consequence of its connection with the mind. Indeed, without such stimuli or demands, without, in other words, the power of fantasy and its corresponding wish for fulfilment, the body could hardly be said to 'work' toward experiencing a gamut of effects ranging from the orgasm to the psychosomatic symptom. Lying on the frontier between the psychical and the somatic; the drive must, in principle at least, allow for a passage in two different directions, each communicating its own set of demands to the other; its 'source' is as much psychical as it is 'a somatic process which occurs in an organ or part of the body and whose stimulus is represented in mental life by an instinct' (Freud, 1915, 123). Most importantly, the drive brings together a 'representing' mind and a 'working' body; without it, the mind knows nothing of lack, fantasy or difference and the body is incapable of anything beyond need or survival.

Freud did not explicitly identify the frontier as a central motif in his understanding of the drive till the mid-1910s. It was only after he had completed his text on the instincts' metamorphoses that he went back and transplanted the notion of the drive as operating along the frontier between the mental and the physical into the third (circa 1915) of the five editions of the *Three Essays on the Theory of Sexuality* (Freud, 1905, 168). Still, Freud had been quite taken with the concept of the frontier from his earliest days. Consider, for instance, the dream book (Freud, 1900) as it elaborates a topography that belongs to the dream as much as it does to the psyche and its three systems (conscious, pre-conscious and unconscious). The essence of a dream resides in the distortions it performs based on, again, 'a measure of the demand made upon the mind for work' in consequence of its connection, in this case, with both reality (as stimulus and/or daily residue) and the unconscious (as wish). The space or, more accurately, the image of the dream is the *Zwischenreich*, a term Freud had already used in a letter to Fliess (Freud, 1985, 181),[9] that references less an intermediary kingdom and more the inter-kingdom, the *interregnum*, as a mechanism of wish-fulfilment nestled in between, seemingly, a primordial hallucination and an irremediably frustrating reality.

This notion of an animated *interregnum* is echoed in Freud's declaration from the same period as 'Instincts and their Vicissitudes' that the transference is simultaneously an 'artificial illness' as well as a 'piece of real experience' that 'creates an intermediate region between illness and real life through which the transition from the one to the other is made' (Freud, 1914, 154). Last but not least, construction, which Freud identified as 'by far the more appropriate description' for much of what goes under the title of interpretation (Freud, 1937, 251),[10] emerges somewhere between fact and fiction, truth and falsehood. Construction is hardly a presentation in speech whose value lies in its ability to plumb the psychic depths and accurately summon a remote and otherwise inaccessible history; as a generative dynamic, construction deploys the doubled lenses of reality and fantasy, utility and pleasure in order to fuel the analytic process and reconfigure the psychic agencies that participate in it. As with repression and finding, construction is far from being a consciously intentional project; it is a mechanism that gathers and sustains various drives, objects and fantasies into a series of unexpected productions that may, intermittently and unpredictably, give rise to a semblance of deliberation and/or intentionality.

What is key about drive, dream, transference and construction is that each tells not only of a space between two otherwise incongruous realms but also of a set of rules often borrowed from both realms but invariably made particular by that space. This is entirely consistent with the nature of the *interregnum*, as not simply an intermediary kingdom but as an inter-kingdom and hence the kingdom between two kings, itself without a king as Jean-Bertrand Pontalis once pointed out.[11] The 'inter' here is potentially temporal (as much an *aevum*[12] as a mere midway phase between the end of one reign and the beginning of another), spatial (as a border territory seemingly created by two adjoining provinces but in effect creating these spaces insofar as it delineates and potentially fixes their contents and contours) or procedural (as a translation and/or mediation between two otherwise incongruous systems or processes). In all three, multiplicity, as both a danger and a prospect, outside and beyond the purity of the mutually exclusive either/or, is the order of the day. Tellingly, we recognize there is hardly anything unitary about the polymorphous drive, over-determined dream, multilayered transference and ever-producible construction[13] (Figure 5.7).

Interregnum

Mind	Drive	Body
Wish	Dream	Residue
Neurosis	Transference	Health
Fiction	Construction	Fact
...	...	...
Hallucination	Transitional space	Reality
Subject	Found object	Object

Pleasure Principle		Reality Principle
Hallucination	Play	Perception
Creativity		Utility

Figure 5.7 Transitionals.

Winnicott's privileging of the tripartite structure reality/play/hallucination is in line with this logic of the in-between. His most singular contribution to the psychoanalytic apparatus, the notion of the found object—as neither delusion nor materiality, neither will nor inertia, as instrument and occasion of play in the so-called transitional space, nestled somewhere between primary creativity and objective perception, animated and animating—is yet another instance of the *interregnum*. With this contribution, Winnicott opened out one of Freud's most iconic pairings, pleasure and reality (Freud, 1911), in order to uncover an extensive ground for play as more than merely a buffer between rest and work, as, indeed, a distinct principle of mental functioning with specific jurisdiction and processes. Depending on the level and purpose of the inquiry, play takes place somewhere between pleasure and reality, hallucination and perception, creativity and utility. In each instance, as with all similar arrangements, play is grounded in both sides of whatever divide it joins, bound by neither and arrogating from each whatever materials or strategies it deems necessary for its continuity. At this point, Freud's other equally iconic though significantly more controversial of pairings, Eros and Thanatos (Freud, 1920), demands a similar intervention.

As he tried to understand the psychological traumas suffered by survivors of the First World War, Freud looked beyond the principle of life and its pleasure and recognized the death drive as another, primary, organizing principle of the psyche. It is Thanatos, Freud proposed, that fuels the compulsion to repeat all manner of events, recollections and fantasies 'which include no possibility of pleasure, and which can never, even long ago, have brought satisfaction even to instinctual impulses which have since been repressed' (Freud, 1920, 20). Central for Freud's exploration of Eros/Thanatos as a duality of the mutually exclusive (Freud, 1925, 239) was the category of the border separating the one drive from the other, the wonted from the exceptional, the within from the beyond. As such, Freud could only attribute to this category the narrowest of liminal widths and, correspondingly, the barest of dynamic functions. Although he hypothesized it, Freud did not genuinely grasp this territory to its fullest as yet another instance of the much richer and more extensive *interregnum*.

I do not dismiss Freud's move in this context as an oversight or abandonment of the psychoanalytic investment in the in-between; rather, I consider it a reflection of the extent to which he held the two drives as imbricated and, indeed, woven into one another so much so that, by the end of his treatment, Freud erased the border and redrew these drives as mostly indistinguishable the one from the other. Witness, for instance, how Eros and Thanatos are separable according to their means rather than the ends they pursue: the former seeks to ensure that the organism shall follow its own path to death (Freud, 1920, 39) while the latter rushes foolishly toward that same end (41); or how Freud eventually concluded that the ego, once recruited to the task of self-preservation in opposition to the otherwise untamed sexual instincts (Freud, 1910, 214), is henceforth the seat of the destructive instincts (Freud, 1920, 60-1n1); or how an investigation initially propelled by recurrences of nightmares, painful experiences and flashbacks seems to culminate in an assessment of the death drive as it does its work rather 'unobtrusively.' (Freud, 1920, 63); or, last but certainly not least, how research into what is presumably excepted from pleasure's domain proceeds through a reversal of the structural and topographical relations in order to reach the troubling conclusion that pleasure is, after all, subsumed by that over which it has no say: 'the pleasure principle seems actually to serve the death instincts' Freud concluded (Freud, 1920, 63).

As he was plumbing the philosophical depths (Deleuze, 1989, 111), Freud failed to recognize that what lies beyond pleasure's principle is no mere singular dynamic, aka the death drive, against which it is defended by the thinnest of shields, but both a 'beyond' as well as that which stands between pleasure and its beyond, an *interregnum* that extends far beyond what Freud deployed under the heading of border. Between the domains of Eros and Thanatos lies much less a frontier than a lateral field upon whose expanse *Ludens* may skim or slide, rather than an abyss into whose depth the psyche and its interpreter may plummet. *Ludens* is a drive on an equal footing to Eros and Thanatos, a drive that unequivocally shares in, all the while remaining unreservedly distinct from, both. *Ludens* is neither a deployment of Thanatos in the service of Eros (as in a fort-da or a proverbial unbinding and delinking in order to bind and link again) nor a 'playful,' somewhat less damning or damaging variation on Thanatos (as in a sublimating sadism or militarism). While the workings of both Eros and Thanatos seem strikingly pragmatic, validated decidedly in terms of their goals and/or applied values, *Ludens* remains steadfastly irredeemable. *Ludens* is play once play has been recognized as pleasurable and hurtful, to the point of being cruel, enlivening and deadening, and sometimes even deadly, freeing and dissociating, at the risk of severing, innocent and guilty, to the extent where its guilt may be unfathomable.

While play is an experience toward which one may be led (in line with the Winnicottian definition of psychoanalysis as a process that leads the analysand to play) and away from which one may move, one is always already steeped in *Ludens*. Put differently, *Ludens* affords us no outside beyond that which is immanent.

I close with an observation from Jean Améry regarding some among those that survived Auschwitz:

> the time in the camp was not entirely without value for us (and when I say us, I mean the nonreligious and politically independent intellectuals). For we brought with us the certainty that remains ever unshakeable, that for the greatest part the intellect is a *ludus* and that we are nothing more—or, better said, before we entered the camp we were nothing more—than *homines ludentes*.
>
> (Améry, 1980, p. 20)

With the identification of the intellect as play and of the human species as ludic comes the recognition of silence not as evidence of the absence of play but as the epitome of an all-encompassing reality in which *Ludens*, as was the case with Abu Ghraib, becomes tantamount to a two-step program of torture that reduces a detainee to mere flesh and goes on to refigure him as, much as I am loath to admit, something akin to a found object invested with its finder's wishes and phantasies at the expense of all others, including, and most especially, its own. At the end of the day, if play and culture are not innocent, then neither is finding. In the Abu Ghraib photographs, the detainees are reduced to the barest in human terms; they are almost always hooded and stripped of all personal identifiers (Spens, 2014). Their terror is inaudible as it too is trapped within the walls of the prison, cell block or interrogation room. When a detainee speaks that terror, if he ever speaks it, he will not be heard; rather, of whatever he does speak only resistance or compliance, both as self-incrimination, may be heard. He is rendered dispensable for he is only the latest in a seemingly endless chain of arrests and transfers; by that same token, he remains virtually inexhaustible. Should he or the chain that brought him to his unbearable present come to an end, his shared and shareable photograph will see to it that he will never truly perish. Ironically, neither will his tormentors for, as is always the case with finding, the subject that finds is also found by the object and transformed to satisfy its needs. The reciprocity increases in magnitude and significance once the scope of what qualifies as a found object surpasses the confines of the nursery: ideas, geographies, technologies, professions, institutions and nations find us and transform us through care, responsibility and/or servitude. And so, the US military personnel from Abu Ghraib are forever woven into the pictures they orchestrated and the worlds of the 'objects' they found and played with; they are redrawn as, among others, bad apples, psychopaths, traffickers in cruelty, agents of imperialist hegemony and/or traumatized veterans. Found, they eventually fade into history's margins from which they may be recruited in the service of the occasional theory, including the current one, that runs the risk of setting yet another 'us versus them' logic that, in turn, affords its audience the feeling that it too might be slightly less complicit.

It is not quite clear whether this dimension to *Ludens* is the symptom of a fixation or a regression to the most rudimentary of encounters with the found object, encounters that we all carry within but can barely speak, encounters that are forever held back from an otherwise genuine reciprocal finding. The view I wish to put forward at this point is that whatever hope we may have rests not on the suppression or surpassing of *Ludens* should it near its crudest and most primitive limit but in the identification of that limit and, echoing Améry, in bridling its desire to expand (35).

Notes

1 All the photographs referenced below may be found at Wikimedia Commons: https://commons.wikimedia.org/wiki/Category:Abu_Ghraib_prisoner_abuse
2 As in, for instance, https://en.wikinews.org/wiki/File:Abu_Ghraib_7.JPG and https://commons.wikimedia.org/wiki/File:251005Abu_Ghraib.jpg
3 https://commons.wikimedia.org/wiki/File:Abu_Ghraib_17a.jpg
4 https://commons.wikimedia.org/wiki/File:Abu_Ghraib_48.jpg
5 https://commons.wikimedia.org/wiki/File:Sabrina-Harman.jpg
6 https://commons.wikimedia.org/wiki/File:Abu-ghraib-leash.jpg
7 https://commons.wikimedia.org/wiki/File:AG-10B.JPG
8 As per, among the many, this photograph of naked detainee staged performing fellatio on another https://commons.wikimedia.org/wiki/File:Abu_Ghraib_49.jpg
9 The letter is dated April 16, 1896. In his translation, Jeffrey Masson renders *Zwischenreich* as 'the in-between realm.'
10 I concur completely with Freud's observation on construction's centrality to the analytic process and refer the reader back to *Series* for a detailed discussion of the matter.
11 Pontalis offered this explanation in the proceedings of a 2000 colloquium in Annecy (Duparc, 2002). This explanation is quoted by Hélène Parat (2007, 131).
12 See *Spaces* for more on the *aevum*.
13 See, respectively, Freud (1905), (1900), (1912) and (1937).

References

Améry Jean. 1980. *At the Mind's Limits: Contemplations by a Survivor of Auschwitz and its Realities*. Translated by Sidney Rosenfeld and Stella P. Rosenfeld. Bloomington: Indiana University Press.

Coates, Ta-Nehisi. 2009. "Torture." In *The New York Times*, April 17, 2009, https://www.theatlantic.com/entertainment/archive/2009/04/torture/16292/ Accessed 15-08-2022.

Crowley, Monica. 2009. "'The things that we did' to detainees to extract information 'happens everyday at an American fraternity'." September 13, 2009. CBS https://www.mediamatters.org/monica-crowley/monica-crowley-things-we-did-detainees-extract-information-happens-everyday-american Accessed 15-08-2022.

Danner, Mark. 2004. *Torture and Truth: America, Abu Ghraib, and the War on Terror*. New York: The New York Review of Books.

Deleuze, Gilles. 1989. *Coldness and Cruelty. In Masochism*. Translated by Jean McNeil. New York: Zone Books, 1989. Pp. 7–138.

Duparc, François (ed.). 2002. *Fenêtres sur l'inconscient: L'Oeuvre de J.-B. Pontalis*. Paris: Delachaux & Niestlé.

Fair, Eric. 2016. *Consequence: A Memoir*. New York: Henry Holt & Co.

Freud, Sigmund. 1900. "The Interpretation of Dreams." In *The Complete Standard Edition of the Psychological Works of Sigmund Freud* () IV-V. London: Hogarth Press.

Freud, Sigmund. 1905. *Three Essays on the Theory of Sexuality*. In SE VII. London: Hogarth Press. Pp. 125–243.

Freud, Sigmund. 1910. "The Psycho-Analytic View of Psychogenic Disturbance of Vision." In *SE* XI. London: Hogarth Press. Pp. 211–218.

Freud, Sigmund. 1911. "Formulations on the Two Principles of Mental Functioning." In *SE* XII. London: Hogarth Press. Pp. 218–226.

Freud, Sigmund. 1912. "The Dynamics of the Transference." In *SE* XII. London: Hogarth Press. Pp. 99–108.

Freud, Sigmund. 1914. "Remembering, Repeating and Working-Through: Further Recommendations on the Technique of Psychoanalysis II." In *SE* XII. London: Hogarth Press. Pp. 145–156.

Freud, Sigmund. 1915. "Instincts and their Vicissitudes." In *SE* XIV. London: Hogarth Press. Pp. 109–140.

Freud, Sigmund. 1920. "Beyond the Pleasure Principle." In *SE* XVIII. London: Hogarth Press. Pp. 7–64.

Freud, Sigmund. 1925. "Negation." In *SE* XIX. London: Hogarth Press. Pp. 233–239.

Freud, Sigmund. 1937. "Constructions in Analysis." In *SE* XXIII. London: Hogarth Press. Pp. 257–269.

Freud, Sigmund. 1985. *The Complete Letters of Sigmund Freud to Wilhelm Fliess: 1887–1904.* Edited by Jeffrey M. Masson. Cambridge: Harvard University Press.

Gourevitch, Philip. 2008. "Exposure: The woman behind the camera at Abu Ghraib." In *The New Yorker*. March 24, 2008 https://www.newyorker.com/magazine/2008/03/24/exposure-5 Accessed: 15-08-2022.

Gourevitch, Philip and Morris, Errol. 2009. *The Ballad of Abu Ghraib.* New York: Penguin Books.

Greenberg, Karen and Dratel, Joshua (eds.). 2005. *The Torture Papers: The Road to Abu Ghraib.* Cambridge: Cambridge University Press.

Huizinga, Johan. 1995. *Homo Ludens: A Study of the Play Element in Culture.* Boston: Beacon Press.

Hersh, Seymour. 2004. "Torture at Abu Ghraib: American soldiers brutalized Iraqis. How far up does the responsibility go?" The New Yorker. https://tinyurl.com/4sxw72j5 Accessed 09-12-2019.

Illouz, Charles and Prétou, Pierre. 2018. *Heur et malheur du joueur.* Rennes: Presses Universitaires de Rennes.

Jones, David. 2009. "Why the hell should I feel sorry says girl soldier who abused Iraqi soldiers at Abu Ghraib prison." In *Daily Mail*. 12 June 2009 https://www.dailymail.co.uk/news/article-1192701/Why-hell-I-feel-sorry-says-girl-soldier-abused-Iraqi-prisoners-Abu-Ghraib-prison.html Accessed 15-08-2022.

Mazzetti, Mark and Shane, Scott. 2009. "Interrogation Memos Detail Harsh Tactics by the CIA." In *The New York Times*. April 16, 2009. https://www.nytimes.com/2009/04/17/us/politics/17detain.html?hp=&pagewanted=print Accessed 15-08-2022.

McKelvey, Tara. 2007. *Monstering: Inside America's Policy of Secret Interrogations and Torture in the Terror War.* New York: Basic Books.

Nelson, Henry. 2004. "Psychological Assessment: Annex 1 to the Taguba Report: AR 15-6 Investigation of the 800th Military Police Brigade." https://tinyurl.com/546fcah4 (accessed 24 April 2019).

Parat, Hélène. 2007. "Le jeu de l'entre-deux ou l' 'effet Pontalis'." In *Passé present: Dialogues avec J.-B. Pontalis*. Edited by Jacques André. Paris: Presses Universitaires de France. Pp. 129–143.

Phillips, Jonathan. 2010. *None of Us Were Like This Before: American Soldiers and Torture.* New York: Verso.

Rampton, Roberta and Holland, Steve. 2014. "Obama says that after 9/11, 'we tortured some folks'." *Reuters*, August 1, 2014. https://www.reuters.com/article/us-usa-cia-obama/obama-says-that-after-9-11-we-tortured-some-folks-idUSKBN0G14YY20140801?feedType=RSSampamp;feedName=topNews Accessed 15-08-2022.

Rejali, Darius. 2009. *Torture and Democracy*. Princeton: Princeton University Press,

Ricks, Thomas. 2007. *Fiasco: the American Military Adventure in Iraq 2003–2005*. New York: Penguin Books.

Shepard, Ryan. 2009. "Toward a Theory of Simulated Atonement: A Case Study of President George W. Bush's Response to the Abu Ghraib Torture Scandal." In *Communication Studies*. 60:5. Pp. 460–475.

Spens, Christiana 2014. "The Theatre of Cruelty: Dehumanization, Objectification & Abu Ghraib." In *Journal of Terrorism Research*. 5:3. Pp. 49–56.

United States Senate Select Committee on Intelligence. 2014. *The Senate Intelligence Committee Report on CIA Torture*. New York: Skyhorse Publishing.

Wildau, Gabe and Seifter, Andrew. 2004. "Limbaugh on torture of Iraqis." In *Media Matters. 05 May. 2004* https://www.mediamatters.org/rush-limbaugh/limbaugh-torture-iraqis-us-guards-were-having-good-time-blowing-some-steam?redirect_source=/research/2004/05/05/limbaugh-on-torture-of-iraqis-us-guards-were-ha/131111 Accessed 15-08-2022.

Winnicott, Donald W. 1971. "Transitional Objects and Transitional Phenomena." In *Playing and Reality*. London and New York: Routledge Books. Pp. 1–25.

Chapter 6

Spaces

Limbo

When at times animated and at others inert, at times the focus of intense psychodynamic investments and at others utterly inconsequential, an object may not be bound by a set of codifiable characteristics. As found, Winnicott located this object in the space of creative illusion, cushioned between the heavenly omnipotence granted by hallucination and the hellish impotence suffered at the hands of external reality. In this space, one may 'exist for a time without being either a reaction to an external impingement or an active person with a direction of interest or movement' (Winnicott, 1958, 34). This then is a space of purposelessness and disinterest, of floundering and fragmentation. It is in this very same space identified as no more than an obsolescent limbo where, Winnicott declared, the found object is bound to spend its irrelevant and thoroughly decathected days (Winnicott, 1971, 5). Should it, after a rich and extended journey, return to its place of origin and, hence, to the site of its founding, where precisely did the found object live its intervening vibrancy and resilience? What of its itineraries, traces and machinations? Presumably, these are all to be found neither in heaven nor in hell but in the transitional space where the object itself was initially found. While the question and answer here may seem rhetorical, they, nevertheless, signal the overdetermination of the space of the transitional as more than a topological third somewhere 'neither here nor there,' 'in between here and there' or even 'on the way from here to there.' On this note, though the simplest and most obvious, the third of these scenarios is also the most obviously over-simplifying of the Winnicottian category in so far as it reduces the space of the found object to a mere way station when, in fact, it is the pivot for much of what Winnicott valued in the workings of the human psyche. At the end of the day, under consideration is the space of 'both here and there, and everywhere else in between,' of the space of the found object whose reality is both inner and empirical, enlivening and deadening, resilient and aggressive, vital and irrelevant. At stake then are the implications and ripples of the *coincidentia oppositorum* throughout the Winnicottian field.

DOI: 10.4324/9781003352488-6

To speak of *coincidentia* and, as in this context, of overdetermination is to speak of dreams, of their components' recurrences, frustrations, distortions, even horrors as much as of their seemingly expedient and unobtrusively gratifying functions.[1] Similarly, and safe as one may wish it to be, the space of the transitional is hardly a space of safety; it is a space where the teddy bear, the parent, the analyst or whatever other found object is involved can very well be the originator of aggression as much as the target of the subject's persecution. To put it differently, the found object's aggression need not always be reduced to a mere by-product of its finder's fantasy or projection. As we have already seen, the very presence of the found object is founded on an injurious 'abrogation of omnipotence' and the grave disillusionment it precipitates.[2]

To complicate things further, Winnicott underscored the found object's ability and, at times, indeed, responsibility to frustrate and inflict what the subject justifiably suffers as an injury. And so, presumably, once she has recovered from her 'primary maternal preoccupation' (Winnicott, 1956b), a mother ought not do all the right things at the right moments and without failure for she otherwise risks limiting her child's developmental options to either a permanent merger (with the seemingly all-good and infallible mother) or a total rejection (of the apparently domineering and all-devouring mother) (Winnicott, 1960). In a similar vein, Winnicott held it as the analyst's responsibility to deploy the objective though negative and potentially hurtful counter-transference as an indispensable tool in the analytic process (Winnicott, 1947). Winnicott believed that the injuries such a counter-transference may inflict on the analysand make sense and have a purpose and, indeed, may be exercised in the spirit of 'optimal frustration,' according to the sanitizing coinage of some in North American psychoanalytic circles.[3] Setting aside its veracity and clinical effectiveness,[4] Winnicott's position brings to light the assumption that, in spite of its harm, an injury may be recuperated and redeemed in the mind of the one that carries it out as but a necessary misfortune, a detour or perhaps a mere bridge on the road to a greater and healthier gain. In a reasoned and reasonable context, such an assumption need not cause much by way of a concern or a challenge; in contrast, the overdetermination of dreams and, by extension, of the transitional space lends less sensibility and even less convenience to the 'short-term pain for long-term gain' or 'the end justifies the means' calculus. Overdetermination has not quite suffered, at least not fully and not yet, the censorial machinations of secondary revision; under its aegis, not everything is necessarily intelligible, good or useful; nor, conversely, is it unequivocally incomprehensible, harmful or futile. Some of what it makes possible may actually have nothing whatsoever to do with an advancement or a gain; at stake, after all, is the space of illusion as it encompasses much of human activity, including not only play, creativity and imagination, but also, as Winnicott himself understood it, their often wasteful, useless, misguided and misguiding detours—to wit, lying, stealing, lack of affection and obsessionality (Winnicott, 1971, 5).

Much, it seems, happens in this limbo that is the transitional. It is hardly a repository of the lost and found or a junkyard for the un-found or the un-founded. It is a fount, if you will, of all that has yet to be found, or found anew, and the very site that gives finding its occasion. Limbo is the pile of second-hand goods, theories, facts, toys, hallucinations, of, in sum, all that has been judged as dross or rubbish and subsequently relegated to the outskirts, the landfill or the basement; it is also precisely all that psycho-analysis rediscovers as memories, fantasies, wishes, objects, demands and bungled actions, as, ultimately, the productions that speak the heart of the unconscious and upon which psychoanalysis as a practice and a science has been founded. The metaphor of a depth of field deployed in the previous discussion of construction[5] is henceforth supplanted by one of a peripheral vision that hones its focus on the outlier, the marginal, at or beyond the border, in the nether region, on the rarely acknowledged and even less often explored yet, psychoanalytically, of potentially the highest import.

Though Winnicott may have deployed the term in its most quotidian usage and thereby wished to sever it from its religious connotations,[6] or sever it again—after, presumably, Henry VIII had severed England's ties with Roman Catholicism and Freud had wrested psychoanalysis from all mythology and illusion—limbo as the middle ground remains a peculiarly evocative term, both conceptually and functionally. Aside from its structural echoes to the transitional space, limbo is the territory reserved not only in some versions of the Christian afterworld for those who are neither sinners nor saints, but also for, on the one hand, all those on earth who may benefit the most from a psychoanalytic cure since they are neither 'psychotic' nor healthy enough, as well as, on the other hand, for Winnicott and his fellow members of the Middle Group in the British Psycho-Analytical Society who, as neither Freudian nor Kleinian, do nevertheless qualify for the title of psychoanalyst.[7]

Much, it seems, thrives in limbo. What follows are thoughts that explore this space and its times; they are presented tentatively, as hypotheses rather than confirmed conclusions, less on what Winnicott actually advanced and more on what his perspective may help enliven.

Aevum

Go ahead and look closer. It is right there, next to where just about ev-erything Greek had been trashed before it got cleaned up and anointed the Cradle of Western Civilisation. Yes; there, in that very same pile where we just dug up limbo, the same one from which Freud, following in the foot-steps of Krafft-Ebbing (1998) and Moll (1898), had salvaged libido. The pile is marked 'Medieval' though its signpost is far afield one can easily miss it.

(Evidently, there are rankings and gradations even in rubbish.) It is the pile that predates the ascendency of modernity's much cherished autonomous subject. Nestled in between the Greco-Roman and the Renaissance, the Medieval is also, literally, the anglicized Latin *medium aevum*, the 'Middle Ages.' That's it, right there. Here we are again precisely where Winnicott wants us—in the middle.

The Middle Ages can be a bit disappointing for those in search of debates re fabulous angelic dances on heads of pins as none actually did take place in that or, for that matter, any other period. However, there is enough in those Ages of the deliberations on the varieties of time and being worth revisiting, especially since such deliberations often rediscovered and traversed 'the middle.' The Ancients, Plato and Aristotle included, had essentially identified two measures of duration: eternity and time. Eternity is a quality of being in its actuality, of that which is and is always already perfect; time, on the other hand, connotes change and potentiality; it belongs to that which becomes and is hence lacking. In this context, duration is as much a quality of being, and hence pertains to ontology, as it is an external standard of reference by which one may track an entity's movements and/or transformations. Fuelled by the concerns of a theology of salvation set to bridge the gap between the eternal and the timely, the intellectuals of Medieval Europe took upon themselves the task of reconfiguring their philosophical heritage in order to accommodate a new classification of beings, a new topography and, by extension, a new time. Henceforth, man's relationship to God was to be rethought in terms of analogy rather than the discreet categories of identity and difference. Thus, angels, considered to be neither godly nor human, needed to be accounted for; the souls of the innocent who, because of accident or history, had not been baptised (who, in other words, were neither saved nor lost) deserved a dwelling that, while not quite heavenly, is nonetheless at a reasonably safe distance from the fires of eternal damnation. Ultimately, as a quality of being, time had to be re-calibrated in such a way as to reflect the emerging ontological diversity.

Along with a *medium aevum* buffered between the ancient and the modern, entered the *aevum* as a radically new category of time itself.

It was mostly the Scholastic texts of the thirteenth century (beginning with the commentaries of Alexander of Hales and extending into the reflections of Bonaventure, Albert the Great, Giles of Rome, Henry of Ghent and, finally, William of Ockham) that undertook this recalibration by introducing, debating, fine-tuning and eventually completely abandoning the idea of the *aevum* as a time quality in between and hence distinct from the eternal and the worldly.[8] The following excerpt from Bonaventure captures well the core of the concept:

> [S]piritual (beings) have measure diverse from time, not only in the genus of the measure, but even in the genus of being ... Wherefore if you

ask, what that (measure) is; one must respond according to the Saints and philosophers, that it is called the *created eternity* or the *aevum*, but since *eternity* is properly accepted for the uncreated, and *aevum* is frequently accepted for time, for that reason it can be called with a proper name *the eviternity* ... [T]he *aevum* is the measure of incommutable *being* alone.

(Bonaventure, 1885, 56–57, emphasis in the original)

Bonaventure stands here for an episode in the history of philosophy that mimics the experience of a 'set situation'—to use a term of Winnicott's whose appearance in print anticipates that of the transitional object by roughly a decade (Winnicott, 1941). In such a situation, the child (philosopher) discovers—or, in the case of Bonaventure, re-discovers[9]—the shiny tongue depressor (*aevum*), uses it and makes it its own by picking it up, sticking it in its mouth, dropping it and picking it up again (by conceptualizing, debating and mulling it over, writing it and debating it some more) till, at a certain point, it loses its appeal as disinterest—or decathexis, as in the language of the found object—sets in and attention moves on to another object nearby. For the outside observer, this is a 'total happening,' an experience complete with a beginning, middle and end. Meanwhile, the subject that participates in such a happening is effectively immersed in a malleable and creative play that unburdens it from all manner of mutually exclusive disjunctions, including not only eternity and finitude, inside and outside, hallucination and reality, but beginning and end, middle and periphery too. It is thus that, in handling the tongue depressor, the six-month-old baby reveals itself to its environment as hardly a bundle of needs and reflexes and more a subject, and a playing subject at that, totally engaged in its object and world (Winnicott, 1991, 75–79). While relieved from the strictures of clashing disjunctions, this subject does not so much venture out of the one side of any given polarity and into the other as it instead opens for itself a space that partakes of both, simultaneously. Here, the subject may take hold of a time at once eternal and finite; it may 'now' take hold of itself as a new subject. And so, in between *aeternitas*, an abiding and indivisible eternity without beginning or end, and *tempus*, a limited and ever flowing time of change and decay, the *aevum* is a created perpetuity; it has an origin but is infinite in duration. The found object is our modern reformulation of this rather awkward logic of beginnings that do not end and departures without destinations: the onset of its time coincides with the moment the object is found; since it never truly dies, this object's time seems to have no end.

As a theological category of neither the godly nor the human, the *aevum* belongs to the angels who are eternal in their substance but finite in their actions.[10] It is, as it were, a 'diminished' eternity whose time moves, in succession, in *vicissitudo*, and where each moment tells of a totality rather than a transient passage. The *aevum* is thus akin to the audible time-stop

(Tick. Tick. Tick ...) as sounded by the mechanical clock first produced in the late thirteenth century and hence from the same period when the *aevum* had acquired its renewed theological and ontological significance.[11] At this point, I want to draw an affinity between ontological categories and mechanical innovations, an affinity that runs counter to what Carlo Cipolla once identified as the much larger cultural surround of a medieval Europe on the move away from an artistic technology and toward pragmatism, instrumentality and production (Cipolla, 1978, 20–21).[12] Understood by all that heard it, the ring of a bell in the thirteenth century did not simply tell the hours; it communicated a social, economic, religious and/or military world as its messages ran the gamut from sounding a fire alarm or announcing an approaching enemy to calling the people to arms or to a peaceful assembly, 'telling them when to go to bed and when to get out of it, when to go to work, when to pray and when to fight, marking the openings and closings of fairs, celebrating the elections of popes, the coronations of kings, and victories in war' (Cipolla, 1978, 38). Similarly, and ever since it displaced the flow of sundials or candle, water and fire clocks as a standard of measure, the ticking of the mechanical clock has come to mark time rather than simply measure it. Each such mark is a time-stop that forces time to stand still, that holds all the parts that may make up a world as it weaves them into a seemingly infinite moment, passing from without but 'forever after' from within. In marking a separation between a before and an after as two distinct worlds, and hence two distinct ways of being, this time-stop opens onto a much-needed, perhaps quintessentially human, third. Between sleep and wakefulness is the world of dreaming; between work and rest is the world of playing, between hallucination and practical reason is the world of desiring. In all this, one ought recall that dreams go hand in hand with nightmares, that games easily exceed a pleasure calculus and that desires are often threatening. One ought then extend the observation here and recognize that between peace and war, celebrations and cannon balls, is the world of both dread and hope, excitement and anxiety, certainty and misgiving, the world where much has yet to happen and just about all seems to have already been fated. Seen through the lens of finding, this is the world of the transitional, of constructions that demarcate the real from the hallucinated, of solitudes ever entangled in loneliness, of cruel games and playful cruelties. In some of its other contexts, psychoanalysis has taken to referring to the time of such a world, to, in effect, the *aevum*, as a time that is other, a time that 'does not pass,' or a time that 'explodes.'[13]

Interregnum

As a marker of time, the *aevum* opens onto a revamped limbo in which, as it turns out, much of the found object's adventures take place. If the found object is nowhere near possible without its finder, which is to say without the subject whose presence imbues it with all manner of vibrancy and potential, then the subject in whose nature it is to find must at the very least make a passage through if not indeed be a resident of said limbo. In order then is a digression on this subject and its emergence in time.

I once again return to Deleuze and Guattari's conjunctive synthesis, 'ah, so that's what it is, that's who I am!' (Deleuze and Guattari, 1977, 16–22), the synthesis that grounds the subject in the moment where affect, experience and thought converge. One gets the impression that, in positing this synthesis, Deleuze and Guattari were arguing for a chronological order to the emergence of the subject—post affect, post experience and post thought. Such an order is at the very least counter-intuitive; some may even say nonsensical, since, presumably, love, hate, sight, touch, reason and imagination are among the faculties that require an agency by which they may be brought about, an agency that has already acquired the capacity to feel, to sense or to contemplate. What then may seem nonsensical is precisely that which, for not only Deleuze and Guattari but, indeed, for the entire psychoanalytic tradition, undermines the subject that declares itself sovereign over its various skills and powers, the subject of reason and fact, of philosophy and technology, of, in sum, sense. This subject sees itself the ground of action and understanding; it may feel, experience or think this or that but, so goes the Cartesian claim, it is neither this nor that; it is, in principle at least, greater than both and capable of the manipulation and/or fulfilment of both.

With psychoanalysis, we have come to appreciate the subject as less conscious, less autonomous, less reasonable; it does not so much repress or forget as it is founded by an act of primary repression (Freud, 1915b, 148) or forgetting (Lacan, 1992, 43–70), an act that sets up in the psyche a complex and enduring structure as much as it enacts what is typically identified as repressing or forgetting. In a parallel move, specifically with Winnicott this time, it may be declared that finding is the *sine qua non* of the subject as much as it is of the found object, that the subject can hardly count finding as merely one among the many talents it may call upon whenever necessary or convenient; on the contrary, the subject is founded by, and as, finding. This is a reiteration of the point I already put forward in *Findings* above: finding is a reciprocal relationship that ascribes to both subject and object their identities, qualities and functions within specific times and relations. A subject will find itself being found not only by other subjects in its surround but also by the very objects it has found; henceforth, it will be incorporated into these objects' worlds, governed by their times and transformed to satisfy their needs. As the scope of what qualifies as a found object surpasses the confines of an individual's earliest experiences with bears and blankets to encompass not only subjects but communities, institutions, professions, and/ or, indeed, ideas, finding will increase in both subtlety and significance.

With this very same sensitivity to shifting origins and doubling sequences, the subject does not enact feeling, experiencing and thinking; it is produced by and as feeling, experiencing and thinking—hence the 'ah, so that's what it is, that's who I am!' that marks the 'I' as a product of the confluence of the three registers of affect, experience and thought. As such, the 'I' is not simply influenced, troubled or perplexed by these registers or the changes they undergo; it is also re-configured, re-defined and re-produced, in sum found by them. She may no longer see herself a woman after a radical hysterectomy in her late twenties; he may rethink his masculinity now that he is sexually attracted to another man; they may never regain their sense of self since their last tour of duty; and they may experience themselves as a doctor differently now that they are an analytic patient. As so-called crises of identity we witness as well as suffer—and at times even relish—such turning points bespeak an ongoing process of being found as well as finding—perhaps less explicit or abrupt but no less transformative.

Since affect, experience and thought are no mere qualities or extensions of a pre-existing subject but the ground that makes the feeling, experiencing, thinking 'I' possible, the time of this 'I,' the time in which it is found, modulated and lived is a time of eruption. Ah! So that's who I am! The exclamation marks both a pre and a post to neither of which, strictly speaking, it—I—belongs. The exclamation is somewhere on a border between the two types of time we have already encountered, one timeless—the *aeternitas* of the immovable Subject (with the S capitalized, if you please)—and the other timely—the *tempus* of the ever so mundane and finite subject. The exclamation belongs to an *interregnum*[14] whose time, the *aevum*, is the time of finding.

'She sees light,' 'he envies her' and 'they contemplate travel' may reference completed facts or settled states of being; more importantly, they point to findings that set up relationships between any given number of entities and invest in each its temporary status as subject or object. 'Seeing,' envying' and 'contemplating' are more than bridges that allow pre-existing subjects to cross over and relate to their corresponding objects—bridges that, by their very nature, may be as conveniently forgotten as they are crossed. Each of these verbs designates a finding and is hence far more complex than a buffer or border agreed upon by some external entities that precede and/or exceed it in power and value. Each is a weaving that, momentarily at least, accords subject and object certain powers and imbues them with specific functions as it both defines the gap that separates them and shapes its possibilities.

The (Other) Set Situation

In between, on the one hand, primordial psychic goo that knows nothing of negation or death, that, in other words, is thoroughly oblivious to the fact and logic of opposites, and, on the other hand, an ego that abides by a commonsensical reality whose law of the excluded middle is indifferent to these selfsame opposites—which is another way of saying an ego that confirms the inevitability of opposites so that it may declare it inadmissible—lies a subject that thrives in the *coincidentia*. In between the newborn's presumed oceanic feeling in which there is no room and even less need for subjectivity and the adult's sense of a coalesced conscious self distinct from all that surrounds it we encounter an 'I' that is the effect of the Deleuzo-Guattarian conjunctive synthesis, an 'I' for which much of psychoanalysis has erroneously prescribed a developmental, conflict-free, depressive or oedipal standard, an 'I' that is more accurately understood as produced, situational, transitional. It is to this 'I' that belong drive, dream, transference and construction as well as, by extension, the found and the playful. In turn, it is to these that the 'I' as the *interregnum* between the timeless and the timely must belong.

It is no coincidence that, as the time that enlivens limbo and reconfigures it as an *interregnum*, the *aevum* is the time of the libido, if not Augustine of Hippo's with its connotations of power[15] then definitely Freud's and its investments in pleasure. Although he tirelessly advanced the thought that the drive has a history—a radical thought for his time and, indeed, ours still—Freud also held that such a history does not unfold in smooth developmental phases. In fact, the passages from narcissism to object love (via the ideal ego and the ego ideal), from a supposedly repudiated homosexuality to paranoia (via negation and projection),[16] from, effectively, any one given modality, object or aim of the drive to another and from any one bodily locus to another all occur in a spasmodic, paroxytic fashion. The drive does not waft in elegant seamlessness from one configuration to another so much as it hops in 'fits and starts' (Deleuze and Guattari, 1977, 1). Here, there and there again. Tick. Tick. Tick … At each location and within each interval, the components are assembled, if not indeed found, in such a way as to make sense and to lend sense. The drive moves through eruptive and discontinuous yet self-contained totalities in the style of a vicissitude. Addressing its itinerary, Freud wrote: 'We can divide the life of each instinct into a series of separate successive waves, each of which is homogeneous during whatever period of time it may last, and whose relation to one another is comparable to that of successive eruptions of lava' (Freud, 1915a, 131).[17] The time of the drive is hence altogether different from, on the one hand, that of the arrow, river or wheel (the metaphors are aplenty here), of the time of the empirical as becoming, chaos, repetition, lack, progress and/or decay and, on the other hand, the still and indivisible time as a hallucinated omnipotence or an abstracted perfection (as Instinct, Soul or Nature). The time of the drive is the time of volcanic eruption; it is the time of enumerating in integers, in staccato. The time of the drive is the time of the *aevum* and of its *vicissitudo*.

Not surprisingly, the *aevum* is also the time of the transference. What stands out from among his many observations on the phenomenon is Freud's warning that, as the driving force in the clinical setting and effectively a factor of 'undreamt-of importance' (Freud, 1940, 174), the transference comes about 'suddenly' and is 'bound to surprise' the analyst. Whether it manifests as love or hate, the phenomenon's 'extraordinary powers' will recast the entirety of the clinical setting and give it a new meaning that may potentially 'blow away' the success of the work and make it vanish (176). The dream too operates along similar lines: it is only as an effect of secondary revision that its images acquire a semblance of chronological order, of meaning, no less conjunctive than the Deleuzo-Guattarian synthesis but much more prone to ossification than Deleuze and Guattari thought it ought to be. With the dream, we in fact find ourselves not only in the space of the transitional as Winnicott understood it, but also in the space of the *aevum*, with a beginning but without an end. For what is a dream but a 'diminished' hallucination, a psychosis (Freud, 1940, 172), that grows 'like a mushroom out of its mycelium' and whose meaning is never a single abiding wish but a 'meshwork' of latent thoughts with no definite ending (Freud, 1900, 525)? Such thoughts do not accrue into an ever-higher or reach into an ever-deeper organization. Freud himself insisted on the necessity of over-interpretation as a clinical disposition that, contrary to what its 'over' (its *'über'* in *'Überdeutung'*) may suggest in terms of primacy or hierarchy, manifests such a meshwork and, in so doing, undermines the hegemony of the one overarching and immutable meaning over all others.

It is in this context that Freud wrote his now-famous metaphor of the dream's navel as a tangle of thoughts that cannot be unravelled at the spot where the dream is supposed to reach down into the unknown (Freud, 1900, 525). Curiously enough, Freud himself tangled up two distinct thoughts at this point: the first is that the multitude of interpretations brings the interpreter face to face with the limit of interpretation (as an 'unknown'); and the second is that, since interpretation is the process that presumably untangles the elements of the dream-work (displacement, condensation and secondary revision) in order to uncover the distorted wish, the 'unknown' in this case is no less the opening from which the dream emerges than it is the gap into which it reaches. While its images may appear chaotic and incomplete, the latent time of the dream is none other than the time of the *aevum* for it too is a created perpetuity, with a grounding in a wish though infinite in meanings. Interpretation brings to light the succession of such meanings (Freud, 1900, 214) and, in so doing, clarifies the *vicissitudo* in its limitless series of thoughts, each as a consistent and useful totality in its own right. Tick. Tick. Tick …

It, therefore, seems to me that, semantic liberties notwithstanding, James Strachey's rendering of Freud's title *'Triebe und Triebschiksale'* as 'Instincts and their Vicissitudes' rather than, say, 'Drives and the Fate of Drives,'[18] is a faithful capturing of the spirit of the text's central and most intriguing contribution. Obviously, the notion that the drive has both a history and an aim is a notion Freud had been tirelessly advancing for at least a decade, ever since the first, 1905, edition of the *Three Essays on the Theory of Sexuality*. However, the idea that this history does not always unfold in developmental stages but that it often involves eruptive, discontinuous and yet self-contained and coherent totalities[19] in the style of a *vicissitudo*, totalities that, on their own, lack nothing and lead nowhere, the idea then that the drive's 'history' need not be purposeful or that it may not even be fatefull, is an idea he had rarely treated as forcefully or as unambiguously.[20]

The farther we stray from Winnicott's cultural and clinical surround the closer, I believe, we touch upon the core of his metapsychological sensibilities. Limbo, *aevum* and *vicissitudo* as I have so far deployed are in essence variations on the theme of the set situation Winnicott introduced not long after he qualified as a child psychoanalyst (Winnicott, 1941). While designed as a tool of observation and prognostication, and particularly instructive in its carefully implemented clinical minutia, the set situation is striking in its ability to convey in the most vivid of ways the subject's experience of its space and its relationship to time at the point of play. Ideally, the subject seems absorbed in the activity at hand, radically oblivious to whatever may lie beyond its peripheries—both spatial and temporal. As it plays with the object it has found, it pays no heed to the space beyond its scope and perhaps even less to whatever may lie in its close vicinity; it has lost track of chronological time for while it may remember when it entered the situation it seems to spare not a thought to the moment when it will leave. The world it shares with its object is whole, meaningful, self-sustaining; the rules it follows are the ones it has created. Ideally, again, any disruption to its experience will go unnoticed for the threat will have been neutralized swiftly by the seemingly invisible hand of some guardian (parent, analyst, deity...).

'Ideally ...' since this world does eventually betray its own *coincidentia*, and not only of the kind willed by the subject as it inevitably loses interest in what it had found, or the one that comes about once the resources that sustain the situation are depleted or the guardian gets distracted or the disruption emanating from the outside is too abrupt, forceful or persistent. Playing is not as boundless and certainly not as coherent as it may seem.

Timings

My aim so far has been to propose a framework that ascribes to the drive a location, time, status and rhythm. While these categories also shed light on a dream, a session and an analysis, they are not without their limitations. They remain much too gathered and much too organized to accommodate not only the meanderings and experimentations but also, and especially, the excesses and disruptions that mark the drive and its work, the *coincidentia* of play and cruelty, healing and hate, solitude and loneliness. Though heuristically useful, the so-called time of angels is far removed from the struggles and uncertainties at the core of the human psyche. This time's internal consistency leaves little room for identifying let alone working through conflict and chaos. And the little room it does leave is often hijacked by the language of 'exception' (nightmare), 'problem' (masochism) or 'failure' (negative therapeutic reaction), a language dear to the heart of many an analyst since it speaks reassuringly of often avoidable hazards rather than systemic barriers on the way to a distant though attainable all-curative clinic and all-encompassing theory.

Equally troubling is this language's inability or unwillingness to allow for endings, for the psychodynamic and material fact that the 'this and that' of Winnicottian finding eventually does reach a finality rather than a mere decathexis, that the beginning of an *aevum* is actually the mark of a conclusion or even abrupt breaking off of whatever may have preceded it, that something did precede it and is no longer, that such a no longer is neither the effect of an illusion nor the telltale sign of disinterest but an ever so trenchant condition for the subject seizing hold of itself.[21]

The category of endings seems to be altogether jettisoned, perhaps even disavowed as modern psychoanalysts follow medieval philosophers in buckling at their finitude and the prospect of their passing. Thus, we read Freud declaring that negation has no place in the unconscious (Freud, 1925, 239), that death cannot be represented in the system Ucs.[22] "Our unconscious [he wrote] does not believe in its own death; it behaves as if it were immortal. What we call our "unconscious" ... knows nothing that is negative and no negation; in it *contradictories coincide*' (Freud, 1915d, 296; emphasis added).[23] *Coincidentia oppositorum* indeed! I would argue that it is precisely because contradictories do coincide that we may not so readily absent the unconscious from any representation of its own demise, that death is no mere negation, that life and death, the representations as well as the drives, are as constitutive of the unconscious as any duality we have encountered so far. Here, Freud's confidence, if not indeed naiveté, is betrayed by his recurring use of the negative in his declarations; his insistence that the unconscious 'does not believe' in its own death is undermined by what he himself came to recognize in the work of negation—as that which operates only on what has already been confirmed (Freud, 1925)—and flies in the face of what he came to understand of the nature of Eros and Thanatos—as drives that differ in means while sharing death for an aim (Freud, 1920, 38–9).[24]

Winnicott, it seems, may be exempted from some of these concerns. Rather than insisting on an exhaustive and coherent account of the psyche, he acknowledged the paradox at the heart of what it means to be human and judged its acceptance as a defining feature of his cornerstone concept of the found object (Winnicott, 1969, 89). It is no surprise that, in the spirit of such paradox, his treatment of endings gives rise to as many tensions as it dispels. On the one hand, Winnicott considered the experience of ending, of the passage of time, as an often invaluable source of relief 'from almost anything, however intolerable, provided someone who is understanding and familiar is present, keeping calm when hate, rage, anger, grief, despair, seem to be all' (Winnicott, 1988, 57). Although meant to counter the oft un-bearable absence of an end in sight, the impression that, in a clinical setting, such intense and unpleasant emotions are the prerogative of the one re-ceiving care ought not go unchecked, Indeed, Winnicott did not hesitate to identify the analyst's call for the end of the session as a hatred enacted (Winnicott, 1954, 285). Troubling as it may be, this hatred is somewhat redeemed by the concurrent unspoken though not any the less assumed 'till the next time' promise when the analytic task will be taken up again. Along the interruption then comes the putative guarantee of time's continuity as an available resource (Winnicott, 1988, 69–70). By time's analytic standards, and lest the entire clinical frame collapse under the weight of uncertainty, suspension and constancy must be co-extensive.

A tally of these and many of the other Winnicottian instances of ending reveals them as situational and hence understandably disparate—as opposed to principled, unalterable. That said, the singular ending in which Winnicott was particularly invested, the one that signals a turning point in the subject's relationship to a particular found object, is, as it turns out, a non-ending. The found object never truly dies, or so we are told and so we have come to accept, in almost as scriptural a faith as the one we have adopted toward Freud's assertions on death. Decathected, the found object is neither re-pressed nor destroyed; it is fated to rest on the proverbial shelf, useless, collecting the dust of its memories as the subject's cathexis is directed else-where. Since nothing has died, no irreversible forfeit has been suffered and no grief need be endured. Not only is the work of mourning the now lost object forestalled, so is the reckoning with the subject's responsibility or guilt for whatever its moving on toward a new chapter in interests and in-vestments may have precipitated.

The basics of finding tell a different story. Found and finding are dynamic states governed by *coincidentia oppositorum* rather than occurrences or traits meant to complement one another. As found, the object is vital and resilient; it has the capacity to reconfigure the subject's world into which it has been drawn and not simply bear it or fit in it. In other words, the object is en-livened enough to find the subject that found it and alter its workings as it draws it into its own vision. Once decathected, the object loses its capacity to participate and, therefore, to find. Contra Winnicott's claim, this object no longer belongs to the transitional space but is relegated back to the deso-lation of objective reality. Neither found nor finding, this once subjectivized object is now lifeless as its relationship with the subject is severed—until, or unless, it may be found again.

Against this background, whatever in the subject was shaped by the decathected object will feel deadened as the cliché 'part of me died' response to loss carries a bit more truth than is bearable. The Winnicottian assertion regarding the presumed immortality of the object mitigates this truth as metapsychology counters old adage in the service of a manoeuvre designed less to negate the demise of the object and more to defend against the threat that whatever in the subject that had been enlivened by that object is now no longer. Contra the fantasy that the subject may saunter off in the direction of better, greener, more playful pastures all the while inured to the effects of its relinquishment of the object—or, heaven forbid, its relinquishment by that once subjectivized object—is the transitional reality of a subject not only deeply shaped by its findings but indeed sustained as a subject by its capacity to find and be found. The survival of the subject thus depends on it having found more than one object; otherwise it is deadened once its sole finding partner has been decathected.

Returning to the arithmetic with which these essays have been framed, to the axiom that counting begins with the number 2, before us is a Winnicottian reformulation of subtraction: $2-1 = 0$. In disabusing itself of its belief in the object's immortality, the subject must come to terms with an 'abrogation of omnipotence' (Winnicott, 1971, 5) far greater than the one it suffered in its initial encounter with the object beyond its control. Ambiguities and complications notwithstanding, 0 is not nothing; 0 is a representation. In this context, 0 points toward an existential abrogation that surpasses the reliance on any one particular object: without an entire world beyond its grasp, a world it gets to find, the subject must confront its finality as well as the very basis of its subjecthood.

The upshot then is that time operates as more than an objective and verifiable measure. In mediating the subject's relationship to its object, it too becomes an object, a found object more specifically. As it bears directly on the subject's experience of itself and its world, time is animated, periodized and/or disrupted to fit the subject's psychodynamic requirements. Control, recovery, nostalgia or a belief in immortality are among the many projects for which it may be recruited. The varied modalities of time (*tempus*, *aevum* and *vicissitudo* among them), if not indeed time itself as a modality, are refashioned by the psyche in order to circumvent, adapt or defend against the experience of irredeemable endings, not only those suffered but, more poignantly, more dangerously still, those inflicted. Perhaps then it is the experience of endings itself that gives rise to time, of a before and an after that render of eventless time a no time at all.[25]

The circular logic governing time's relationship to endings echoes the one previously highlighted between play and culture.[26] It underscores the extent to which endings may not be experienced without time. Freud would have been in complete agreement with this observation since he stressed the indifference the unconscious experiences in relation to both: timelessness is one of the main characteristics of a primary process (Freud, 1915c, 1887) according to which 'nothing can be brought to an end' (Freud, 1900, 577); and if there is nothing in the id that could be compared with negation, there is even less in it that might correspond to the idea of time (Freud, 1933, 74). However, as the thread of timelessness ran through much of his metapsychological output, Freud's elaborations of the drives' vicissitudes, at times developmental and at others eruptive, introduce a countermeasure of timeliness to his account of the primary process. Neither a failure nor a contradiction, at work yet again is an irreducible *coincidentia* that renders utterly futile any attempt to capture the unconscious in a singular relationship to time. Instead, since it seems to produce as well as obey a number of dynamics, the ground is now opened to rethink time as one of the functions of the unconscious rather than a static far off reality to whose tactics it may be immune, to expand time's layers and trajectories in favour of many timings indeed.

Barzakh

To acknowledge in time a number of components—eternal, eruptive, developmental, decaying ...—is to echo Freud's recognition of libido's own constitution as polymorphous, incorporating diverse, seemingly chronologically progressive though structurally simultaneous, perversions. Since one of the implicit threads in the discussion so far has been that time and space are mutually determining, an awareness of time's internal heterogeneity helps reframe the Winnicottian transitional as equally multiple. The barzakh, a category flourishing since around the same time as the medieval *aevum* though in a different turf, may shed further light on the topic.

Much of what the Christian theologians of Medieval Europe knew of the philosophical tradition that came to structure and sustain their intellects they had learned from the translations and commentaries prepared by their Muslim counterparts. As the former were beginning to harness the recently transmitted intellectual legacies of classical Athens, exploring, expanding and sometimes even distorting them in the manner of what we may now identify as found objects, some among the latter were already well at work weaving these selfsame objects into their own intellectual tapestries. Interestingly enough, and regardless of pedigree or concern, the efforts of key figures from both currents seem to have coalesced around, among others, the notion of the in-between. Even more interesting is how the specifically Sufi from among these efforts strongly resonates with some of the most central principles and sensibilities in the otherwise hardly theistic and far from mystical psychoanalytic tradition.

Addressing this resonance, William Chittick has interpreted the West's more recent interest in certain Islamic traditions as an attempt at recuperating imaginative modes of understanding lost with the 'Age of Reason' (Chittick, 1989, xi). Chittick's own studies (1989, 1994, 1998) go a long way toward articulating a Sufi version of such modes. One wonders whether, having already abandoned all faith in the primacy of the rational mind, psychoanalysis, albeit unwittingly, has found its own way back to these very same roots via certain far from direct or obvious itineraries—possibly through Jewish mysticism and all the way back to Maimonides and the Muslim scholars and mystics whom he considered his peers and interlocutors.[27] Generally speaking, the recent rise in research on the intersection between psychoanalysis and Islam attests to a fruitful though ambiguous tension between the two currents.[28] Rather than a mapping of trends and traditions, I will continue with my focus on some of the ways in which the notion of the in-between has been framed and deployed; throughout, my concern will remain psychoanalytic.

From the many intellectuals bequeathed us by the Andalusia of the thirteenth century, Ibn al-'Arabi stands out as one of Sufism's most eminent masters and theoreticians. Chief among Ibn al-'Arabi's technical categories is *wujud*, a concept whose semantic polyvalence in Arabic extends to being, presence, discovery and finding. While noting this polyvalence has become common practice among the translators and researchers, it is of particular relevance in the present context for two interrelated reasons: first, its striking echoes in a Winnicottian understanding of being as grounded in a relationship to the other (*as* found object)—more specifically of being as finding rather than as a static identity that precedes or facilitates any activity—finding included; and, much more fruitfully, second, its grounding of being and finding in the liminal space of the *barzakh*.

Of the *barzakh*'s three occurrences in the Koran,[29] the first defines it as a barrier prohibiting a human from returning to earth after death: the concept acts here as a counter to the belief in reincarnation widely held in pre-Islamic Arabia.[30] The second and third occurrences, meanwhile, underscore the *barzakh*'s function as an often invisible division or marker of distinction. The prevalence of this understanding has since paved the way for the notion of 'a bridge linking our lives and actions on earth with the final dispensation of justice at the eschaton' (Idelman Smith and Yazbeck Haddad 2002, 48). It is while crossing this one-way bridge that an individual is confronted with a heightened awareness of all of their deeds, wishes, anxieties and aspirations during life on earth; it is there that the individual's innermost moral and spiritual structures, their '*nafs*' (spirit), is made manifest by means of archetypes, representations and imaginations. Much as with a dream, the *barzakh* is a recapitulation in images of those wishes and deeds that may otherwise remain elusive or ineffable. It is there, this particular elaboration adds, where lays bare before one's eyes all the evidence that will predict the final judgement. 'Imagined' as it may be, the *barzakh* is hence no interim delusion; it is the 'cold sleep' of the grave—often referred to in the tradition as the 'punishment' or 'torment' of the grave—where a non-corporeal reenactment of an entire earthly history and, by extension, a foretelling of, as well as a preparation for (Chittick, 1994, 102), a coming eternity and its judgement unfold. In the broader context of the tradition's investment in a correlation between space and probity, or lack thereof, the *barzakh* takes on the form of either an expansive garden of paradise or an ever-narrowing cave of fire (Bashier, 2004, 79). Constant throughout is the recognition that the *barzakh* belongs to a series and is clearly demarcated by indelible experiences of endings—of life on earth as its preamble and of itself as an overture to the eternal.[31]

While Ibn al-'Arabi's understanding of the *barzakh* is rooted in the classic belief in an intermediary world between the visible and the invisible, his revaluation and deployment of the concept go far beyond the notions of bridge, barrier or grave or, for that matter, the realms of dreams and fantasies. Indeed, Ibn al-'Arabi expanded the *barzakh* from the world of spirits and what lies between man and God into a limitless quality of existence that, he contended, is itself limitless: 'There is nothing in existence but *barzakhs*, since a *barzakh* is the arrangement of one thing between two other things ... and existence has no edges' (quoted in Chittick, 1989, 14). Consider, within this framework, Ibn al-'Arabi's description of the nine spheres (divine or human) that, together, make up all of creation; each such sphere is itself a *barzakh* and an in-between; the world of the senses too is a *barzakh*; ditto the world of 'Power' and that of the 'Inner Realm.'[32] Though alone in being fully accomplished, God too, declared Ibn al-'Arabi, is a *barzakh* 'between the degrees of Paradise and the degrees of Hell. Indeed, He has described Himself as having two hands (Kor. 5:64). Now what is between two hands is the isthmus relative to them' (Ibn al-'Arabi, 1995, 92).[33] Following in the Sufi philosopher's footstep, Chittick has suggested that if God and all of his creation are indeed *barzakhs* then 'The Book [the Koran] is the *barzakh* or isthmus between man's intelligence and God's knowledge of things as they are in themselves. It provides the God-given and providential means whereby man can come to know things in themselves, without the distortions of egocentrism' (Chittick, 1989, 15–16). Seen through this lens, the Koran manifests divine reality through language as a distinguishing feature of human existence; it is no mere translation from one mode into the other since translation installs a distance between source and outcome, original and derivative; the Book is an original that engages, rather than merely connects, both the divine and the human.

Regarding the *barzakh* that is a thing 'between two other things,' what is most useful for our present purposes is less its theological legitimacy or import and more the Sufi appreciation of its inter- and intra-dynamics. The *barzakh* upends the classic bias of a hierarchy that marks the border as secondary in relation to the entities it demarcates. Although not an essential reality independent of its surroundings, the *barzakh* as 'between' is hardly the mere effect of, say, the juxtaposition of two pre-existing entities; it is, for Ibn al-'Arabi at least, that which '*separates* two things without ever becoming either of them' and, while being neither, nonetheless 'has in itself the powers of each' (1995, 106, emphasis in the original). Much like the transitional's relationship to materiality and hallucination, the *barzakh* is the space of an internal unification and unity of an external separation and duality. It resists the classic intellectual sensibilities according to which a marker of difference is by extension, and inevitably, a marker of separation—presumably, distinguishing one entity from another goes hand in hand with consolidating for each its own domain and attributes. The *barzakh*, however, is a boundary that unites; it is an indivisible partition whose single-sidedness gathers the elements of a difference and insists on their co-incidence. The *barzakh* is an *interregnum* of overdetermination situated somewhere between the two sides of a polarity that it nevertheless incorporates. Ibn al-'Arabi put it thus:

> So the reality of the *barzakh* is that within it there be no *barzakh*. It is that which meets what is between the two by its very essence. If it were to meet one of the two with a face that is other than the face with which it meets the other, then there would have to be within itself, between its two faces, a *barzakh* that differentiates between the two faces so that the two do not meet together. If there is no such *barzakh*, then the face with which it meets one of the two affairs between which it stands is identical with the face with which it meets the other. This is the true *barzakh*. It is, through its own essence, identical with everything that it meets. Hence the separation between the things and the separating factor become manifest as one in entity. Once you come to know this, you have come to know what the *barzakh* is.
>
> (quoted in Chittick, 1998, 334–35)

As a one-sided divide, the *barzakh* is akin to a Moebius strip, a trope Lacan often deployed to illustrate the quasi-imperceptible continuity between inside and outside, conscious and unconscious, love and hate (Lacan, 1965–66 and 1976–77).[34] That said, the figure also emphasizes the starker and more tense simultaneity of the components that make up these as well as other dualities: a found object that belongs to both the real and the illusory; an object that is always already subjectivized; a construction bourn out of the concurrence of two radically different visions, an artificial transference that is not any the less real; the list goes on.

Quite a few, no doubt, will be comfortable relegating the *barzakh*'s structural and functional reverberations with key elements of psychoanalysis to some category of the accidental or coincidental in the history of ideas, to the trifle, secondary or derivative, to, in other words, the intellectually and hence, seemingly by reasonable extension, the meta-psychologically, if not, most definitely, the clinically, irrelevant. If, by any chance, this were the case, it is precisely for that reason, as I have been suggesting all along, that these reverberations merit the attention, rather than the indifference, that urges us to pursue their psychoanalytic significance and import. It seems to me instead that the notion of the *barzakh* leads us away from the ever-looming and seemingly unbridgeable differences, of the hierarchies among the offshoots and accidents—of Babylonian Towers collapsed and heights unscaled—and, toward the Freudian scenario of a night's multiple dreams that grapple with a common phenomenon, though with differing biases and priorities. And as is the case with the basics of Freudian dream interpretation, we encounter the in-between as a node at which different series of associations (staged here as intellectual paradigms) on the theme of duality and opposition intersect. Recently reworked by Henry Corbin, the *barzakh*, I would suggest, is not merely one among the many versions of this node, it is also one of its most vivid and generative.

Mundus Imaginalis

Henry Corbin, one of the twentieth century's eminent European scholars of Islam, and Sufism in particular,[35] expanded the interpretation of the *barzakh* and defended it against the 'rational dilemma' sustained by such polarities as matter or spirit, history or myth (Corbin, 1989, 79). Corbin articulated an imaginal world (*mundus imaginalis*), both intermediary and intermediate, neither imagined nor non-existent and as ontologically real as any other.[36] 'This world [he wrote] is behind the very act of sense perception and has to be sought underneath its apparent objective certainty' (Corbin, 1972, 11):

> Just as the Latin word *origo* has provided us in French with the derivatives *originaire* (native of), *original, originel* (primary), the word *imago* can give us the term *imaginal* in addition to the regular derivative *imaginary*. We would thus have the *imaginal* world as an intermediary between the sensible world and the intelligible world.
>
> (Ibid; emphasis in the original)

No matter where it might be wedged—whether between the real and the intellectual (theosophy) or, I would argue, the real and the delusional (psychoanalysis)—to the *mundus imaginalis* corresponds an imaginative, rather than sensible or intellective, cognition that circumvents the limits of shallow dualisms (Corbin, 1972, 7). Corbin's re-interpretation of the *barzakh* takes up and extends the logic of the transitional as 'limiting and conjoining time and eternity, space and transspace' (Corbin, 1989, 80), as the 'incarnation of thought in image and the placing of the image *in being*' (Corbin, 1969, 407; emphasis in the original), as, in sum, what 'immaterializes' the Sensible ... [and] 'imaginalizes' the Intellectual (Corbin, 1989, ix).[37] This interpretation points back to the earliest elaborations in *Findings* as it foregrounds the imaginal's *coincidentia* and transforms it into a more accessible, more, dare I say, useful, category beyond Ibn al-'Arabi's ubiquitous formulations.[38] The imaginal, indeed, dovetails with the Winnicottian transitional in two respects: on the one hand, as it enlivens the objective world through the imagination and renders the imaginary in material form and, on the other hand, as it constitutes a divided unity and a unified heterogeneity (as subjectivized object and found subject, as lonely solitude and cruel play ...).

As imagination, the *mundus imaginalis* will remain out of focus so long as it is conceived in exceedingly rationalist and oppositional terms; as finding, it will continue to strike a so-called paradoxical note—enigmatic, not quite commanding, timid—so long as it is construed primarily as a way station along the path to the consistent, the reliable, the mature. In a deft and insightful reversal of the customary warning that the imagination is a betrayal of truth, Corbin concluded his presentation of the imaginal by suggesting that the degradation of the image to the status of a mere perception combined with the over-valuation of the intellect as the sole standard of truth are precisely the dangers to counter (Corbin, 1972, 12): 'with the loss of the *imaginatio vera* [imagination in the true sense] and of the *mundus imaginalis* nihilism and agnosticism begin' (Corbin, 1989, xii). This, to me, strikes a most familiar note, not only insofar as it encapsulates the position I have been advancing all along that in the absence of finding and its (transitional) space one is left with stagnation (of so-called objectivity, of secondary revision, of the law of excluded middle ...), but also because of its concordance with Freud's most trenchant insight into an inner reality irreducible to both the material and the delirious, the same reality that psychoanalysis has identified as the core of the human.

That said, Corbin was keen to articulate a complex hierarchy of worlds and abilities in line with his theosophical sensibilities.[39] Interestingly, Winnicott himself often argued for a similar order. Although emphatic in his advocacy for the legitimacy of the illusion that is the transitional object (Winnicott, 1971, 12), the same illusion that allows the psyche to play as it shields it from collapsing into a deadening materiality or a horrifying delusion, Winnicott nevertheless identified weaning as a required process of disillusionment along the way toward affective and cognitive maturity. The assumption here is that, unlike finding where the decathected object may be rediscovered and invested with all manner of new potential, weaning adheres to a developmental model according to which a return to a past object is most likely to be marked as a regression. Presumably, the same sequence of illusion-disillusionment must obtain in the development of any practice, from its earliest stages of intuition, conjecture and experimentation and all the way toward a fully formed model that delivers a coherent and verifiable perspective as well as a reliable and effective technique. Anything short of such a sequence compromises reality testing and opens the gates onto pathology and/or quackery. However, as it encourages a back and forth between illusion and fact, all the while correcting, adjusting, and fine-tuning the former in light of the latter with the aim of producing as accurate a match as possible, this sequence subordinates transitionality and finding to the demands of a super-ordinate law of correspondence according to which, at the end of the day, illusion must cede to science as the image is reduced to a mere perception. And yet, Winnicott was very careful in discerning pathology and indeed madness not in the presence of subjective phenomena but in their unwavering claims to objectivity (1971, 14), in the peculiarities of the one becoming the standard for all—in, essentially, the universalization of singularity. I want to suggest that an instance of such madness is the claim that illusion must suffer the fate of breastfeeding, that finding ought to be subject to the same laws as physiological growth, that, ultimately, the concerns and procedures of psychoanalysis are the same as those of science or technology. It would be convenient to limit Winnicott's endorsement of illusion to the intermediary areas and experiences that belong to either the infant who has yet to grow or the adult engaged in 'art or religion or philosophy' (Winnicott, 1971, 14); psychoanalysis, so the claim might be made, is neither art nor religion nor, most especially, philosophy. The fact remains, such a limit is not only a blatant disregard of all that Winnicott had to say about psychoanalysis as fundamentally a form of playing, in terms of both method and aim, it is also the type of madness that obviates transitionality and classifies every human practice as, at the end of the day, either fact or fiction, either science or quackery.

Without losing site of the concrete and the delusional, the sensory and the intellectual, nay, while fully aware of the strength and validity of all that lies on either side of the divide, the imaginal helps set in even greater relief the challenge of co-incidence. It is both revealing and unsettling for the way in which, as a unifying Moebius strip, it expands on the logic of the *vicissitudo*, contained, self-sufficient and hardly ever aware of an outside. Much as it brings to mind something in the order of a reassuring and sustaining containment and proximity, a *claustrophilia* as Fachinelli once put it (1983), this scenario carries with it all the elements of an impermeable claustrophobic design, a holding now synonymous with confinement, rest with stagnation, satisfaction with dependency, all as overwhelming from within as they are inscrutable from without. Before us then is the outline of a wholly different type of 'set' situation tantamount to the troubling antithesis of what Winnicott had in mind when he deployed the term, a situation that has no beginning, middle or end, one that consists instead of endless, nonorientable and hence potentially agonizingly confusing loops.[40]

Hence, the need for a recognition of the outside, under the guise of the two opposing sides of the divide, as materiality and hallucination or as life and death for instance, not as limits, containers or respites, not even as dangers, but as constitutive of all that unfolds under the heading of the inside, the transitional, the imaginal. This effectively recognizes the finality that classic analytic theory has for the most part tried to elide. Death is no mere 'principle;' with the imaginal, its sensible experience as well as its status as a category become the representations from which psychic reality may not be exempted.

Notes

1 For the purposes of this discussion, the overdetermination of dreams is as heuristic as it is psychological, as per the multiplicity of constructions advanced in the *Series* text.

2 As per the discussion in *Findings*.
3 The term is originally Heinz Kohut's. It emerged out of the analyst's work on empathy from the late 1950s and subsequently became a key concept in his writings (Kohut, 1984, 2009). One can hardly overstate the extent to which Winnicott's work has been appropriated by Kohut and his school of self-psychology.
4 Brett Kahr recounts the unease with which Winnicott's text on the psycho-analyst's hate was met when first presented to colleagues at a meeting of the British Psycho-Analytical Society in 1947. Kahr also notes the paucity of refer-ences to the text in the analytic literature for roughly four decades after its initial publication. (Kahr, 2011, 175 and 207n1)
5 In *Series*.
6 Though not official church doctrine, limbo was for many in Medieval Europe part of hell as its edge, as opposed to the purgatory which, strictly speaking, is a territory in its own right separating heaven from hell. In Canto IV of *Inferno*, Dante iden-tified limbo as the first of the nine circles of hell, past the Acheron where, along with the unbapitzed, such luminaries as Homer, Ovid, Plato, Avicenna, Virgil, Lucretia, Cicero, Julius Caesar, Saladin, Euclid, Electra and Averroes reside.
7 For more on the 'Middle Group,' see Raitt (2004) for a history of the very early days of psychoanalysis in Britain; see also Hinshelwood (1995, 1999) for an account of the history's subsequent developments. Rodman (2003) provides a good overview of Winnicott's involvement in that history.
8 The accounts of Porro (2001), Jaritz and Moreno-Riaño (2003) as well as Althoff et al. (2002) are very useful access points to the study of this period's treatment of time. Although the scholastic theologians eventually abandoned the notion, the *aevum* did not disappear irrevocably from the theologico-philosophical lexicon. See Calcagno (2008) for an assessment of the notion at work in the philosophy of the early twentieth-century German phenomenologist Edith Stein.
9 D. P. Simpson cites a number of first-century BCE references (including Cicero, Virgil, Ovid and Lucretius) as instances of the *aevum*'s use in his presentation of the term as 'eternity' (Simpson, 1979, 29). The *aevum*'s most notable occurrence for our purposes dates back to the Latin Vulgate of Verse I of the first chapter of *Ecclesiasticus*, believed to have been written by the Alexandrian Ben Sira at some point between 180 and 175 BCE. According to Ben Sira,'*Omni sapientia a Deo Domino est et cum illo fuit semper et est ante aevum*,' ('All wisdom is from the Lord, and is with him for ever'), as per Oesterley's edition (Ben Sira, 1916, 14). While only fragments of the Hebrew text have survived, the Latin Vulgate edition is based on a Greek translation of the original prepared by the author's grandson. Although not included in the Hebrew Bible, *Ecclesiasticus* is one of the books of what later became the Septuagint edition of the Old Testament; the Latin Church Fathers eventually dubbed it the 'Church Book.' It is safe to assume that the medieval philosophers I am referencing here were well aware of the earlier epi-sodes in the *aevum*'s theologico-philosophical history.
10 This definition picks up on an earlier but not fully explored concept proposed in the *Book of Causes* from the fifth century AD: 'between the substance, whose substance and action is in the moment of eternity, and the substance, whose substance and action is in a moment of time, there is an intermediary [*media*] substance, whose substance is in the moment of eternity, and (whose) action (is) in a moment of time' (Anonymous, 1984, Proposition 31). See also Propositions 205 and 210 in the same text. Initially attributed to Aristotle, the *Book of Causes* is now accepted as most likely the work of the Neo-Platonist Proclus.
11 Also of note in this history of audible eruptions is the introduction of the cannon into Europe—from China, via the Middle East—at around that very same time.

This might explain the fact that the earliest clock makers were often drawn from the ranks of blacksmiths and gun founders (Boorstin, 1985, 67–68 and Cipolla, 1978, 50–51).

12 My disagreement notwithstanding, Cipolla's text provides an invaluable introduction to the history of clock production and its impact on culture and technology. On this topic, David Landes (1982) is a rich and equally essential read.

13 As per the titles of texts written by, respectively, Pontalis (1997) and Green (2000).

14 See *Games* for more on this category.

15 Augustine's elaborations on the *libido dominandi* (Augustine, 2005) date back to the fourth century AD and hence long before the Medieval investment in the *aevum*, an investment to which, had he witnessed it, Augustine most certainly would have been opposed, considering his strictly dualistic stance in matters theological and philosophical (Augustine, 1998).

16 See, respectively, Freud (1914) and Freud (1911).

17 Just as he understood dream interpretation as the reverse of the dream work, Freud's archaeological model of psychoanalytic investigation is also the reverse of the instincts' volcanic stratigraphy. On this score, the references in Freud's text are numerous; they span from his earliest elaborations to Fliess in 1896 (Freud, 1985, 207), and all the way to the late 1930s when he underscored the parallels and differences between psychoanalysis and archaeology (Freud, 1937, 259). I have already touched on this topic in *Series*; meanwhile, O'Donoghue (2004) and Bowdler (1996) are very worthy springboards into the extensive psychoanalysis-archaeology literature.

18 Graham Frankland opted for the straightforward 'Drives and Their Fate' in the recent Penguin re-translation under the general editorship of Adam Phillips (Freud, 2005).

19 As with, in one regard, the drive's reversal into its opposite, turning around upon the subject's own self, repression, and/or sublimation, and, in another regard, libido's surges from one bodily locus to another (mouth, genitals, skin, anus, eyes, etc.).

20 The clarity of Freud's treatment did not pass without its own consequences as its author eventually metamorphosed his writing of the lava metaphor into a volcanic writing. No sooner had the ink that wrote in favour of the self-sufficiency of discontinuous moments, and hence of the *aevum*, dried on the page than it was overtaken by a dread of *tempus* and a wish for *aeternitas*, a dread and a wish that would pin the fate of such moments to the laws of succession, accumulation and usurpation, to, among other dynamics, rivalry—oedipal or otherwise. In a manoeuvre designed to pre-empt any eventual questioning of these latter laws, Freud's pen did not hesitate to retrace its steps back a decade—as per Strachey's editorial dating (Freud, 1905, 168n2)—and write into the *Three Essays* a new passage that would try to cover over any preceding hint of the *aevum* by confirming, again and in the spirit of secondary revision's definitive 'once and for all,' that the instinct is indeed a 'continuously flowing source of stimulation, as contrasted with a "stimulus," which is set up by *single* excitations' (Freud, 1905, 168, emphasis in the original).

21 It is worth noting here that the Deleuzo-Guattarian elision of endings is no less defining than the Winnicottian. The conjunctive 'ah, so that's what it is, that's who I am' does not hint at any possible 'ah, so that's what it was, that's who I used to be!' On this question, see Abou-Rihan (2008) reviewing Lampert (2006).

22 Razinsky has already noted the enduring nature of this point of view and its tremendous influence on subsequent generations of theorists: 'Although so many of Freud's ideas regarding the nature of the unconscious or psychic life have been

revised in subsequent developments of psychoanalysis, there has been little opposition to his views about death' (Razinsky, 2011, 334). The literature on this
topic is vast and the following are useful points of entry: Eigen (2004), Klein
(1948), Searles (1965) and Lifton (1979).

23 Note that the blind spot here pertains to one's appreciation of one's own finitude;
Freud had no trouble acknowledging that 'for strangers and for enemies we do
acknowledge death, and consign them to it quite as readily and unhesitatingly as
did primaeval man … Our unconscious does not carry out the killing; it merely
thinks it and wishes it. But it would be wrong so completely to undervalue this
psychical reality as compared with factual reality. It is significant and momentous
enough. In our unconscious impulses we daily and hourly get rid of anyone who
stands in our way, of anyone who has offended or injured us' (Freud, 1915d, 297).

24 At this point, I cannot but wonder as to how much Freud's sure-footedness regarding this matter has less to do with either clinic or metapsychology as it
perhaps does with whatever struggles he may have had confronting his own
mortality.

25 'From nothing to nothing is no time at all' John Steinbeck once mused: 'A time
splashed with interest, wounded with tragedy, crevassed with joy—that's the time
that seems long in the memory. And this is right when you think about it.
Eventlessness has no posts to drape duration on.' John Steinbeck (1979, ch. 7)

26 See *Findings*.

27 David Bakan (2004) spoke of a 'basic mood' and an 'atmospheric similarity'
linking Freud with the Jewish mystical tradition; relevant here is also the study by
Bakan, Merkur and Weiss (2010). On the topic of Maimonides and Islam, see
Pines (1963), Kraemer (2003, 2008) and Stroumsa (2009).

28 See in this regard Pratt Ewing (1997), Akhtar (2008), Benslama (2009), Copjec
and Jöttkandt (2009), Jöttkandt and Copjec (2009) and el-Shakry (2017).

29 In order of their appearance in the text, these are: 'In falsehood will they be until,
when death comes to one of them, he says: "O my Lord! Send me back (to life)—in
order that I may work righteousness in the things I neglected"—"By no means! It is
but a word he says"—Before them is a partition [*barzakh*] till the day they are raised
up' (Kor. 23: 99–100); 'It is He Who has let free the two bodies of flowing water,
one palpable and sweet, and the other salty and bitter. Yet has He made a barrier
[*barzakh*] between them, a partition that is forbidden to be passed' (Kor. 25:53);
and 'He has let free the two bodies of flowing water, meeting together: Between
them is a barrier [*barzakh*] which they do not transgress' (Kor. 55:20).

30 Alongside the monotheistic Jews, Christians and Hanifs, pre-Islamic Arabia was
a fertile ground for many indigenous sects animated by gods and goddesses,
eternities and returns. For more on this history, see Hoyland (2001) and Burkey
(2002) as well as the highly informative Bowersock (1998).

31 See Jeffery (1938), Widengren (1955) and Karbassian (2017) for more on the
barzakh's history and meanings.

32 I cite a passage of Ibn al-'Arabi's in its entirety here to convey his allusive style
and numerological approach:

> The nine spheres are at the same time seven spheres. Actually, the world of the
> senses is in itself an intermediate world (*barzakh*); that makes one. It has an
> inner face, which makes two, and an outer face; which thus makes three. The
> world of Power (*jabarût*) is an intermediate world, and thus the fourth. It has
> an outer face that is the inner side of the world of the senses, and an inner face,
> which is the fifth world. And finally, the world of the Inner Realm (*malakût*)
> is, in itself, an intermediate world; the sixth. Its outer face is the inside of the
> *jabarût*; its inner face is the seventh world, and there is no other. Such is the

form of the heptad and the ennead (*is-sab'iyya*, *al-tis'iyya*). If we now take the three, and multiply them by seven, we get twenty-one. When we take away the three that belong to Man, we are left with eighteen, the station of the Angel, that is, the set of spheres from which man receives inspiration (*mawârid*). Let us proceed likewise with the three divine worlds; their multiplication by seven gives the spheres from which God projects toward His servant the knowledge that it pleases Him to inspire (*wâridât*) ...

(Ibn al-'Arabi, 2004, 156)

33 The widespread though not quite accurate rendering of *barzakh* as isthmus is worth flagging here.

34 The clearest illustration of this structure is a strip of paper glued end to end after a half-twist. The result is a loop with a single surface and a single edge. Drawing a line down the middle returns a pencil to its starting point without it lifting off or puncturing the paper. Along a Moebius strip, the signposts of inward and outward, up and down, left and right are now reversed as the strip itself is designated a 'nonorientable' surface. For more on Lacan's investments in topology, see Hewitson (2015) and Ragland (2015).

35 Aside from being a friend and colleague of Lacan's and the earliest translator of Heidegger into French (Heidegger, 1938), Corbin was also a regular presence at the Eranos Circle in Ascona, along with Carl Jung and Gershom Scholem.

36 As Bottici rightly points out, the imaginal refers to a world and not a faculty (Bottici, 2014, 55); it lies somewhere between imagination as an individual faculty and the imaginary as a social context. Contra Bottici, the world to which the imaginal refers is not made of images. The essays collected in Fleury (2006) and Bertin and Guillaud (2020) offer exceptionally useful overviews of the concept.

37 Corbin (1969, 179) credited this formulation to Alexandre Koyré's insight into the Renaissance (Koyré, 1971).

38 As previously noted, everything according to Ibn al-'Arabi is a *barzakh*; it is an all-pervasive characteristic of a limitless existence.

39 Corbin flagged his presentation with the clear intention 'to circumscribe a very precise order of reality, which corresponds to a precise mode of perception' (Corbin, 1972, 1).

40 Here, the parallel may be drawn with the all-knowing non-disillusioning parent and the danger they pose for the offspring. (Winnicott, 1960).

References

Abou-Rihan, Fadi. 2008. "'Why No Longer?' Review of Jay Lampert's *Deleuze and Guattari's Philosophy of History*." In *Symposium*. 12:2. Pp. 53–56.

Akhtar, Salman. 2008. *The Crescent and the Couch: Cross-Currents Between Islam and Psychoanalysis*. Lanham: Jason Aronson.

Althoff, Gerd, et al. (eds.). 2002. *Medieval Concepts of the Past: Ritual, Memory, Historiography*. Cambridge: Cambridge University Press.

Anonymous. 1984. *Book of Causes: Liber De Causis*. Translated from the Latin with an introduction by Dennis Brand. Milwaukee: Marquette University Press.

Augustine of Hippo. 1998. *Confessions*. Translated by Henry Chadwick. Oxford: Oxford University Press.

Augustine of Hippo. 2005. *De Civitate Dei, The City of God, Books 1 and 2*. Edited and translated by P. G. Walsh. Liverpool: Liverpool University Press.

Bakan, David. 2004. *Sigmund Freud and the Jewish Mystical Tradition*. Mineola, NY: Dover Books.

Bakan, David, Merkur, Dan and Weiss, David. 2010. *Maimonides' Cure of Souls: Medieval Precursor of Psychoanalysis*. Buffalo: SUNY Press.

Bashier, Salman. 2004. *Ibn al-'Arabi's Barzakh: The Concept of the Limit and the Relationship Between God and the World*. Albany: SUNY Press.

Ben Sira of Jerusalem. 1916. *Ecclesiasticus*. Translated by W. E. O. Oesterley. D.D. London: Society for Promoting Christian Knowledge. https://archive.org/details/wisdomofbensirae00oest Accessed: 15-08-2022.

Benslama, Fethi. 2009. *Psychoanalysis and the Challenge of Islam*. Minneapolis: University of Minnesota Press.

Bertin, Georges & Lauric, Guillaud. 2020. *Topologies de l'imaginal*. Lyon: Éditions du Cosmogone.

Bonaventure, Doctoris Seraphici. 1885. *Opera Omnia Quaracchi Vol 02, Commentarii Sententiarum, Liber II*. http://www.documentacatholicaomnia.eu/20vs/221_Bonaventura/1221-1274,_Bonaventura,_Doctoris_Seraphici_Opera_Omnia_(Quaracchi)_Vol_02,_LT.pdf Accessed: 15-08-2022.

Boorstin, Daniel. 1985. *The Discoverers*. New York: Random House.

Bottici, Chiara. 2014. *Imaginal Politics: Images Beyond Imagination and the Imaginary*. New York: Columbia University Press.

Bowdler, Sandra. 1996. "Freud and Archaeology." In *Anthropological Forum*. 7:3. Pp. 419–438.

Bowersock, Glen. 1998. *Roman Arabia*. Cambridge MA: Harvard University Press.

Burkey, Jonathan. 2002. *The Formation of Islam: Religion and Society in the Near East*. Cambridge: Cambridge University Press.

Calcagno, Antonio. 2008 "Being, *aevum*, and nothingness: Edith Stein on death and dying." In *Continental Philosophy Review*. 41:q. Pp. 59–72.

Chittick, William. 1989. *The Sufi Path to Knowledge: Ibn al-'Arabi's Metaphysics of Imagination*. Albany: State University of New York.

Chittick, William. 1994. *Imaginal Worlds: Ibn al-'Arabi and the Problem of Religious Diversity*. Albany: State University of New York.

Chittick, William. 1998. *The Self-Disclosure of God: Principles of Ibn al-'Arabi's Cosmology*. Albany: State University of New York Press.

Cipolla, Carlo. 1978. *Clocks and Culture:1300–1700*. London and New York: W. W. Norton & Co.

Copjec, Joan and Sigi Jöttkandt (eds.) 2009. *Islam special issue of UMBRa: A Journal of the Unconscious*.

Corbin, Henry. 1969. *Alone with the Alone: Creative Imagination in the Sufism of Ibn'Arabi*. Princeton: Princeton University Press.

Corbin, Henry. 1972. "Mundus Imaginalis or the Imaginary and the Imaginal." http://www.bahaistudies.net/asma/mundus_imaginalis.pdf Accessed: 15-08-2022.

Corbin, Henry. 1989. *Spiritual Body and Celestial Earth: From Mazdean Iran to Shi'ite Iran*. Princeton: Princeton University Press.

Deleuze, Gilles and Guattari, Felix. 1977. *Anti-Oedipus*. Translated by Robert Hurley, Mark Seem, and Helen R. Lane with a preface by Michel Foucault. New York: Viking Press.

Eigen, Michael. 2004. *Psychic Deadness*. London: Routledge.

Fachinelli, Elvio. 1983. *Claustrofilia*. Milano: Adelphi.

Fleury, Cynthia. 2006. *Imagination, Imaginaire, Imaginal*. Paris: Presses Universities de France.

Freud, Sigmund. 1900. "The Interpretation of Dreams." In *The Complete Standard Edition of the Psychological Works of Sigmund Freud SE* IV-V. London: Hogarth Press.

Freud, Sigmund. 1905. "Three Essays on the Theory of Sexuality." In *SE* VII. London: Hogarth Press. Pp. 125–243.

Freud, Sigmund. 1911. "Psychoanalytic Notes on an Autobiographical Account of a Case of Paranoia." In *SE* XII. London: Hogarth Press. Pp. 1–82.

Freud, Sigmund. 1914. "On Narcissism: An Introduction." In *SE* XIV. London: Hogarth Press. Pp. 67–102.

Freud, Sigmund. 1915a. "Instincts and their Vicissitudes." In *SE* XIV. London: Hogarth Press. Pp. 109–140.

Freud, Sigmund. 1915b. "Repression." In *SE* XIV. London: Hogarth Press. Pp. 146–158.

Freud, Sigmund. 1915c. "The Unconscious." In *SE* XIV. London: Hogarth Press. Pp. 159–216.

Freud, Sigmund. 1915d. "Thoughts for the Times on War and Death." In *SE* XIV. London: Hogarth Press. Pp. 275–302.

Freud, Sigmund. 1920. "Beyond the Pleasure Principle." In *SE* XVIII. London: Hogarth Press. Pp. 7–64.

Freud, Sigmund. 1925. "Negation." In *SE* XIX. London: Hogarth Press. Pp. 233–239.

Freud, Sigmund. 1933. "New Introductory Lectures on Psychoanalysis." In *SE* XXII. London: Hogarth Press. Pp. 5–182.

Freud, Sigmund. 1937. "Constructions in Analysis." In *SE* XXIII. London: Hogarth Press. Pp. 257–269.

Freud, Sigmund. 1940. "An Outline of Psychoanalysis." In *SE* XXIII. London: Hogarth Press. Pp. 144–207.

Freud, Sigmund. 1985. *The Complete Letters of Sigmund Freud to Wilhelm Fliess: 1887–1904*. Edited by Jeffrey M. Masson. Cambridge: Harvard University Press.

Freud, Sigmund. 2005. "Drives and Their Fate." In *The Unconscious*. Translated by Graham Frankland and edited by Adam Phillips. London: Penguin Books.

Green, André. 2000. *Le temps éclaté*. Paris: Les Éditions de Minuit.

Heidegger, Martin. 1938. *Phénoménologie de la mort fin § 52 & § 53, Sein und Zeit*. Halle am Saale, M. Niemeyer, 1927. Traduit de l'allemand par Henry Corbin. Paris: Hermès. Pp. 37–51.

Hewitson, Owen. 2015. "From the Bridges of Königsberg – Why Topology Matters in Psychoanalysis." https://www.lacanonline.com/2015/01/from-the-bridges-of-konigsberg-why-topology-matters-in-psychoanalysis/ Accessed: 15-08-2022.

Hinshelwood, Robert D. 1995. "Psychoanalysis in Britain: Points of Cultural Access." In *International Journal of Psychoanalysis*. 76:135–151.

Hinshelwood, Robert D. 1999."The Organising of Psychoanalysis in Britain." In *Psychoanalysis and History*. 1: 87–102.

Hoyland, Robert. 2001. *Arabia and the Arabs: From the Bronze Age to the Coming of Islam*. London: Routledge.

Ibn al-'Arabi. 1995. "The Meccan Revelations chapter 63." In Morris, James Winston "Devine 'Imagination' and the Intermediate World: Ibn 'Arabi on the '"Barzakh'." Translated by J. W. Morris. In *Podesta* 2:15. Pp. 104–109. Available at https://dlib.bc.edu/islandora/object/bc-ir:100505/datastream/PDF/view Accessed: 15-08-2022.

Ibn al-'Arabi. 2004. *The Meccan Revelations volume 2*. Edited by Michael Chodkiewicz and translated by Cyrille Chodkiewicz and Denis Gril. New York: PIR Press.

Idelman Smith, Jane and Yazbeck Haddad, Yvonne. 2002. *The Islamic Understanding of Death and Resurrection*. Oxford: Oxford University Press.

Jaritz, Gerhard and Moreno-Riaño, Gerson (eds.). 2003. *Time and Eternity: The Medieval Discourse*. Turnhout: Brepols Publishers.

Jeffery, Arthur. 1938. *The Foreign Vocabulary of the Qur'ān*. Baroda: Oriental Institute.

Jöttkandt, Sigi and Joan Copjec (eds.). 2009. *Islam and Psychoanalysis, a special issue of S: Journal of the Circle for Lacanian Ideology Critique*. http://www.lineofbeauty.org/index.php/S/issue/view/6 Accessed: 15-08-2022.

Kahr, Brett. 2011. "Winnicott's '*Anni Horribiles*": The Biographical Roots of 'Hate in the Counter-Transference'." In *American Image* 66:2. Pp. 173–211.

Karbassian, Malihe. 2017. "The Meaning and Etymology of *Barzakh* in Illuminationist Philosophy." In *Illuminationist Texts and Textual Studies: Essays in Memory of Hossein Ziai*. Edited by Gheissari Ali, et al. Leiden and Boston: BrillAcademic Publishers. Pp. 86–95.

Klein, Melanie. 1948. "On the Theory of Anxiety and Guilt." In *The Collected Works of Melanie Klein vol. 3*. London: Karnac. Pp. 25–42.

Kohut, Heinz. 1984. *How Does Analysis Cure*. Chicago: The University of Chicago Press.

Kohut, Heinz. 2009. *The Analysis of the Self: A Systematic Approach to the Psychoanalytic Treatment of Narcissistic Personality Disorders*. Chicago: The University of Chicago Press.

Koyré, Alexandre. 1971. *Mystiques, Spirituels, Alchimistes du XVIème siècle Allemand*. Paris: Editions Gallimard.

Kraemer, Joel L. 2003. "The Islamic Context of Medieval Jewish Philosophy." In *The Cambridge Companion to Medieval Jewish Philosophy*. Edited by Daniel H. Frank and Oliver Leaman. Cambridge: Cambridge University Press. Pp. 38–68.

Krafft-Ebbing, Richard von. 1998. *Psychopathia Sexualis With Special Reference to the Antipathic Sexual Instinct*. Translated with an introduction by Franklin S. Klaf. New York: Arcade Publishing.

Lacan, Jacques. 1965-66. *The Object of Psychoanalysis. The Seminar of Jacques Lacan, Book XIII*. Translated by Cormac Gallagher. http://www.lacaninireland.com/web/wp-content/uploads/2010/06/13-The-Object-of-Psychoanalysis1.pdf Accessed: 15-08-2022.

Lacan, Jacques. 1992. *The Ethics of Psychoanalysis. The Seminar of Jacques Lacan, Book VII*. Edited by Jacques-Alain Miller and translated by Denis Potter. New York: W. W. Norton & Company.

Lampert, Jay. 2006. *Deleuze and Guattari's Philosophy of History*. London and New York: Continuum Books.

Landes, David. 1982. *Revolution in Time: Clocks and the Making of the Modern*. Cambridge, MA: Harvard University Press.

Lifton, Robert J. 1979. *The Broken Connection: On Death and the Continuity of Life*. New York: Simon and Schuster.

Moll, Albert. 1898. *Untersuchungen über die Libido Sexualis*. Berlin: H. Kornfeld.

O'Donoghue, Diane. 2004. "Negotiations of Surface: Archaeology within the Early Strata of Psychoanalysis'." In *Journal of the American Psychoanalytic Association*. 52:3. Pp. 653–671.

Pines, Shlomo. 1963. "Translator's Introduction: The Philosophical Sources of The Guide of the Perplexed." In *The Guide of the Perplexed*. Edited by Moses Maimonides. Translated by. S. Pines. Chicago: The University of Chicago Press. Pp. lvii–cxxxiv.

Pontalis, Jean-Bertrand. 1997. *Ce temps qui ne passe pas*. Paris: Editions Gallimard.

Porro, Pasquale (ed.). 2001. *The Medieval Concept of Time: The Scholastic Debate and its Reception in Early Modern Philosophy*. Leiden, Boston, Köln: Brill.

Pratt Ewing, Katherine. 1997. *Arguing Sainthood: Modernity, Psychoanalysis, and Islam*. Durham, NC: Duke University Press.

Ragland, Ellie. 2015. *Jacques Lacan and the Logic of Structure: Topology and Language in Psychoanalysis*. New York: Routledge.

Raitt, Suzanne. 2004. "Early British Psychoanalysis and the Medico-Psychological Clinic." In *History Workshop Journal*. 58. Pp. 63–85.

Razinsky, Liran. 2011. "Against Death's Representability: Freud and the Question of Death's Psychic Presence." In *Psychoanalytic Study of the Child*. 65. Pp. 332–357.

Rodman, F. Robert. 2003. *Winnicott: Life and Work*. Cambridge, MA: Da Capo Press.

Searles, Harold F. 1965. "Schizophrenia and the inevitability of death." In *Collected Papers on Schizophrenia and Related Subjects*. New York: International Universities Press.

Shakry, Omnia. el-. 2017. *The Arabic Freud: Psychoanalysis and Islam in Modern Egypt*. Princeton and Oxford: Princeton University Press.

Simpson, D. P. 1979. *Cassell's Latin-English Dictionary*. London: Cassell Limited.

Steinbeck, John. 1979. *East of Eden*. London: Penguin Books.

Stroumsa, Sarah. 2009. *Maimonides in His World: Portrait of a Mediterranean Thinker*. Princeton; Oxford: Princeton University Press.

Widengren, Geo. 1955. *Muhammad: The Apostle of God and his Ascension*. Uppsala: Lundequistska bokhandeln.

Winnicott, Donald W. 1941. "The Observation of Infants in a Set Situation." In *Through Paediatrics to Psychoanalysis: Collected Papers*. New York and London: Brunner-Routledge. Pp. 52–69.

Winnicott, Donald W. 1947. "Hate in the Contertransference." In *Through Paediatrics to Psycho-Analysis: Collected Papers*. New York and London: Brunner-Routledge. Pp. 194–203.

Winnicott, Donald W. 1954. "Metapsychological and Clinical Aspects of Regression Within the Psycho-Analytical Set-Up." In *Through Paediatrics to Psycho-Analysis: Collected Papers*. New York and London: Brunner-Routledge. Pp. 278–294.

Winnicott, Donald W. 1956b "Primary Maternal Preoccupation." In *Through Paediatrics to Psychoanalysis: Collected Papers*. New York and London: Brunner-Routledge. Pp. 300–305.

Winnicott, Donald W. 1958. "The Capacity to Be Alone." In *The Maturational Processes and the Facilitating Environment*. London: Hogarth Press and the Institute of Psycho-Analysis. Pp. 29–36.

Winnicott, Donald W. 1960. "The Theory of The Parent-Infant Relationship." In *The Maturational Process and the Facilitating Environment*. London: Hogarth Press and the Institute of Psycho-Analysis. Pp. 37–55.

Winnicott, Donald W. 1969. "The Use of an Object and Relating Through Identification." In *Playing and Reality*. London and New York: Routledge Books. Pp. 86–94.

Winnicott, Donald W. 1971. "Transitional Objects and Transitional Phenomena." In *Playing and Reality*. London and New York: Routledge Books. Pp. 1–25.

Winnicott, Donald W. 1988. *Human Nature*. London: Free Associations Books.

Winnicott, Donald W. 1991. *The Child, the Family and the Outside World*. London: Penguin Books.

Chapter 7

Properties

In The Middle

'It's not easy to see things in the middle, rather than looking down on them from above or up at them from below, from left to right or right to left: try it, you'll see that everything changes.' (Deleuze and Guattari, 1987, 23). Deleuze and Guattari's challenge to shift perspective strikes at the very nature of being. To be in the middle is to be on the inside looking out and back again toward that very same inside; it is to be self-analytical and, at times, self-preoccupied, in the best though by no means most comfortable of ways. This is also to say that to be in the middle is to deploy on oneself the tools and strategies one is all too keen to apply to the other from the outside in, to bear the other in mind, to, effectively, bare oneself as other. The middle, as Deleuze and Guattari deployed it, is the *milieu* in reference both to the middle, as an in-between, and to the environment, as a surround or context, and hence that which connotes the core as well as the periphery. The middle is a midpoint and an after-effect that will often reveal itself as the hub around which all else is organized and without which all else may come undone.[1]

To be in the middle is to find oneself on a plateau as a 'continuous, self-vibrating region of intensities whose development avoids any orientation toward a culmination point or external end' (Deleuze and Guattari, 1987, 22).[2] This plateau is far removed from the familiar stasis—frequently registered as accomplishment though more often than not experienced as stagnation. Here, the plateau is a plane of continuous intensity, of attention captured and released, of focus shifted, de-centred, externalized though all the while reclaimed, a plane of time passing yet devoid of the anguish or hope that carry the hint of an end or a resolution, of another time and, better still, of a time that is other, of a time installed, of a time endured.

With self-reflexivity as part and parcel of what it means to be in the middle, I want to reconfirm my earlier assertion that psychoanalysis is as much a practice as it is a theory of transitionality, that while it speaks of transitional objects and spaces it also speaks (through) them. Bearing in mind their

DOI: 10.4324/9781003352488-7

differing qualities and scopes, I consider the child's play, Winnicott's play with that play and my own manipulations of these phenomena—my play—as part of a string, or series, of associations and constructions with which one may not simply tie up or confine (Winnicott, 1960a) but, through tugs or knots, also communicate by pointing toward new terrains, thus leaving behind a trail of constructions once produced and held as vital but since, for one reason or another, displaced, overridden or altogether decathected.

Consider, for example, the string to which belongs Winnicott's recapitulation of a vignette he had already written up twice before (in 1960 and 1965) as an addendum to the final version of his transitional objects essay. Labelled an 'application' to his theory of transitionality, the vignette focuses on a boy's struggles negotiating separation from mother (Winnicott, 1971, 15–20). The clinical details here matter less than the fact of Winnicott's iterations as they underscore the vignette's highly overdetermined evidentiary uses:

- first, to testify to Winnicott's unshakeable investment in the validity of the theory he had been espousing for over two decades, in spite of all difficulties, whether theoretical or clinical;
- second, to warn against the costly repercussions of the failure to implement that theory as, in this case in particular, a stagnation in libido's development in terms of both object and aim, and hence, as it were, its derailment from a productive dreaming into a sterile fantasying;
- third, to justify the clinical usefulness of a specifically psychoanalytic approach to the customary, but otherwise un-analytic, treatment of a number of disorders including, in this case, drug addiction;
- fourth, to illustrate Winnicott's drawing on his own previously published clinical material as one would on a found object, deploying it anew and weaving it into a fresh schema, recapitulating its most salient features while expanding on previously unexplored others;
- fifth, to confirm Winnicott's continued deployment, as, for lack of a better term, 'conceptual' found objects the classic Freudian categories of inversion and perversion—this in spite of the Object Relations school's break with Freud in favour of Fairbairn's reformulation of libido as object-seeking rather than pleasure-seeking and all of that reformulation's attendant ramifications for thinking libido and its vicissitudes;
- sixth, to communicate, in the style of a symptom, Winnicott's own defensive manoeuvres against the anxiety regarding the potential tenuousness and subsequent relinquishment of his clinical assessment of the case, much as, by his own reckoning, a child's use of a transitional object communicates a defence against, at best, an anxiety of the depressive type (Winnicott, 1971, 4) or, as is with this vignette in particular, the debilitating prospect that child suffered at having to separate from mother.[3]

This is hardly an exhaustive list of the purposes the vignette may endorse or of the effects it may trigger. No doubt, other readers will extrapolate other meanings and consequences and will go on to prioritize them according to their own investments or concerns. Partial as it may be, the list does highlight the invariable multiplicity of the vignette's uses and effects. In the process, it testifies less to any awkwardness or indeed limitation in the Winnicottian theory of the transitional in the face of clinical evidence, and more to its author's experience of that theory as itself a transitional object or, to put it differently, as a meshwork of meanings that speak an imaginative planning of Winnicott's metapsychological and clinical acumen.

I would therefore suggest that Winnicott need not have spilled much ink tolerating, justifying or begging his reader's patience as regards the so-called paradoxical nature of his theory, or the equally paradoxical quality of the text elaborating on that theory, since what is at stake here is a theory and a text that are themselves transitional, which is to say found, conjured, woven, appropriated and/or relinquished. As such, and much like the found object's, the theory and the text's relevance and legitimacy depend neither on their internal consistency (as with the logic of the hallucinatory core) nor on their concordance with an external observable reality (as with the demands of hard science) but on their potential to extend the string further by accruing future objects, theoretical, textual and otherwise—equally found, equally useful.

The question before us then is a question of the use rather than the meaning of a symptom, an object, or a theory.[4] Indeed, and whereas the Winnicottian parental privileges the symptom's efficacy at referencing and conveying to the outside world an internal wish or experience and at communicating a corresponding demand, in other words the symptom's symbolic functions (that it can mean), the Winnicottian psychoanalytic is more focused on the symptom's ability to participate in a course of playful action—whether psychic or motor—whose itineraries it has not entirely predetermined, in other words, the symptom's productive possibilities (that it can do). Such a transformation cannot but promote its own specific set of theoretical and clinical priorities away from the simple satisfaction and/or frustration of demands, whether they are justifiable or infantile, and toward the facilitation and sometimes even instigation of unpredictable productions. Consequently, this transformation must render highly problematic the quasi-collapsing of psychoanalysis onto a science, and in this case a science of parenting, as it has been customarily understood and often endorsed by most psychoanalysts, including Winnicott. The transformation must shift the focus of the psychoanalytic process away from a hermeneutics of fantasy and toward a pragmatics of desire.

Property

And so, we return to the Winnicottian insistence that any given found object must be decathected, fully aware of the fact that such an object can be as much an idea, an interpretation or a theory as it can a toy, a blanket or a teddy bear. In this context, it is worth recalling Winnicott's recognition that the found object's eventual decathexis does not so much privilege the crucial experiencing (Winnicott 1971, 2) that takes place in the region between inner fantasy and outer reality over and above the found object as it grounds the one in the other. Indeed, without a found object, the experiencing cannot take place, and the subject is left with either hallucinations that are essentially unfulfilling or sensory perceptions that are foreign and jarring. Likewise, without the experiencing, any object that may be found and potentially enlivened remains precisely nothing but an object—concrete, meaningless, inert. The same dynamic can be claimed of a text and its readings, a thought and its procedures, a practice and its implementations. This reciprocal grounding safeguards against the possibility of either object or experiencing being privileged at the expense of the other, against, in this case in particular, the reduction of the Winnicottian project to a vulgar and failed form of either fetishism (of object) or vitalism (of experience).

Seen through this lens, psychoanalysis is a practice in which the session and the elements that comprise it (analysand, analyst, couch, associations, constructions, slips, durations, finances, etc ...) constitute potential found objects. Initially, most found among these is the analyst's invitation for the analysand to speak whatever comes to mind, an invitation that expresses a possibility rather than a directive, a curious and titillating invitation, not entirely familiar and certainly not without its dangers and anxieties, an invitation that the analysand may accept as both gravitas and caper, an invitation, finally, crucial for the analytic process precisely because it is genuinely extended all the while quite fantastical in its possible outcomes. That such an invitation, conflicted in its workings and resonances, is found and not merely granted or assumed is evidenced by the myriad of inevitably diverging ways in which it is enacted and lived, by its polymorphous nature as to purposes and processes (including, for instance, unravelling, obscuring, complying, confessing, dumping, fantasizing, fantasying, distracting, revealing or soothing). Thus the invitation to speak freely cannot be simply delivered in the opening sessions of an analysis and then taken for granted. It needs to be reiterated and confirmed, whenever and however needed. Depending on context and timing, each such instance is likely to trigger its own peculiar responses and uses, which is also to say non-uses.

Most enlivening, the invitation to associate and speak freely not only points to a rarely encountered world somewhere between private psyche and public space, it also serves as the pivot for a new field of the 'speaking' ('celui du dire') (Laplanche and Pontalis, 1998, 24) rather than of, say, 'language' or 'the symbolic.' Though neither real nor imaginary, this space is where 'the difference of the real and of the imaginary' ('la difference du réel et de l'imaginaire') maintains its value (24). At one level, the difference Laplanche and Pontalis were highlighting is the one between the real and the imaginary as constituted by speaking. However, the awkward sentence structure ('the difference of the real and of the imaginary' rather than the difference between the two) also communicates that speaking is what sets the real and the imaginary apart from all else. Contra Lacan then, the engine of difference *par excellence* is speaking as experience and not language as structure. Not surprisingly, Laplanche and Pontalis went on to explain that the 'homology between the analytic domain and the unconscious domain to which it elicits is not based on their common "subjectivity" but in the profound kinship of the unconscious with this field of speech: it is not "it is *you* who says so," but "it is you who *says* so"' (25; emphasis in the original). Incidentally, this passage first appeared in 1964, five years after the publication of the French translation of Winnicott's seminal essay on transitional objects (Winnicott, 1959). The lines of exchange and influence between London and Paris were unfolding in subtle and unexpected ways. Laplanche and Pontalis's favouring of the rather ambiguous 'kinship of the unconscious with the field of speech' and their rupture with the oft-invoked Lacanian dictum that 'the unconscious is structured like a language' bear witness to the incipient fissure between the Master and two amongst the soon-to-be recognized as the most important figures in the French psychoanalytic pantheon.[5]

As a found object, the invitation to speak and associate freely is not an invitation to build a bridge between the hallucinatory and the concrete but, more importantly, to expand the bridge that playing, finding and dreaming had already built and forever declare its world a most useful habitat. It is on this bridge that one encounters the analysand's unrestricted uttering of associations (as a saying and an experiencing) as it meets the analyst's sustained invitation to speak freely (as a found object). The uttering operates between private fantasy and public pronouncement; it brings forth the working through of yet undisclosed or differently disclosed thoughts and affects; it relocates personal torments and treasures in a space that is no longer private (in its inclusion of the analyst), though not quite public either (in its commitment to confidentiality). While transitional insofar as it opens to and neighbours both the private and the public, this space is under the sign of co-incidence since it is fantastic as well as lived, and fantastic as lived, private as well as public, and private as enunciated. It is a space of suspension, a plateau which is anything but a space of stillness.

Winnicott showed how, as experiencing is gradually displaced and/or dispersed from one particular found object, and henceforth decathected and relinquished, onto newer and possibly broader objects and structures, it opens up from the singular illusion of play to the plural collusion (as in the co- and hence shared illusion) of culture (Winnicott, 1971, 5–6), from the other-than-me to the more-than-me. Presumably, the subject of this experiencing has shifted from a sense of itself as solitary, autonomous, even omnipotent, to experiencing and recognizing, which is to say, collaborating or colluding with, resisting or seducing the other as subject. This, in a nutshell, is what the analytic transference brings into relief.

The shift from omnipotence to collaboration brings out yet another layer to Winnicott's understanding of the found object as eventually decathected and relinquished. While an adult subject may come to recognize that a particular found object is not a possession in the true sense of the word but the seed and/or pivot for a broader cultural experience (an idea, a relationship or a community for instance) that no one person can genuinely possess or control, a much younger subject is likely to reject even the slightest suggestion that the teddy bear or blanket it has found is not entirely its own. It may not look kindly upon the adult's attempts to mend, clean or in any way alter said bear or blanket; it may tolerate even less the prospect of having to share it with those around. As the first other-than-me possession, the found object is not necessarily registered as an other-than-mine. Two provisional implications arise here, and both need to be put to the test. The first is that the ability to move from the other-than-me to the other-than-mine is one that the subject will have to develop if it is to look both forward and backward in time on the objects it encounters, experiences and relinquishes in order to recognize them as found as opposed to simply appropriated, guarded and/or discarded. The second implication is that Winnicott may very well have paved the way, although perhaps inadvertently, for an assessment of the experience of the static and acquired object as, in part at least, inherently childish.

As these thoughts promote a cohesive and unified theory of a developmental journey from object recognition (as objectification and possession) to subject recognition (as subjectivization and collaboration), they are not entirely convincing. If, indeed, the found object is found by virtue of the fact that it is experienced as more than a mere object, if, in other words, it has already been subjectivized, however partially, then the subject's capacity to recognize and experience the subject-hood of the other—even at the most elemental levels of vitality and animation, and in its most rudimentary capacities to soothe, comfort or protect—is a concurrent condition for the very possibility of an event such as finding rather than its subsequent developmental consequence or achievement. Perhaps, then, a major fault line in the Winnicottian paradigm has to do not only with its unsubstantiated investment in a developmental model, as many (especially Lacanians) have argued,[6] but also with its (and its detractors') investment in a murky and, I would suggest, not entirely warranted language of static and discrete subjects and objects, at least as far as the psychodynamic underpinnings of finding and experiencing are concerned.[7]

If, to its finder's mind, the found object begins as animated and vital and only later is decathected so that it may become an object in the most quotidian sense of the word and potentially, a *bona fide* possession whose value lies not in its specific nature, which is to say in the markers that animate it and differentiate it from all other objects, but in the measure to which it may be saved, traded, spent or circulated, in the measure to which it is presumed to be similar or even identical to other objects that will eventually come to take its place, thus erasing its memory, including the fact that, at one point, it did have a memory, then property and the corresponding experience of privacy may not be entirely childish. Property and privacy are the products of a process of concretization and a rendering static, as in 'this is mine and you may not have it, use it or change it,' which the subject brings to bear on the object, a process that may recognize the fact of a neighbour but only on the condition that the lines separating the territories, the objects as well as the subjects that may lay claim to them have been properly identified, demarcated and registered, on the condition that a presumably indisputable outside authority has already been installed and may be called upon to adjudicate a conflict, an intrusion or a misappropriation, on the condition that, finally, any room for the middle as co-incidence has been unequivocally and irrevocably eradicated. Needless to say, the exceptionally complex and subtle apparatuses and procedures that produce this state of affairs can hardly be qualified as childish, whether psychologically, structurally or chronologically.

Intelligibility

To my mind, this process of concretization runs parallel to the systematizing secondary revision Freud identified in his work on dreams. Following in the footsteps of waking thought's manipulations of perceptual material, secondary revision's distinguishing function is to lend cohesion to the otherwise fragmentary content of a dream, to 'establish order in material of that kind, to set up relations in it and to make it conform to our expectations of an intelligible whole' (Freud, 1900, 499). Secondary revision, then, seeks to mould the material offered to it 'into something like a day-dream' (492);[8] it edits and re-writes that material so as to produce a sequential, self-evident and presumably definitive story, an, as it were, official story whose pleasure depends on its ability not only to gratify, for that is what (day-)dreams supposedly do, but also to pre-empt the need for further explanation, and hence further work, by the dreamer or anyone else for that matter. This is a story whose pleasure lies in the fact that it does not stimulate, that it does not produce other, which is to say different, potentially unsettling and transformative, stories.

Therein lies secondary revision's status as a form of censorship; it is a revision that may not be further revised and a process whose aim is not only the production of an 'intelligible whole,' but, more importantly, the consolidation of that whole and the prohibition against anyone else having, using, changing or dismantling it. As is the case with any other prohibition, this consolidation betrays its own efforts as it exposes the revision's underlying disorder and unintelligibility and, equally dangerously, recognizes in it an opportunity for new and unforeseeable uses or transformations, (dis) orders or (un)intelligibilities. Ultimately, secondary revision is an injunction against movement and mutation; it is the imposed *terminus* to the work of association. Therein also lies secondary revision's radical distinction from the work of, say, construction. Much as it imbues an otherwise chaotic constellation of objects and drives with a graspable meaning, construction is by its very character preliminary and mutable (Freud, 1937, 260); it is both a re-construction of whatever may have preceded it as well as a pre-construction that prompts and promotes further work. Meanwhile, secondary revision attempts to foreclose all that has to do with stages, series or processes, including finding. Beyond the realm of the unconscious, secondary revision becomes a critical stratagem for that strain of the self-anointed revolutionary spirit whose vision aims not only to redress the chaos of a preceding illness, injustice or illusion (whether clinical, theoretical, institutional or political) but to do so with the promise of completion, of the 'once and for all.' As it strives to consolidate for itself the status of the new order and the new truth, this spirit will judge any threat to its authoritative finality as pathological, seditious, regressive, counter-revolutionary.

Secondary revision and private property are essentially meant to secure the wish for, respectively, incontrovertible intelligibility and possession beyond doubt; together, they authorise the ownership of intelligibility and the intelligibility of ownership. Utterances such as 'this is so' and 'this is mine' are not statements of fact but demands (Freud, 1900, 500) meant to eliminate any and all room for change, fragmentation and, most importantly, most threateningly perhaps, for loss—which is to say any and all room for movement, experiencing and, most importantly, most unfortunately perhaps, for finding. Everything ought to fit at the end of a secondary revision; if the story is to be retold, the same elements must be recounted in the same order and in the same tone; otherwise, a jarring distortion and a disquieting falsehood, in the guise of a false claim to ownership, will result. Similarly with private property, the record ought to be clear as to where and to whom everything belongs so that the proprietary right to exclusivity may be enforced and the deeply unsettling disorder of theft, including the theft of intelligibility, may be prevented.

And yet, the upshot here is that neither private property nor secondary revision may be reduced to the expression of a virtually intractable repetition compulsion. On the contrary, such classifications are meant to preclude repetition insofar as each is an attempt to fulfil a defensive wish to preserve a certain state and defend against anything that might be perceived as threatening its survival. Constancy and stasis are the principal concerns here. This might explain why Freud not only appreciated the pleasurable yield of such defences, inasmuch as he understood pleasure as a principle of constancy, but also why he went so far as to identify pleasure itself as a yield that serves the death drive (Freud, 1920, 63), a drive which, after all is said and done, is the most forceful instantiation of constancy and stasis. Secondary revision's wish for finality, its attempt to hold its product 'as is' and 'once and for all,' captured, motionless, in other words silent, runs counter to the found object's eventual loss of meaning as never truly definitive and whose decathexis is neither a death nor a rejection nor, even, an irrevocable abandonment of the object (Winnicott, 1971, 5).

Although the found object's meaning is eventually displaced onto other domains, its reappearance can and often does trigger a charged fund of memories of people and places, thoughts and activities, all of which may now be found anew, differently. In the context of the everyday, the keepsake, the memento, the trace, the relic and the gravestone are among the many objects that can illustrate well this process. In a clinical setting, it is the availability of the erstwhile decathected object as a potential link in a series of constructions, syntheses and associations, between one neighbour and the next and between one neighbourhood and the other, its ability to reinvigorate and be re-invigorated by that series, to boost, bend and derail it and, in so doing, become subject to the same effects it is capable of producing, however unwillingly, that propels the analytic process as an engagement with the return of the repressed, an engagement possible only on the condition that it disabuse itself of the fantasies of efficacy and verifiability.

On the other hand, the found object is relinquished not only when it becomes irrelevant or when its destruction is of no consequence to its finder, but also when its destruction no longer looms as a danger, when the other (individual, institution or environment) to whom it is relinquished is now invested with the hope and entrusted with the care and responsibility to not destroy it and, along with it, those parts of its finder that have become intertwined with, or 'woven' into, it. Perhaps, then, the subject's possessiveness, its 'this is mine and you cannot have it, use it or change it,' may be, in some contexts at least, better understood as a 'this contains and hence is a part of me and I do not trust you (or at least not yet) not to destroy it and me in the process.' When relinquished to an other, the object is susceptible to manipulation and transformation, to mutation. While the subject may be confident, even if mistakenly, that it can survive the loss of the object it has found or that, in turn, the object can survive its aggression, it may be less than certain that both can survive the aggression of that other. Herein lies the quasi-existential anticipatory anxiety familiar to most creators (artists and artisans, theorists and scientists) as they prepare to open up their works to the experiences of the world at large. The objects these creators have found and with which their thoughts, passions and imaginations have become intertwined—the words, colours, thoughts and experiments they have playfully re-constructed into new outputs—are now on the verge of being, at best, interpreted, assessed and revised or, at worst, dissected, attacked and discarded. Since these objects implicate not only the creations but also the creators in them, the prospect of such manoeuvres and reactions only exacerbates the conflicts, pains and dilemmas surrounding critiques, proprietary rights and authorial intentions.

Consequently, decathexis and relinquishment need not be confined to the unidirectional and/or sequential order in which they present themselves. Although one may relinquish one object that has been deemed meaningless (as refuse, debris or residue), one may relinquish another only on the condition that its continued relevance and/or sustenance is guaranteed. One may also come to recognize as less vital, differently vital or perhaps even more vital, that object over which one has already released one's proprietary grip. Nowhere are such dynamics more evident than in the analysand's frequent relief upon disclosing treasured private thoughts and fantasies to an analyst before whose interpretative manipulations and/or normative evaluations, be they actual or projected, one may feel defenceless.

The Irrelevance of Psychoanalysis

I want to turn to the scenario in which psychoanalysis itself acquires the status of a found object, the scenario in which the practice becomes no more and no less than an animated, resilient and eventually decathected object. The most obvious and frequent strategy for exploring this issue has been to elaborate on the clinical and psychodynamic factors that allow for the analysand's associations to take on the qualities of a found object, for the expression of dreams, memories and affects to occupy the intermediate space between hallucination and external reality, flight of fancy and demand and, in turn, for the analyst's intervention to meet such an expression on its own terrain instead of functioning as a correction according to a scientific fact ('This is what actually happened') or an injunction in the name of a psychomythology ('This is what should have happened')—for, in other words, the analyst's intervention to take on the qualities of a found object as well.

Contra the strategy advocated by a narrow reading of Freud and Klein according to which every phenomenon that arises from the couch—be it a sound, a shift, a stutter, a slip or a sigh—ought to be identified, understood and eventually interpreted as the enactment of some pre-existing unconscious pattern, Winnicott's elaborations have prompted many clinicians to encourage and focus the analysand's use of their own words, wishes and predicaments, of the analyst's person, presence and utterances, of the frame, the couch and the money that exchanges hands—of in sum, the entire range of components that make up the analytic situation—as a found object. Transference, aggression and resistance are no longer the unconscious puppet masters that must be exposed, resolved and/or neutralized. They are addressed as the effects of the analysand's attempts to utilise, as best they can, the current analytic situation and all that runs through it as found objects that will satisfy certain dynamics while thwarting others (Modell, 1968 and Ogden, 1994), or, following the Deleuzo–Guattarian terms previously elaborated, as machines embedded in specific series of production and consumption, demands and exchanges. Never truly original and even less frequently definitive, such objects and machines are redrawn, re-produced, redeployed; their itineraries and transformations belong at the centre of the analytic focus. A similar understanding has been advanced regarding the phenomena and dynamics that belong to the analyst, among them counter-transference, projective identification and, to a certain extent, supervisory pull.[9]

What emerge as crucial at this point are the analyst's responsibilities in the face of these deployments, not to mention the interpretive, counter-transferential and extra-transferential[10] factors that correspond to and fur-ther them. Such responsibilities require the analyst's recognition that every single aspect of the analytic situation that has acquired the status of found object and/or machine is not only animated and resilient, but, sooner or later, decathected—that, in other words, each such aspect will, in time, be-come irrelevant and cede its place to something not only more-than-itself but also other-than-itself. The found object that is a dream, a construction, a transference, an analysis and even—or, perhaps, most especially—an ana-lyst, will not simply pale in comparison with a deeper, richer or truer other of its own kind, it must ultimately open onto an altogether different and broader experience, a non-clinical and/or extra-analytic part of 'the whole cultural field.' To put it bluntly, for psychoanalysis to qualify as a found object, as indeed it must, not only can it not be its own end, it must also foster its own eventual dissipation, otherwise, as Deleuze and Guattari have warned, it becomes a 'limp rag' (Deleuze and Guattari, 1977, 5) committed to its own endless circulation, a fetish—less as the substitute for the mother's non-existent penis, as per the classic Freudian definition, and more as the singular permissible object and/or aim of desire.[11] Obviously, the fact that a specific process of production merits an end does not undermine the poten-tially boundless nature of producing, constructing, playing. The distinction that needs to be underscored here is between a procedure and/or an event on the one hand, as in a game, a book or an institutionally sanctioned analysis, and, on the other, an activity, as in playing, reading or analyzing; while the finitude of the former preempts its derailment into a fetish, the latter is less reliant on the prospect of an end and may, in fact, be greatly harmed by it.

The interpretation I propose sets Winnicott apart from those orientations that identify the end of the analytic process in terms of the analysand's identification with or internalization of the analyst, thus consolidating the latter's position as the instantiation of an erstwhile absent good-enough mother, father, doctor, friend, judge, mentor, etc. and foreclosing the pos-sibility of such a figure ever becoming irrelevant. Nevertheless, there is nothing inherently unique or original about Winnicott's call for the dis-sipation of analysis. Indeed, many a Freudian has argued that the resolution of the transference and, with it, all of the analysand's entanglements with the person of the analyst must be the measure of clinical success. One finds a resonant, albeit dated, version of this disentanglement in Janet Malcolm's infamous account (1981) of the clinician comfortable in sorting through his case histories and ranking their success on the basis of his patients' avowed indifference to their analyst and analysis. Collapsing psychoanalysis onto surgery, Malcolm's clinician explained: 'When you're through with the operation, you sew up the patient, you hope that the scar isn't too conspicuous, and if everything afterward goes as it should—fine, that's enough' (62). The protocol that once was but is now concluded may lay claim to legitimacy and success against the background of, among other dynamics, a healthy dose of ingratitude in the analysand and an equally healthy dose of humility in the analyst. Presumably, both parties have proven themselves capable of decathecting and moving on; neither is beholden to the other as each has shed the yoke of transferential expectations and responsibilities.

What sets Winnicott apart here is that, while the clinician in him equips us with the category of the found object as yet another instrument that fosters the psychoanalytic process, the philosopher in him opens up for us the possibility of transforming that object into a meta-clinical reference in relation to which we may understand and assess the practice and its purposes not only from within the analytic situation, and hence according to the needs, demands or expectations of those that participate in it, but also, and, I believe, much more fruitfully, from without.

Indeed, in giving us the found object, Winnicott has given us not only a tool of analytic inquiry that will no doubt come to be replaced by other, more useful though no less analytic tools, but also a standard grounded in analytic theory and practice and by which both theory and practice (rather than any particular analytic instance or technique) can be assessed. To put it differently, Winnicott has given us direct access to a moment of psychoanalytic self-reflexivity in which we may not only simultaneously participate and observe, but in which we may also participate and observe in the observation itself.[12] Psychoanalysis, Winnicott maintained, does not stand outside the history of that quintessentially human phenomenon, play; it is only its 'most recent form' (1967, 41), and, though he described it as a 'highly specialized' type of play, nowhere did he intimate that the practice is the definitive and crowning achievement of play and its history. In fact, there is every reason to believe that Winnicott would have agreed that it is playing that endures, whereas, much like any other found object in the life of the individual, psychoanalysis as a theory and a method is nothing more and nothing less than a found object in the life of the species, an object with which we play, an object that will neither die nor be repressed but will nevertheless lose its meaning in favour of potentially broader, more exploratory, more subtle and maybe even more collective (more 'cultural') objects and/or forms of 'play.'[13]

While the literature on the topic of termination as a clinical phase is extensive, psychoanalysis as a discipline seems to have entirely sidestepped the

Winnicottian challenge to work through its own decathexis, to, both clinically and meta-analytically, elaborate, suffer, survive and, perhaps, even
take a certain pleasure in the otherwise unbearable co-incidence that underscores its own termination. Freud could not have conceived of civilization's future without analysis as the method best qualified to contain
humanity's psychological ailments.[14] And although Lacan and Klein appeared to disagree on much within the analytic field, it seems to me that they
would have been in complete accord over the virtually insurmountable
difficulty of thinking humanity's continued growth without a psychoanalysis
that would not only temper but also resist culture's relentlessly distorting
effects on the psyche.[15]

The prospect of its decathexis confronts psychoanalysis with one of its
sharper moments of *coincidentia*—fading away into a background of irrelevance while being propelled in the direction of a rich and invigorating
outside. Although desirable as the 'fine, that's enough' index of one particular scenario where ingratitude meets up with humility, as per the Malcolm
example above, *coincidentia* in the broader context may be experienced as an
outright threat to the discipline's integrity should it be exposed to interests
and priorities beyond its control. At stake here is an abrupt and radically
transformative process far more unsettling than a collegial meeting across
disciplinary boundaries meant to foster an exchange of findings or techniques. Indeed, as it ventures beyond the practices of illustration or corroboration and into a world that is truly other, the passage from analytic
couch to academic podium, gallery wall or cultural laboratory triggers a
vicissitude potentially no less jarring than the passage from the commonsensical to the instinctual or from the rational to the libidinal. Of vicissitudes, Freud spoke of the successive waves that make up the life of an
instinct (1915, 131). Cumulative, these waves are no less abrupt, untimed,
disruptive.[16] As much unpredictability and turbulence faces the psychoanalytic sensibility as it encounters its disciplinary others; as many ruptures
and losses it must endure as it expands its outlook and reserves.

The Psychoanalysis of Irrelevance

A while ago, a Winnicottian colleague wondered if my thinking psychoanalysis as a found and hence eventually decathected object meant that I was
contemplating abandoning the profession. When I responded in the negative,
she gingerly requested that I defer expressing my thoughts til after she had
retired. Understandably, there is little that is comfortable and even less that is
humorous about an analyst having to consider the possibility of relinquishing
the very practice that has enlivened them in the most fundamental ways,
personally and professionally. For many of us, psychoanalysis has been an
animated and animating practice, a perspective and a procedure that have
withstood our most demanding idealizations as well as our harshest critiques

and a discipline that has grown into a familiar and virtually indispensable foundation for our sense of who we are in the world, how we can contribute to it and how we might matter in it—little as we may. The thought that, at the end of the day, psychoanalysis, by its own nature and according to its own findings rather than through invalidation, conquest or attrition will necessarily come to nought is deeply unsettling.

Armed with the idea of a 'life without analysis,' some detractors may be eager to declare, yet again, the irrelevance of psychoanalysis, and to try to bury, yet again, and, no doubt, once and for all, a practice that seems to contain within its very logic the inevitability of its own irrelevance.[17] If only things were that simple. Since Winnicott identified for us a tool that functions both within and without the analytic situation, a tool that allows us to pursue the relevance of psychoanalysis in light of finding, which is to say, to track the discipline's relevance to the limit—which is also to say, to the point of its own irrelevance—we can and certainly must, with the help of that very same tool, reconsider psychoanalytically the very notion of irrelevance itself, of how it has been conceived and practised, of its scope and dynamics and of the radicalizing momentum Winnicott's contribution can impart to it.

In principle, an object's irrelevance is the outcome of the subject's indifference to it, of the experience that neither its presence nor its absence deters that subject from a task or influences their function and position. Irrelevance is the limit imposed by a specific subject on an object's ability to make a difference in a given context and at a given point in time. Irrelevance is therefore a situational effect rather than an inherent characteristic that the object must suffer. It is in the nature of its experience of the subject's indifference and its response to it that the object manifests some of its more salient features: the extent of its vulnerability, its endurance, its need for occasional validation and/or reprieve, or, ultimately, the measure and quality of its investment in relationships, including the relationship to the subject by and for whom it has been rendered irrelevant.

Given such a definition, irrelevance here echoes what Winnicott identified as the found object's capacity to survive whatever attributes the subject projects into it (passivity, vitality, longevity...) and whatever treatment that subject heaps upon it (love, possessiveness, affection, mutilation) (Winnicott, 1971, 5). Irrelevance is then bound up with an object's resilience within a particular relationship to a particular subject, with that object's ability to sustain its existence in the face of whatever is thrown at it—be it love, hate or, perhaps most especially, indifference. Needless to say, this point is predicated on the distinction between irrelevance and non-existence which may parallel Winnicott's own distinction between decathexis and death. That life continues for the subject as if the irrelevant object is not present does not necessarily entail the object's actual absence or demise. Conversely, and all along, one ought to be equally mindful of the underlying distinction between resilience and indestructibility: that an object may prove pliable and/or hardy under certain circumstances is no guarantee against its destruction under others; likewise, that an object may be indestructible is quite often the symptom of ossification and lifelessness rather than of dynamic resilience.

When Winnicott spoke of that aspect of the object I am labelling irrelevance, he was accounting for the requirement that, in due course, the found object is decathected, that it is 'not so much forgotten as relegated to limbo' (1971, 5). As the eternal in-between, Winnicott's deployment of limbo evokes that other, earthly, human, and maybe even, and most vitally, humane in-between in which and by which the analyst's theoretical imagination as much as his clinical orientation was captured.

Wedged midway between the seemingly heavenly omnipotence of hallucination, of instant and boundless gratification, and the supposedly hellish limitations of the physical world, of frustration and helplessness, it would appear that limbo is a forever irrelevant realm where no reasonable person would want to be trapped. After all, limbo is hardly the hoped-for eternal dwelling for oneself, one's loved ones or even one's enemies; heaven or hell tend to be the preferred destinations. As a desolate and senseless landscape that has been stripped of all desire and anticipation, as the endlessly grey atmosphere of apathy and unresponsiveness, limbo, it would seem, is the home of pure neutrality, of that which is neither good nor bad, neither loving nor hating, neither near nor far.[18] Many a psychoanalyst has taken up this so-called neutrality and elevated it to the gold standard of clinical rigour as discretion, unobtrusiveness and inconspicuousness. Winnicott's transitional, his limbo, could not be any further from such a space. Or, it may very well be located within that space, but only for those who have already decreed that it ought to belong there, those who look upon it from the outside, those who, in heaven or hell, in hallucination or empirical reality, in mythology or science, justify the merit of their own positions by sustaining an attitude of seeming indifference toward limbo, thereby stripping it of its ability to make any difference and ultimately dismissing it as irrelevant.

I have pursued this notion of limbo further in *Spaces*. At this point, I would like to explore the implication of the category of found object for the practice of psychoanalysis, specifically for the principle of clinical neutrality, of the 'neither good nor bad ...' vested in every analyst by virtue of having been properly and sufficiently analyzed. For it is this very principle that allows the clinician to work through rather than act out, at least within the confines of the session and the consulting room, their own histories and predicaments, thus enabling them to genuinely extend to the analysand the invitation to associate freely. As a clinical requirement, this sufficiency may be traced back to Freud's original and much stricter prescription for a so-called purification (Freud, 1912, 116) to which every clinician must submit and without which the clinical setting would be contaminated. While it still retains currency amongst the most classic of Freudians, this purification has given way to a seemingly more lax yet actually much more layered self-awareness, to an as thorough as possible recognition of one's own limits and resistances coupled with the measure of psychological strength necessary to either curb such limits and minimize their interference or, instead, reclaim and harness their effects.

Winnicott, on the one hand, did not seem to stray too far from the Freudian guideline as he advocated for a strong ego that allows the analyst to 'remain *professionally* involved, and this without too much strain' (Winnicott, 1960b, 162; emphasis in the original).[19] However, the extent to which such professionalism may be maintained at the expense of all else is seriously undermined once neutrality as a self-sustaining and unequivocal imperative to avoid correcting or directing, influencing or judging becomes a responsibility to provide the context and tools that make it possible for the analysand to move through the transitional space, transform whatever they may encounter into something other than an intractable fact or an immutable fantasy— associating, constructing, finding, experiencing. Henceforth, Winnicottian neutrality restructures the clinical space as it declares 'yes' to the investment in the animated and the unscripted, and 'no' to the collusion with or subjection to the rigid demands of mythology (as confabulation and so-called autonomy) or science (as observation and disinterest). One need only peruse the opening pages of *Holding and Interpretation* (Winnicott, 1986) for an illustration of this overhauling of so-called neutrality. Here, one encounters Winnicott intervening as often as twelve, fifteen or twenty times in the course of a single session,[20] recognizing and often inquiring about certain aspects of his analysand's concerns without becoming embroiled in them (21, 34, 37), trying to clarify matters for him (22), reminding him of material from previous sessions (24, 25, 27, 30, 33, 35, 38, 40, 41, 42) and sorting through and connecting with his various experiences and associations (22, 26, 27, 29, 34, 39, 41). At times, Winnicott did not hesitate to acknowledge his own mistaken interpretations, mindful of their effects (23—twice in a row, 39), or to admit his ignorance (38) as well as his interest in and, albeit moderate, excitement about his analysand's improvement (30, 31). At least with this particular analysand, Winnicott could have hardly been accused of adopting the silent stillness of objectivity or the presumed impartiality of disinterest underscored in Freud's exhortation that the analytic practitioner follow the model of the surgeon who 'puts aside his feelings, even his human sympathy, and concentrates his mental forces on the single aim of performing the operation as skilfully as possible' (Freud, 1912, 115).[21]

However much this redefinition of neutrality runs counter to the attitude reserved for that which presumably makes no difference, the logic of indifference follows in negation's footsteps by first affirming what it will later come to deny (Freud, 1925). Indifference is constituted through the recognition, nay, the experience of difference—as an encounter with that which is deemed other and for which one may reserve all manner of future responses, including coldness or lack of interest. In the analytic situation, neutrality thus redefined is the environment, the *milieu*, of what might be better characterized as 'in-difference,' as the heterogeneity that marks the object as found rather than consumable or unattainable, as the foreignness that distinguishes a construction from an interpretative equivalence, and as the differentiation that expands within the analysand a space from which a finding and founding voice, an other, which is to say, a difference, may emerge.[22] It therefore behoves us as psychoanalysts to speak of in-difference unabashedly and distinguish ourselves from the advocates of aloofness and apathy. In so doing, we recognize that our stance will be less tolerated, and likely judged unwelcome, no less by some among our peers than by the practitioners of both mythology and science, who will respond to it with indifference and relegate it to the status of the irrelevant.

Obviously, my advocacy here is in no way meant to suggest that the history of psychoanalysis is the history of a movement that has steadfastly resisted any and all aspirations to mythological comfort or scientific conformity—far from it. In fact, although each and every analyst has been required to abide by the classic principle of neutrality and assume the 'position' of analyst as opposed to other available positions (parent, judge, doctor or mentor, to name but a few), they have been enjoined, repeatedly, uncritically, to think of themselves as anything but an analyst (good-enough mother, benign super-ego, competent purveyor of health or expert tradesman), and, correspondingly, to think of the work as anything but an analysis (nurture, absolution, cure or apprenticeship), as well as to assess their function in terms of anything but an analyzing (feeding, acquitting, treating or training). One could patiently, even generously, explain this phenomenon as telling of a discipline that, having just begun its second century, is struggling through its adolescence and thus still seeking to model itself in terms of its similarity and difference with respect to some of the more established and familiar functions or trades, as telling of a psychoanalysis that, despite all outward pretensions, has yet to acquire a mature and secure sense of its distinct theoretical and clinical identity, as telling of, in sum, a psychoanalysis that has yet to comfortably claim Winnicottian neutrality and inhabit the position of in-difference among the various sciences.

As a discipline, psychoanalysis has been reluctant often to move beyond an unsophisticated attachment to, on the one hand, the practice of the select few who are presumably fit to analyze after having been sufficiently analyzed themselves, and, on the other, the principle of the universalizing law (as prohibition) or language (as structure). This attachment speaks a core contradiction that continues to plague the practice and inhibit its development—namely, that it assumes for itself the instrumental position of a bridge to a healthier, freer or truer existence while steadfastly holding itself up (whether as a principle, a practice or a group of individuals that promotes either) as the healthiest, freest or truest; in other words, it privileges the mutability of the transitional without relinquishing the aspiration for the constancy of its self-assured superiority—in health, freedom or truth. Many other disciplines suffer from the selfsame contradiction. One may legitimately mock those teachers of critical thought who are adamant about the orthodoxies of bureaucratic pedagogy, the preachers of piety who indulge in the most ostentatious displays of authority and the scientists who invest their faith in the redeeming powers of fact. It is the psychoanalysts, however, on whom the most unsettling effects of this contradiction befall, for it is none other than psychoanalysis that has set itself up, and understandably so, as a model of unwavering critical introspection.[23] And yet, it is precisely to the psychoanalysts that the fertile tensions of in-difference as co-incidence rather than contradiction, fallacy, double standard or failure belong. In-difference fosters the singularity of a voice that nonetheless utters a recognizable speech, a voice whose speech may be the least relevant to both hallucination and reality but is, all the same, crucial for the assumption of responsibility for what is conscious and all the meanings it might make and endorse. Herein lies the empathy psychoanalysis lives as a disciplinary characteristic rather than an individual accomplishment. In acknowledging itself as a found object, as vital, resilient and, eventually decathected, psychoanalysis mourns its fantasy of the eternal (as truth or health) and approximates like no other discipline the lived experience of its participants.

It is precisely in its contradictoriness and finitude that psychoanalysis may find its distinction, legitimacy and potential.

Notes

1 When not paralleling the *milieu* in reference to both content and context, the medium, one of the middle's nearest cousins, is no less muddled as it invokes a more balanced representation of what is most quotidian as well as that which is uncommon on the grounds that it supposedly communes or at least facilitates the communion with what is other or beyond. The mean, yet another member of the family, references both the average as well as the exceptional.
2 Deleuze and Guattari's use of 'plateau' owes much to Gregory Bateson (1972).
3 The slide from "mother" to "theory" and vice versa is not a necessarily far-fetched manoeuvre as each is capable of reproducing, enveloping, nourishing, safeguarding, and disillusioning. For some, the separation from the one may not necessarily be any more, or any less, poignant and/or freeing than the separation from the other.
4 In one of the talks he recorded for the BBC in the 1950s, and hence from the period shortly after the first appearance of the transitional objects essay, Winnicott identified abnormality in a child as neither a statistical deviation nor a behavioural aberration but as the stagnation in that child's ability to grow in personality and character. An abnormal child is a child that gets 'hung up at some spot' (Winnicott, 1991, 124) and can go no further in his or her movements and interactions; a normal child, on the other hand, '*can* employ any or all of the devices nature has provided in defence against anxiety and intolerable conflict' (126–7; emphasis in the original). Thus, bed-wetting is often an effective protest against strict management while the refusal of food may be a rejection of what is experienced as bad. 'Abnormality shows in a *limitation* and a *rigidity* in the

child's capacity to employ symptoms and a relative lack of relationship between the symptoms and what can be expected in the way of help' (127; emphasis in the original). Winnicott's concern was hence focused not on any one particular type or category of behaviour but on the extent to which one may use a behaviour and communicate through it.

5 While Laplanche's thought pursued its own post-structuralist path (Laplanche, 1987, 1997, 1999, 2007), Pontalis' original reworking of the Winnicottian point of view lasted an entire career (Pontalis, 1983, 1988, 1997, 2007).

6 For more on the Winnicott–Lacan connection, see, among others, André Green (2011) and Deborah Anna Luepnitz (2009).

7 See *Findings* where I have already addressed the extent to which these categories are dynamically inscribed onto one another.

8 We encounter this day-dreaming effect in Winnicottian 'fantasying' and its logic of the dead end. It is worth recalling that Freud had already coined 'phantasying' as the split-off thought activity 'kept free from reality-testing,' and 'subordinated to the pleasure principle alone' (Freud, 1911, 222). Freud went on to state that phantasying 'begins already in children's play, and later, continued as day-dreaming, abandons dependence on real objects' (222).

9 Winnicott (1947) was among the most notable to address, publicly at least, aggression in the counter-transference, head-on and without much self-recrimination. James Grotstein's (1981) remains a foundational text on projective identification. Supervision, however, has been often relegated to the status of a training concern; on this score, and though far afield from object relations, Jean-Paul Valabrega's observations on the four analyses (the analysand's, the analyst's, the training analyst's and the supervising analyst's) at work in every analytic session (1994) are, I would suggest, richly relevant.

10 As in the institutional, ethical and legal standards and/or guidelines that further define the clinical function of the analyst.

11 On this score, Deleuze and Guattari speak of the 'fantastic law,' the 'objective movement' and the 'quasi cause' as synonyms for the fetish (1977, 154).

12 The reference here is to the practice of participant observation which extends from the anthropological researches of Abu-Rihan al-Biruni (1952) in India in the early eleventh century to the work of Frank Hamilton Cushing at Zuni in the nineteenth century (Green, Green et al, 1990) and Bronislaw Malinowski in Melanesia (1929), Margaret Mead in Samoa (1928), and the Chicago School of Sociology in the twentieth century. For the psychoanalytic variant, the texts of Chrzanowski (1979) and Brenner (1987) offer a good introduction.

13 Winnicott would likely have agreed, unless, of course, he or his followers were to invoke the category of paradox with which the threat of an unsettling thought can always be contained, disciplined and minimized and even, preferably, altogether annulled.

14 That civilization is effectively the Petri dish of much of humanity's psychological ailments is the position Freud confirmed in a number of contexts (Freud, 1908, 1930).

15 For Lacan, the subject of the unconscious struggles against a culture that adamantly tries to fix it onto an 'alienating' destination (Lacan, 2006, 76); psychoanalysis allows us to recognize that such a subject nevertheless remains 'at an indeterminate place' beneath culture's networks, chains and history (Lacan, 1981, 208). Though Klein saw in culture an indispensable vehicle of reparation, she nonetheless insisted on the need for a psychoanalysis that would influence the development of sublimation, inhibition and neurosis and redirect them away from mere societal accommodation or collusion (Klein, 1923, 105).

16 More on the topic of vicissitudes is in the *Timings* essay.

17 This burial reference is to Raymond Tallis's 'Burying Freud' (1996), a favourable review of Richard Webster's *Why Freud Was Wrong* (1995), which launched a series of seemingly unending attacks and rebuttals.
18 The eerie echo here is to Wilfred Bion's classic 'neither memory nor desire,' 'neither history nor future' recommendation (Bion, 1967, 272).
19 On this note, Louis Althusser once proposed that 'counter-transference is transference, in principle like others, except that it is the transference of an individual A who has been analyzed, and who, in his relations with B, respects the rules of analytic practice. *That's all.*' (Althusser, 2020; emphasis added).
20 One may count twenty-five interventions made by Winnicott during the session of Friday, 18 March (64–68).
21 Freud went on to justify his requirement for such an 'emotional coldness' on the grounds that 'it creates the most advantageous conditions for both parties: for the doctor a desirable protection for his emotional life and for the patient the largest amount of help that we can give him' (Freud, 1912, 115).
22 It is with this difference in mind that the clinician may circumvent the seemingly inevitable trap of a counter-transference oscillating between empathic exhaustion and heartless separation when working with a difficult population. (Cf Willson and Lindy, 1994).
23 While learning, faith and information have presumably become more 'democratic' insofar as they have become, in principle at least, accessible to all those who seek them, psychoanalytic understanding, much like some versions of its predecessors philosophical wisdom and spiritual truth, still tends to set itself apart as the purview of a select few. The danger in such selectivity is that it carries within it the demands of often unattainable, if not, indeed, deadening standards.

References

Abu-Rihan al-Biruni. 1952. *Tarikhu-l Hind/The History of India.* New Delhi: Susil Gupta.

Althusser, Louis. 2020. "On Transference and Counter-Transference." In *Décalages.* 2:3. https://docplayer.net/189137985-Volume-2-issue-3-article-2.html Accessed: 15-08-2022.

Bateson, Gregory. 1972. *Steps to an Ecology of Mind.* New York: Ballantine Books.

Bion, Wilfred. 1967. "Notes on Memory and Desire." In *The Psychoanalytic Forum, vol. 2.* Edited by John Lindon. Pp. 271–280.

Brenner, Charles. 1987. "Notes on Psychoanalysis by a Participant Observer: A Personal Chronicle." In *Journal of the American Psychoanalytic Association.* 35:3. pp. 539–556.

Chrzanowski, Gerard. 1979. "Participant Observation and the Working Alliance." In *Journal of the American Academy of Psychoanalysis.* 7:2. Pp. 259–269.

Deleuze, Gilles and Felix Guattari. 1977. *Anti-Oedipus.* Translated by Robert Hurley, Mark Seem, and Helen R. Lane with a preface by Michel Foucault. New York: Viking Press.

Deleuze, Gilles and Felix Guattari. 1987. *A Thousand Plateaus.* Translated by Brian Massumi. Minneapolis: University of Minnesota Press.

Freud, Sigmund. 1900. "The Interpretation of Dreams." In *The Complete Standard Edition of the Psychological Works of Sigmund Freud SE* IV-V. London: Hogarth Press.

Freud, Sigmund. 1908. ""Civilized" Sexual Morality and Modern Mental Illness." In *SE* IX. London: Hogarth Press. Pp. 177–204.

Freud, Sigmund. 1911. "Formulations on the Two Principles of Mental Functioning." In *SE* XII. London: Hogarth Press. Pp. 218–226.

Freud, Sigmund. 1912. "Recommendations to Physicians Practicing Psycho-Analysis." In *SE volume XII*. London: Hogarth Press. Pp. 111–120.

Freud, Sigmund. 1915. "Instincts and their Vicissitudes." In *SE* XIV. London: Hogarth Press. Pp. 109–140.

Freud, Sigmund. 1925. "Negation." In *SE* XIX. London: Hogarth Press. Pp. 233–239.

Freud, Sigmund. 1930. "Civilization and its Discontents." In *SE* XXI. London: Hogarth Press. Pp. 59–145.

Freud, Sigmund. 1937. "Constructions in Analysis." In *SE* XXIII. London: Hogarth Press. Pp. 257–269.

Freud, Sigmund. 1920. "Beyond the Pleasure Principle." In *SE* XVIII. London: Hogarth Press. Pp. 7–64.

Green, André. 2011. "The bifurcation of contemporary psychoanalysis: Lacan and Winnicott." In *Between Winnicott and Lacan: A Clinical Engagement*. Edited by Lewis A. Kirshner. London and New York: Routledge. 29–49.

Green, J., Weiner Green, S., and Cushing, F. H. 1990. *Cushing at Zuni: The Correspondence and Journals of Frank Hamilton Cushing, 1879-1884*. Albuquerque: University of New Mexico Press.

Grotstein, James. 1981. *Splitting and Projective Identification*. Northvale, NJ: Jason Aronson Inc.

Klein, Melanie. 1923. "Early Analysis." In *Love, Guilt and Reparation and Other Works 1921–1945 The Collected Woks of Melanie Klein vol. 1*. London: Virago Press. Pp. 77–105.

Lacan, Jacques. 1981. *The Four Fundamental Concepts of Psychoanalysis. The Seminar of Jacques Lacam, Book XI*. Edited by Jacques-Alain Miller and translated by Alan Sheridan. New York: W. W. Norton & Company.

Lacan, Jacques 2006. "The Mirror Stage as Formative of the *I* Function as Revealed in Psychoanalytic Experience." In *Ecrits*. Translated by Bruce Fink in collaboration with Héloïse Fink and Russell Grigg. New York: W. W. Norton & Company. Pp. 75–81.

Laplanche, Jean. 1987. *Nouveaux fondements pour la psychanalyse*. Paris: Presses Universitaires de France.

Laplanche, Jean. 1997. *Le primat de l'autre en psychanalyse*. Paris: Flamarion.

Laplanche, Jean. 1999. *Entre séduction et inspiration: l'homme*. Paris: Presses Universitaires de France.

Laplanche, Jean. 2007. *Sexual: La sexualité élargie au sens freudien*. Paris: Presses Universitaires de France.

Laplanche, Jean, and Pontalis, Jean-Bertrand. 1998. *Fantasme Originaire, Fantasmes des Origines, Origines du Fantasme*. Paris: Hachette Littératures.

Luepnitz, Deborah Anna. 2009. "Thinking in the space between Winnicott and Lacan." *The International Journal of Psychoanalysis*. 90:5. Pp. 957–981.

Malcolm, Janet. 1981. *Psychoanalysis: The Impossible Profession*. New York: Alfred Knopf.

Malinowski, Bronislaw. 1929. *The Sexual Life of Savages in North-Western Melanesia: An Ethnographic Account of Courtship, Marriage and Family Life Among the Natives of the Trobriand Islands, British New Guinea.* New York: Halcyon House.

Mead, Margaret. 1928. *Coming of Age in Samoa: A Psychological Study of Primitive Youth for Western Civilisation.* New York: William Morrow & Co.

Modell, Arnold. 1968. *Object Love and Reality.* Madison, CT: International Universities Press.

Ogden, Thomas. 1994. "The Analytic Third: Working with Intersubjective Clinical Facts." In *International Journal of Psychoanalysis.* 75:1. Pp. 3–19.

Pontalis, Jean-Bertrand. 1983. *Entre le rêve et la douleur.* Paris: Editions Gallimard.

Pontalis, Jean-Bertrand. 1988. *Perdre de vue.* Paris: Editions Gallimard.

Pontalis, Jean-Bertrand. 1997. *Ce temps qui ne passe pas.* Paris: Editions Gallimard.

Pontalis, Jean-Bertrand. 2007. *Le royaume intermédiaire.* Paris: Editions Gallimard.

Tallis, Raymond. 1996. "Burying Freud." In *The Lancet,* 9 March 1996 347:9002. Pp. 669–671.

Valabrega, Jean-Paul. 1994. *La formation du psychanalyste.* Paris: Editions Payot & Rivages.

Webster, Richard. 1995. *Why Freud Was Wrong: Sin, Science and Psychoanalysis.* London: Harper Collins.

Wilson, John P. and Lindy, Jacob D. 1994. *Countertransference in the Treatment of PTSD.* New York & London: The Guilford Press.

Winnicott, Donald W. 1947. "Hate in the Contertransference." In *Through Paediatrics to Psycho-Analysis: Collected Papers.* New York: Basic Books. Pp. 194–203.

Winnicott, Donald W. 1959. "Objet transitionnel et phénomènes transitionnels, étude de la première 'Not-me possession." In *La Psychanalyse, N°5.* Paris: Presses Universitaires de France. Pp. 89–97.

Winnicott, Donald W. 1960a. "String: A Technique of Communication." In *The Maturational Process and the Facilitating Environment.* London: Hogarth Press and The Institute of Psycho-Analysis. Pp. 153–157.

Winnicott, Donald W. 1960b. "Counter-Transference." In *The Maturational Process and the Facilitating Environment.* London: Hogarth Press and The Institute of Psycho-Analysis. Pp. 158–165.

Winnicott, Donald W. 1971. "Transitional Objects and Transitional Phenomena." In *Playing and Reality.* London and New York: Routledge Books. Pp. 1–25.

Winnicott, Donald W. 1986. *Holding and Interpretation: Fragment of an Analysis.* Introduction by M. Massud Khan. New York: Grove Press.

Winnicott, Donald W. 1991. *The Child, the Family and the Outside World.* London: Penguin Books.

Index

Moreno-Riaño, Gerson 124n8
mundus imaginalis 121–123
Murdin, Lesley 81n2

'*nafs*' (spirit) 118
Nägele, Rainer 37n11
neutrality: clinical 147; redefinition
   of 148
Newtonian 8
Nichols of Cusa 21
Nietzsche, Frederick 5, 78
Nussbaum, Martha 13n5

object 37n14, 136; decathected 122,
   141–142, 145; found 19–20, 25, 27–28,
   30, 35, 36nn2–3, 43, 45–47, 52, 58, 61,
   63n14, 97, 99, 103–104, 107–109,
   114–115, 120, 134–138, 141–147, 150;
   inanimate 26; principal 69; recognition
   138; sexual 78; subjectivized 25, 31–32,
   115–116; transitional 107, 122,
   134–135
Oceanus Britannicus 10
O'Donoghue 63n13, 125n17
Oedipal drama 46
Oedipal edifice 48
Oedipal triangulation 67
Oedipus 30, 48
Ogden, Thomas 4
Ovid 124n6

The Panama Canal 24
Parat, Hélène 100n11
Parisian culture 24
The Parthenon Marbles 23
patience 5, 55, 135; fortitude and 30; and
   pathology 55
The Pergamon Altar 23
Phillips, Adam 35
Pines, Shlomo 126n27
Plato 106, 124n6
pleasure 5, 12, 34, 50, 52, 55, 57, 61, 67,
   75, 84, 86, 96, 111, 139–140, 145; of
   culture 7; erotism and 27; and reality
   97; utility and 96; world of 3, 76
Pommard, Chateau de 82n10
Pontalis, Jean-Bertrand 14n11, 96,
   100n11, 125n13, 137, 151n5
Porro, Pasquale 124n8
Post-World War II 34
property 13, 34, 135–139; private 140
psychoanalysis 4, 6, 8–9, 12–13, 15n14,

24, 28–30, 33, 35–36, 38n19, 46, 48, 53,
   62, 63nn9–10, 63n12, 70–71, 75, 86,
   94, 98, 105, 108–109, 111, 117–118,
   120, 122–123, 124n7, 126n22, 133,
   135–136, 144, 151n15; applied 2; and
   archaeology 60, 63n13, 125n17;
   central tenets of 3; history of 7;
   irrelevance of 142–150; philosophy
   and 6; principle of 45
psychoanalytic 5, 7–8, 93, 118;
   apparatus 97; approach 87; clinicians
   56; deployment 48; discovery 25;
   experience 14n12, 68; field 11, 34;
   investment 97; moment 35, 72; process
   60–61, 63n12, 135, 144; project 24;
   recognition 76; research 62n7;
   sensibility 85, 145; theory 94; throne
   21; tradition 28, 109, 117;
   understanding 59, 152n23

Raitt, Suzanne 124n7
Razinsky, Liran 125n22
reality 5, 26, 34, 45–46, 58, 72, 76, 79,
   87–88, 95, 99, 103, 122, 136;
   commonsensical 110; concrete 71;
   discourse and 48; divine 119; external
   19, 26, 32, 103, 142; factual 126n23;
   and fantasy 62, 67, 96; hallucination
   and 58, 107, 150; inner psychic 20;
   mimic 84; objective 6, 115; pleasure
   and 97; psychic 123, 126n23;
   transitional 116
reciprocity 27, 43, 99; principle of 57
relinquishment 71, 116, 134, 142
Renaissance 106, 127n37
resistance 4, 37n18, 38n21, 63n12, 68, 87,
   99, 142, 148; resolution of 35
Rodman, F. Robert 124n7
Roman Catholicism 105
The Rosetta Stone 23

Saladin 124n6
Sandler, Joseph 15n13
Saragnano, Gennaro 13n3
Scarfone, Joseph 79
Schlesinger, Herbert 81n2
Schmidt, Dietmar 63n13
Scholem, Gershom 22, 127n35
Searles, Harold F. 126n22
secondary revision 44, 47, 62n3, 104,
   112, 122, 125n20, 139–141
Sell, Christian 13n5

For Product Safety Concerns and Information please contact our EU
representative GPSR@taylorandfrancis.com
Taylor & Francis Verlag GmbH, Kaufingerstraße 24, 80331 München, Germany